Psychology and Crime

Longman Criminology Series

Series Editor: Tim Newburn

Titles in the series:

Psychology and Crime:
Myths and Reality

Peter B. Ainsworth

 LONGMAN

An imprint of PEARSON EDUCATION

Harlow, England · London · New York · Reading, Massachusetts · San Francisco · Toronto · Don Mills, Ontario · Sydney
Tokyo · Singapore · Hong Kong · Seoul · Taipei · Cape Town · Madrid · Mexico City · Amsterdam · Munich · Paris · Milan

Pearson Education Limited
Edinburgh Gate
Harlow
Essex CM20 2JE
England

and Associated Companies throughout the world

Visit us on the World Wide Web at:
www.pearsoned-ema.com

First published 2000

ISBN 0-582-41424-5 PPR

British Library Cataloguing-in-Publication Data

A catalogue record for this book is available from the British Library

Library of Congress Cataloging-in-Publication Data

Ainsworth, Peter B.
   Psychology and crime : myths and reality / Peter B. Ainsworth.
      p.   cm. – (Longman criminology series)
   Includes bibliographical references (p.   ) and index.
   ISBN 0-582-41424-5 (PPR)
   1. Criminal psychology.   2. Crime–Psychological aspects.
   3. Criminal justice, Administration of–Psychological aspects.
   4. Fear of crime.   5. Victims of crimes–Psychology.   I. Title.
   II. Series.
   HV6080.A55   2000
   364'.01'9–DC21   99-36913
                                                              CIP

Set by 7 in 10/12 New Baskerville
Printed & Bound in Great Britian by
T.J. International Ltd., Padstow, Cornwall.

To Gennie, who makes it all worthwhile.

Contents

Series Editor's Preface

Our society appears to be increasingly preoccupied with crime and with criminal justice. Despite increasing general affluence in the post-war period, crime has continued to rise – often at an alarming rate. Moreover, the pace of general social change at the end of the twentieth century is extraordinary, leaving many feeling insecure. High rates of crime, high levels of fear of crime, and no simple solutions in sight, have helped to keep criminal justice high on the political agenda.

Partly reflecting this state of affairs, the study of crime and criminal justice is burgeoning. There are now a large number of well-established postgraduate courses, new ones starting all the time, and undergraduate criminology and criminal justice degrees are also now appearing regularly. Though increasing numbers of individual textbooks are being written and published, the breadth of criminology makes the subject difficult to encompass in a satisfactory manner within a single text.

The aim of this series is, as a whole, to provide a broad and thorough introduction to criminology. Each book covers a particular area of the subject, takes the reader through the key debates, considers both policy and politics and, where appropriate, also looks to likely future developments in the area. The aim is that each text should be theoretically-informed, accessibly written, attractively produced, competitively priced, with a full guide to further reading for students wishing to pursue the subject further. Whilst each book in the series is designed to be read as an introduction to one particular area, the Longman Criminology Series has also been designed with overall coherence in mind.

Crime in general, and criminal investigation in particular, is now the staple diet of television drama and soap opera. Much of this television purports to tell us something about the psychology of 'the criminal', and of those whose job it is to investigate, detect, prosecute and punish those who offend. Needless to say, however, such drama mythologises and confuses rather more than it explains. This book is an attempt to separate some of the myths about psychology and crime from the realities.

In this broad-ranging text, the fifth in the Longman Series, Peter Ainsworth examines the extent of, and fear of, crime, the psychological consequences of criminal victimisation, explanations of criminal behaviour, including the role of mental illness, as well as exploring the nature and role of offender profiling and eyewitness testimony, the behaviour of juries and sentencers, and the role of psychology in (understanding) the effective treatment of offenders.

Peter Ainsworth provides a comprehensive and thoughtful introduction to the ways in which the various branches of psychology can inform and aid our understanding of crime and of criminal justice. This book will be invaluable for undergraduate and postgraduate students of psychology, law and criminology. It will also be ideal for professionals working within the criminal justice system who are looking for an accessible and broad-ranging guide to the subject.

Tim Newburn
August 1999

Acknowledgements

Sincere thanks are due to a large number of people who have helped in a variety of ways to ensure this book's completion. I am particularly grateful to my wife, Susan, and my daughter, Gennie, for their continued help, support and understanding during the writing of this volume. Sincere thanks also go to Ken Pease for his extremely helpful comments on my writing and for his continuing faith in my abilities. I am also appreciative of the help and support offered by Chris Hitchen who provided me with much useful information and not a little encouragement.

Thanks are due to my colleagues at Manchester, especially those whose altruistic gestures allowed me to take a period of study leave to write some of this book. Thanks also to Elaine who encouraged and helped, but also made sure that I did not neglect my other duties. I am also grateful to Tim Newburn and to Longman for providing me with the opportunity to reach such a large audience with this work. I hope that their trust in me is rewarded.

Peter B. Ainsworth
Department of Social Policy and Social Work
University of Manchester

Introduction

Among the posters often encountered on office walls is one which shows a person sat at a desk surrounded by vast piles of paper. The amusing caption reads 'Work fascinates me; I can sit and watch it for hours'. The same appears to be true of crime. Many people seem utterly fascinated by crime and spend hours watching crime series on television (Sparks, 1992; Howitt, 1998). Detective stories and 'murder mystery' novels also attract large numbers of fans. On any given week, British television audiences can choose from an array of fictional and factual crime series, ranging from the soap-like *The Bill* to reconstructions of actual crimes featured in programmes such as *Crimewatch UK*. Perhaps even more popular are series like *Inspector Morse* and *Poirot* in which crimes are solved through the clever deductions of an experienced detective.

In the late 1990s there have been additions to the already large array of crime programmes on offer. These new productions (e.g. *Eye Spy*) show the commission of actual crimes, often filmed by surveillance cameras or by video cameras sited in police cars. These new programmes appear to attract audiences almost as large as the more traditional detective series. The heavy diet of crime programmes is not specific to British television audiences. Most audiences in the Western world appear to share a liking for this form of entertainment (Howitt, 1998).

There is however something of a paradox here. While large numbers of television viewers remain fascinated by programmes dealing with crime, the same individuals might be less enthralled by the subject if they were to become victims of crime themselves. Most people like to think that serious crime is something which only happens to other people. Thus, those who spend hours watching fictional crime series do not necessarily come away fearful that the next victim could be them. Even if viewers do become victims, there may be an expectation that an Inspector Morse-like figure will step in to solve the crime and ensure that the culprit is imprisoned for many years. Although there are many very good detectives working within the police service, few have success rates approaching that of their media counterparts. It must also be acknowledged that even if the police arrest the perpetrator it is by no means certain that he or she will be convicted in court.

We can see, therefore, that there are discrepancies between the portrayal of crime in fictional television series and reality. The notion that most crimes are solved through the clever deductive powers of an inspired mind is a myth (Canter, 1994; Jackson and Bekerian, 1997). The reality is that most crimes are solved by other means. Many arrests result from information given to the police by witnesses and informants. Other apprehensions may be the result of a careful sifting of forensic evidence, including fingerprints and DNA samples. Other crimes are solved by careful, methodical (but often tedious) police enquiries and the following-up of many leads.

Unlike the mythical crimes solved in fictional television series, the solving of real crimes is more often the result of '95 per cent perspiration and five per cent inspiration'. The problem is that much routine police work is boring and ultimately fruitless. If one thinks of the thousands of hours spent trying to catch infamous criminals such as Peter Sutcliffe, the so-called Yorkshire Ripper, then one realises that there is often a great rift between fact and fiction. Of course, television producers should not necessarily be blamed for this – television audiences would quickly switch off (literally and metaphorically) if they were shown the hours of tedious and often fruitless work which goes into the average police enquiry. Many 'fly on the wall' documentary series about the police have to be edited ruthlessly so as to produce a programme which is attractive to an audience raised on the excitement and intrigue portrayed in fictional police television series and films.

The public may well have an unrealistic expectation of what the police can achieve. The myth is that the police are capable of solving the vast majority of crimes to which the general public fall victim. The reality is that the police do not solve most crimes, especially those of a less serious nature. As a result the public may well become disillusioned and become critical of the police's apparent incompetence (Ainsworth, 1995a: ch. 9).

If there is a mismatch between the public's expectations of the police, and what they actually achieve, then the same may also be true in relation to psychologists who help in criminal investigations. The British fictional series *Cracker* may have something to do with this misconception, although recent films such as *Silence of the Lambs* may also have left lasting (but inappropriate) impressions with the general public. In the case of *Cracker*, large audiences watched fascinated as the fictional character Fitz was brought in to solve crimes with which the police were experiencing difficulty. His somewhat unconventional lifestyle and extremely questionable methods proved to be a fascination for the many millions who watched the programmes. Although the series was fictional, many members of the public may have come to believe that Fitz's behaviour was representative of what psychologists have to offer.

Once again, however, the reality is somewhat different from the myth. As we will see in Chapter four, while psychologists have made important contributions in the field of offender profiling, their methods are considerably at odds with those of Fitz. This has not, however, deterred a large number of aspiring eighteen-year-olds from applying to study psychology in the hope of one day working as 'Crackers' for the police. Indeed it was reported that following the broadcast of *Cracker*, applications to study psychology at Manchester University (where *Cracker* was filmed) increased significantly.

While it is undoubtedly true that psychologists can help in the solving of some crimes, their expertise is gained from research and training rather than relying on intuition or hunches. What psychologists can do is to examine carefully all the evidence at the scene of a crime and make predictions as to the likely motive and characteristics of the offender. In some cases, this information is helpful to the police, if only to confirm that their lines of enquiry are appropriate. In other cases, the profile may help the police to follow up important leads or at least allow them to wind down some less fruitful lines of enquiry. The myth may be that large numbers of psychological profilers are employed by the police to help in the detection of crime. The reality is that in Britain in the late 1990s, no police force employs a psychologist as a profiler on a full-time basis. When profilers are brought in, they are usually employed on a part-time basis and asked to provide specific information. Unlike their fictional equivalents, psychologists are not routinely asked to examine a crime scene immediately after the crime has been discovered. Rather a psychologist is often brought in when normal police enquiries appear to be making little progress and when the police are struggling (Copson, 1995; Smith, 1998). Where psychologists are employed by the police, it is more likely to be in the role of occupational psychologist, dealing with matters such as assessment, training or stress counselling (Ainsworth, 2000).

There are, of course, many other areas in which myths about crime and criminals are seriously at odds with reality. One example is the notion that all criminals are fundamentally different from the rest of us 'normal' people. There is a commonly held view that criminals can be identified by means of their appearance or by an examination of their psychological make-up. The reality is that although some criminals do stand out, and perhaps even draw attention to themselves, the majority are not so easily distinguished. There are certainly stereotypes about the appearance of certain types of criminals. Most members of the public would happily provide a description of the likely appearance of a 'typical' child molester, 'flasher', armed robber, burglar etc. There may even be a high degree of consensus about the likely appearance – but consensus does not necessarily equate with accuracy (Bull and McAlpine, 1998).

Few people will have personal experience of a large sample of child molesters, so their presumptions of such offenders' appearance will be largely based on portrayals in the media. Producers of fictional television crime dramas will tend to pick an actor whose 'face fits'. In other words, the person chosen to portray the role will be one who will be recognised by the audience for what he is supposed to be, as he conforms to the stereotype. But this quickly becomes a vicious circle. To put it bluntly, not all 'flashers' are short-sighted rotund old men who wear dirty raincoats! However, the media may perpetuate such a myth by falling back on the hackneyed stereotype. In the same way that the mentally ill are invariably portrayed by the media as deeply disturbed and dangerous (Philo, 1994) so the stereotype of criminals will blind people to the large amount of variation within any sample of offenders.

The notion that criminals all share something in common in their make-up that makes them 'different' from law-abiding citizens may be a flawed, yet widely held perception. There are a number of reasons as to why this simplistic view does not stand up to closer scrutiny. For one thing, society's definition of what are and what are not criminal acts, changes constantly. To take one example, homosexual acts may not in themselves be a crime in Britain today, provided that they take place between consenting adults in private and do not involve physical harm to any participant. Yet if such acts had been committed 30 years earlier, they may well have resulted in the participants being convicted of a criminal offence. In other words, an act committed in the 1960s may have resulted in a person being labelled as a criminal, whereas the exact same act committed 30 years later would not. Would we really expect to find that the person in the former case carried all the stereotypical attributes of a 'criminal' whereas the person in the latter case did not?

The statute books are full of laws which prohibit certain specific acts by members of society. In theory, anyone who knowingly breaks these laws could in theory be branded a criminal. However, most members of the public may commit some illegal acts and yet not come to see themselves as criminals. The person who uses the office telephone to make a private call, or who takes home some office stationery for private use, may be guilty of a criminal act but not see themselves as a criminal. There is an amusing story about a father who chastises his son for having brought home some pencils belonging to his school. The father is heard to say 'Son, you really shouldn't steal the school's pencils – if you want some pencils I'll bring you some from work' (!) Would most people who found that a bank's cash machine had mistakenly given them too much money take the appropriate action and return the money to the bank? The point about such examples is that most people will at some point in their lives have committed a criminal act. It is thus inappropriate to expect that 'criminals' form a homogeneous group which is easily separable from the rest of us 'non-criminals'.

Even if we seek to make a distinction between petty offences and those of a more serious nature, it is not always possible to establish a clear cut dividing line between criminals and non-criminals. In most countries, the killing of another human being is the most serious offence on the statute book, often carrying the most severe of punishments. Yet even here, we may wish to make a distinction between some types of killing and others. The distraught husband who eventually succumbs to his terminally ill wife's requests that he help her to die with some dignity may be guilty of taking the life of another. Yet his 'crime' should surely not be viewed in the same way as that of a person who sets out deliberately to murder another in a planned attack. A momentary lapse of concentration by an experienced driver may result in the death of another motorist, yet such killing may not result in the offender being sent to prison.

We can see from these examples that it is not always easy to make distinctions between criminal and non-criminal behaviours. As we will see in Chapter 1, the dividing line between what is and what is not recorded as a criminal offence is an extremely blurred one. Similarly, whether or not a person really intended their actions to cause harm can lead to differing outcomes. It is a simplistic, and in some cases dangerous, notion to assume that all those who commit an offence do so because they are just 'that sort of person'. Although many people have attempted to come up with a single (and simple) explanation for criminal behaviour, the reality is that the issues are not quite so straightforward. As we will see later, there are a large number of factors, many of which interact in complex ways, which can lead to the commission of a criminal act (see Chapters 5 and 6).

It would appear from the above that there are a large number of myths and misunderstandings about crime. The intention of this book is to address and challenge some of these misconceptions and to explore the reality. In the areas chosen for examination, reference will be made to appropriate psychological research which can help to make sense of criminal behaviour and the criminal justice process.

Chapter 1 will look at the thorny question of the measurement of crime levels in society and the extent to which people's fear of victimisation is directly related to the actual level of crime. As we will see in that chapter, simply measuring levels of crime accurately is not as straightforward as it may at first appear. We will also see that fear of crime is not necessarily related directly to actual crime levels. Chapter 2 will consider why some people and properties become victims of crime while others do not. One myth that will be challenged is that many victims somehow 'deserve' their fate, or at least contribute to their own victimisation. This chapter will also allow us to consider why repeat victimisation is such an apparently robust phenomenon. Finally, this chapter will consider the psychological effects of victimisation.

Chapter 3 will examine how psychologists have contributed to initiatives aimed at preventing crime. Most governments, both in the United Kingdom and elsewhere, have made grand promises to take steps to reduce crime, yet many well-intentioned initiatives have failed. This chapter will consider why some initiatives have been successful while others have not. Chapter 4 will examine why some people appear to choose to embark upon a life of crime while others do not. The simplistic notion that all criminals are somehow 'different' and easily identifiable will be challenged here.

Chapter 5 allows us to consider another area in which the paths of psychology and criminal justice cross, i.e. in the consideration of the mental state of someone who commits a crime. The law often assumes that for a person to be guilty of a crime, they must have had the necessary intention to commit the crime. In this chapter we will also consider, and to some extent challenge, the simplistic notion that there is a clear link between mental illness and crime. Chapter 6 looks at the analysis of crime patterns and trends and the expertise which psychologists have brought to this important area. Although psychologists' roles are somewhat different from those of their fictional counterparts, they do have a considerable contribution to make.

Chapter 7 considers the role of judges and magistrates and examines decision-making by such officials. Sentencing policy will also be considered in relation to its possible effect on crime levels. We will also scrutinise the apparent perversity of some jury decisions and discuss jury processes. Chapter 8 considers what advances psychologists have made in the treatment of offenders. Despite what the public would like to think, prison in itself does not appear to reform most criminals and a significant majority of those sent to prison reoffend soon after release. However, psychologists have developed a number of treatment programmes which appear to be effective and the more successful of these will be reviewed in this chapter.

Chapter 9 will examine some of the ways in which things can go wrong within the criminal justice system and consider the reasons for such errors. It will look specifically at how eyewitnesses can make mistakes and how some police methods might lead to innocent people making confessions. Finally, the Conclusion will pull together the many strands and themes covered in the book, and will consider the future role of psychology in relation to crime and criminal justice.

In a book of this nature it is not possible to give a complete overview of the fields of psychology and crime. Rather, this book tries to draw attention to what appear to be some of the more important areas in which psychology plays a part in the criminal justice process. The selection is essentially a personal one and the reader should be aware that there are other sources which concentrate on different aspects of the psychology/crime interface. It is however hoped that this book will alert the reader to some important areas in which social, cognitive and forensic psychology are relevant to the study of crime. The interested reader may also wish to pursue some of the suggestions for further reading at the end of the book.

Chapter 1

The extent and fear of crime

Any discussion of crime should start with an accurate assessment of the level of criminal activity in society. Every year a large number of statistics are collected and published purporting to show the level of crime in each country. Figures are published (in England and Wales by the Home Office) and an eager media report on the latest trends. However, it has long been recognised that official statistics, while offering some valuable information, may not present an accurate picture of the actual level of crime.

Measures of crime

For many years, official statistics on recorded crime appeared to show an inexorable rise. We also hear almost daily that the prison population is increasing at an alarming rate. The figures assembled in most countries are compiled from returns submitted by the police to a government body. In England and Wales, each police force sends in its returns to the Home Office and an overall picture is produced. However, as we will see below, these figures may be neither totally accurate nor objective. In England and Wales, the statistics include only so-called 'notifiable offences'. There are, therefore, some anomalies. For example, criminal damage under a monetary value of twenty pounds is not a notifiable offence, whereas that above this threshold is.

The statistics suggest that by the mid-1990s, the average number of crimes recorded by the police in England and Wales each year was around five million. This compares with half a million in 1950, 1.6 million in 1970 and 2.5 million in 1980. For the period from 1970 to the early 1990s there was an average annual increase of about five per cent. To put the figures in a slightly different way, the number of crimes per head of population rose from about one per hundred in the 1950s to almost eleven per hundred in the early 1990s. It is perhaps surprising to learn that from the period 1992–97 there was a yearly fall in the number of notifiable offences. The figure for the twelve-month period up to March 1998 was 4.5 million, which represented a fall of 7.8 per cent from the previous twelve months – the largest yearly fall on record. However, an overall fall coincided with an increase in some violent and sexual crimes over the same period (Povey and Prime, 1998).

While the official statistics give one indication of the amount of crime, surveys of members of the public may provide an alternative perspective. For some years, researchers in a number of countries (including the USA and Australia) have carried out victim surveys. In the UK there is a bi-annual *British Crime Survey* (*BCS*) which looks at the public's actual experience of crime (Mirrlees-Black *et al.* 1998). Surveys such as these ask members of the public directly about their own experience of crime over the previous year. It may thus give a more accurate picture of victim-isation than the official record of notifiable offences. It should however be borne in mind that it is not always possible to make direct compar-isons for all types of crime. For example the *BCS* does not include offences such as fraud, homicide, crimes against businesses or crimes against people under sixteen. The *BCS* also includes some categories of offence which are not directly comparable to those used in the officially recorded figures. These include offences such as common assault and 'other household thefts'. There are however a core of offences for which direct comparisons between the two measures can be made. We will refer to findings from the *BCS* throughout this chapter.

The steps from crime to conviction

Between the commission of a crime and the passing of a sentence on an offender, there are a large number of stages to be passed through. At each of these stages, the 'crime' or the conviction may 'disappear' from the official statistics and not be recorded officially. It may be helpful to consider some of these stages in detail.

1. Will the victim notice the crime?

It may be wrong to assume that a victim will always be aware that a crime has been committed. For example, a man may only be aware that his wal-let is missing. He may have been targeted by a skilful pick-pocket, but may incorrectly assume that the wallet has simply been lost and thus not view this as a crime. A motorist may return to her car to find that a wing mirror has been broken. Should this be viewed as criminal damage or as the actions of a careless motorist who drove too close to the parked car?

One of the major research areas within current social psychology deals with the attributions which people make about events that occur or about the actions of others (for example Schneider, 1995). Thus the loss of a wallet may be explained by one 'victim' as unfortunate but an act for which no-one is really to blame. However, a paranoid person experiencing the exact same 'loss' might attribute the cause as being undoubtedly down to one of the many thieves around in society.

Many shopkeepers might also fail to notice individual crimes. They may be aware that over the course of a year they appear to have lost ten per cent of their stock to shoplifters, but will have little idea as to how many crimes this represents. According to recent figures (Home Office, 1998c), there were 274,000 recorded cases of theft from shops in England and Wales in 1997. (This compares with over 710,000 thefts from vehicles.) But surely this is a gross underestimation of the number of such offences. In reality most shopkeepers will not know how many crimes they have suffered over a given year and will only tend to inform the police if a shoplifter is caught. This is reflected in the fact that theft from shops appears to have an amazingly high clear-up rate of 75 per cent. Such figures are however a gross distortion of the actual detection rate for such crimes. If every single case of shoplifting was noticed, reported and then recorded by the police, the real clear-up rate would be significantly lower.

We must also be aware that some crimes are (perhaps mistakenly) referred to as 'victimless', in that they are only 'noticed' (and recorded) if the police target this particular form of activity. Some sexual offences and the possession of small quantities of illegal drugs are viewed by some in this way.

Although there may be no such thing as 'the perfect crime', those which come close to this dubious ideal may go unnoticed by the public. The murder and subsequent disposal of a vagrant's body may be a crime known only to the perpetrator and so remain unnoticed (and unrecorded) by the police.

2. Will the victim report the crime?

Official statistics can only reflect those crimes which are actually reported to, and recorded by, the police. However, the decision as to whether or not a crime should be reported is a complex one. A victim may feel that the incident is so trivial that it does not warrant reporting. The victim might also think that the circumstances of the offence make its reporting embarrassing. For example, a married man whose wallet is stolen while he is with a prostitute may be disinclined to report the offence to the police. Similarly, a husband who is regularly assaulted by his wife may be reluctant to report the matter to the police, perhaps fearing disbelief or even ridicule. Research suggests that assaults by women on their male partners are actually much more common than official figures would suggest (for example Straus and Gelles, 1990).

A drug dealer who has his stock stolen by a rival is also unlikely to draw this to the attention of the authorities. A bank which regularly 'loses' clients' funds through the criminal actions of unscrupulous employees may also be reluctant to report these matters to the authorities for fear of ruining confidence in the bank. The 1998 *BCS* suggests that for those crimes in which comparisons can be made, only 44 per cent became known to the police. In other words less than half of the crimes which victims admitted to (or could remember) having experienced were notified to the police.

Although we are focusing on victims specifically, we must also bear in mind that crimes might be reported by witnesses or bystanders. Many crimes are similar to other types of emergencies in which people may or may not choose to become involved. Social psychologists (for example Latané and Darley, 1968) have suggested that whether or not people do choose to intervene in such situations is not always a rational or logical decision. Kidd (1985) suggests that witnessing a crime creates emotional arousal, which in turn tends to produce unthinking, almost automatic, responses. Thus, if a witness is naturally impulsive, and a victim is screaming for help, the witness may well ignore any danger to themselves and jump in.

If a victim believes that the police will be unhelpful or unsympathetic, or be unlikely to catch the culprit, then again the crime may go unreported. The 1998 *BCS* suggests that almost three-quarters of incidents of vandalism are not reported to the police. On the other hand, if a victim's insurance company insists that all claims must be supported by evidence of reporting to the police, then this leads to an increased likelihood of reporting. Thus some 97 per cent of vehicle thefts and 85 per cent of 'burglary with loss' cases were reported to the police.

Because of the limitations of surveys such as the *BCS*, the overall level of under-reporting may be difficult to assess accurately. However, as we saw above, such figures suggest that less than half of all the crimes suffered by victims are actually reported to the police. There is though a great deal of variation according to the type of crime. Although, as we noted above, some 85 per cent of 'burglaries with loss' were reported, only 50 per cent of burglaries with no loss were reported. Similarly, although over 95 per cent of vehicle thefts were reported, only 43 per cent of thefts from vehicles and 37 per cent of attempted vehicle thefts were subsequently reported.

Whether or not a crime comes to be reported to the police may even be affected by the ease with which a victim can make contact with a police officer. Thus, the increased availability of public and household telephones will tend to make reporting easier. We should also be aware that putting more uniformed police officers onto the streets may paradoxically lead to an increase in the amount of crime reported. The victim who never sees a police officer from one month to the next will be less likely to bring minor crimes to the attention of the authorities. However, the householder who bumps into the local community constable almost every day may be much more inclined to report even minor incidents.

In general, the more serious a crime is, the more likely it is to be reported. However, this does not necessarily mean that all of the most serious crimes are reported. For example, serious assaults by one member of a family on another may go unreported. This might be because there is a belief that the issue is best handled privately, or because the victim fears reprisals. The 1998 *BCS* suggests that less than half of all woundings and only just over half of all robberies were actually reported to the police. As we saw with the recognition of a crime, attributions of responsibility may also affect the likelihood of reporting. Thus the date-rape victim who is persuaded that she should somehow bear some responsibility for what happened to her may choose not to report the matter for fear of condemnation or embarrassment. Such issues will be dealt with in more detail in Chapter two.

There is evidence to suggest that increases in the reporting of crimes in official figures are not necessarily mirrored by equivalent rises in surveys such as the *British Crime Survey*. To take one example, officially recorded figures showed that vandalism of private property increased by 100 per cent in the period from 1981 to 1991. However, the *BCS* showed no significant rise in the number of such offences during the same time period (Mirrlees-Black *et al.*, 1996: 19). By comparison, the *BCS*'s estimate of the increase in the number of acquisitive crimes in the same decade almost exactly mirrored the Home Office statistics. There are of course a large number of factors which will determine the likelihood of reporting, some of which have been discussed earlier. However, it is interesting to note that although official statistics showed a consistent yearly fall in recorded crime from 1991 to 1997, only in 1997 was this fall mirrored by a reported fall in the *BCS*.

A final point in respect of the reporting of crime concerns the fact that victimisation is not equally distributed among all members of society (Pease, 1998a). This aspect will be discussed more fully in Chapter two, but should be acknowledged here. For the young unemployed inner city resident, the experience of victimisation may be an almost daily occurrence and so may not result in a report to the police. However, for the affluent middle-aged rural dweller, crime victimisation would be a much rarer and distinctive experience which would be much more likely to be reported (Mirrlees-Black, 1998).

3. Will the police record the 'crime' as such?

In some cases, the police may not even attend the scene and the disappointed victim not bother to pursue the matter further. It would be naïve to assume that even if the police do attend, they will automatically record all reported incidents as crimes. Taking the example of the broken wing mirror above, the police may view this as a 'failing to stop' traffic accident, a pure accident, or as deliberate (but not necessarily 'criminal') damage. How it is recorded may be affected by a number of factors. For example, if the wing mirror is from an old Ford Escort and will cost only £10 to replace, it may not be recorded as 'criminal damage'. On the other hand, if the wing mirror is from a Ferrari F40 and the replacement cost considerably more, then the damage may indeed be recorded as 'criminal'. This anomaly in recording practices may not be easily understood or appreciated by the motorists concerned. To take another example, police officers called to a house in which a rear window has been broken may record this as a minor (i.e. non-notifiable) incident, as a case of criminal damage or as an attempted burglary.

A change in police recording practices may well account for some apparent increases and decreases in the recorded incidence of some offences. For example, police called to a domestic incident in which a woman has been the victim of a minor assault by her partner, may, until recently, have taken no action, and recorded the incident as 'no crime – parties advised'. However, due to a recent change in policy, British police officers would today be much more likely to record this as a crime and, perhaps, to arrest the perpetrator.

Interesting examples of how changes in recording can affect official crime rates can be found in most years' reports. If we look at the figures for England and Wales for the period April 1997 to March 1998 there are what appear to be some bizarre differences in the number of violent offences. Taking the figures for the whole of England and Wales, there is a five per cent recorded increase in offences of violence against the person compared to the previous twelve months. However, this overall trend hides a great deal of variation between different police force areas. Thus, while Essex showed a rise of almost four per cent, its neighbour, Kent, showed a fall of over seventeen per cent in the same twelve-month period (Povey and Prime, 1998: 14). However, two very large increases are found in the West Midlands and Greater Manchester where offences of violence against the person appeared to rise by 33.3 per cent and 49.4 per cent respectively. Such apparently dramatic rises may cause understandable concern for the residents of these areas, but if one reads further into these figures, the apparently large increase appears mainly to be accounted for by improved crime recording and auditing practices within the two forces (Povey and Prime, 1998: 9).

Pressure on the police to improve their efficiency may also mean that crimes which are easily detectable may be more likely to be recorded than those which are not. Therefore, a householder who reports that he saw someone who he recognised trying to break into his car may receive a more positive response from his local constable than would someone who has little idea as to who may have been responsible. During 1999, evidence came to light that some police forces in Britain may be deliberately under-recording crime so as to appear more efficient (*The Guardian*, 18 March 1999). It also emerged that some police officers routinely made visits to prisons during which they persuaded convicted offenders to admit to other offences. This was done on the promise that the offender would not be prosecuted further, but the arrangement made the police's clear-up rate appear to be better than it was. It was alleged that in some cases, detectives persuaded offenders to admit to large numbers of offences, at least some of which they had not committed. This helped the police to appear more efficient and suggested that they had 'solved' many more cases than they had.

Recording decisions do not just apply to trivial cases. A missing person case may be recorded simply as a missing person, or, even if no body is found, become the subject of a murder inquiry. The 1998 *BCS* estimates that, for those offence types in which direct comparisons can be made, only 54 per cent of reported crimes were actually recorded by the police. As with the reporting of crime, recording practices show wide variation according to the type of offence. Thus while almost 90 per cent of reported vehicle thefts are officially recorded, less than one-third of 'burglary with no loss' are.

Mirrlees-Black *et al.* (1998) do warn that we should not draw simplistic conclusions about these recording levels. They note that there is often difficulty in comparing like with like in terms of *BCS* categories and those used by the police. We should also be aware that police officers have some discretion in deciding whether or not to record a 'crime' as such. For example, the police may feel that an incident is so trivial that it does not warrant recording, or may view the victim's complaint as exaggerated or even malicious. There are a large number of factors which will impinge upon an individual police officer's decision as to whether or not to record the crime and whether or not to take action against an alleged perpetrator (for example Sykes *et al.* 1976; Stradling *et al.* 1990).

In the light of the Stephen Lawrence enquiry it now appears more likely that the police will take seriously, and investigate, many apparently racially motivated attacks. Such changes will undoubtedly lead to apparently large increases in the level of such crimes. Indeed the *Manchester Evening News Metro* (17 April 1999) carried a large front page headline announcing an 'Explosion in Racist Crime'. The article went on to announce that the number of racist incidents had 'almost doubled over the last twelve months'. Perhaps surprisingly, the local police community liaison officer is reported to have welcomed such a rise in the figures as it suggested that an awareness campaign was working and that people were now more willing to make such complaints. However, the banner headline announcing this apparent 'explosion in racist crime' may have done little to help people from ethnic minorities to feel more secure.

4. Will the offender be caught by the police?

It might be an obvious point, but the fact is that the majority of crimes are not solved by the police and the perpetrators remain at large. Statistics suggest that on average only a quarter of recorded offences are cleared up by the police. If one considers the under-reporting high-lighted by the *British Crime Survey*, then the 'real' clear-up rate may actually be only half of this. While the detection rate for crimes such as homicide may appear encouragingly high (it is currently running at over 90 per cent), the rate for crimes such as stealing from vehicles is signifi-cantly lower. There are of course a very large number of factors which will affect the likelihood that an offender will actually be caught, not least of which is the number of resources which the police deploy towards the solving of the offence (Ainsworth, 1995a). We must also be aware of the fact that police officers do have some discretion in their actions and may choose not to pursue a case even if a crime has been committed and an offender identified (Ainsworth, 1995a: 13). We should also note that some types of crime are extremely common, yet rarely result in arrest. For example, Belson (1975) found that 70 per cent of 15–16 year olds had at some point stolen from shops, yet the majority of these had not been arrested.

5. Will the offender be prosecuted?

Once again it would be naïve to assume that all those arrested for a crime will automatically appear before the courts. Figures suggest that of the 25 per cent of officially recorded crimes which are cleared up, less than half result in a person being charged or summoned to appear in court. Of the remaining solved crimes, twelve per cent result in a caution, a further twelve per cent are 'taken into consideration' and, in over 30 per cent of cases, no further action is taken. Many minor offenders are also given fixed penalty notices which remove the need to appear in court.

There are a large number of factors which will impinge upon prosecu-tion decisions. Perhaps the most important criterion will be the seriousness of the offence. Society might reasonably expect that the police will use some discretion when considering whether to prosecute for trivial offences. However, the public might also presume that almost all those who commit the most serious crimes will be prosecuted. A sec-ond consideration may be the strength of the evidence against an accused. In England and Wales, up until the 1980s, it was the police themselves who decided which cases to prosecute and which to drop. However such decisions are now taken by the Crown Prosecution Service (CPS). To the possible frustration of the police officers involved in a case, the CPS may decide that the likelihood of a conviction is quite low and so will decide not to proceed with the case.

6. Will the perpetrator be found guilty if he/she has actually committed the offence?

While no justice system is perfect, there may be an expectation that the guilty will be found guilty and the innocent be acquitted. However, this is a rather simplistic notion which belies the complexity of judicial decision making (see Chapters 7 and 9). The reality is that miscarriages of justice do occur, and some of those who have committed the crime of which they are accused are deemed to be innocent by the court (for example Arce *et al.*, 1995; Fitzmaurice *et al.*, 1995).

7. Will the perpetrator receive an appropriate sentence?

There will often be disagreements about what an 'appropriate' sentence might be. What the victim considers appropriate may be at odds with the view held by the perpetrator and perhaps the judge. Those charged with sentencing the guilty will need to consider a large number of factors in reaching an appropriate decision (see Chapter 7). However, it is interesting to note that in 1997 some 93,100 people were given an immediate custodial sentence. This figure may appear worryingly high, especially when compared to the 1996 figure (84,600) and the 1990 figure (58,100). However, when one considers that there were almost 4.5 million officially recorded crimes in 1997 the numbers may not appear quite so disturbing. We will say much more about sentencing in Chapter 7, though we should note at this point that a casual glance at officially recorded sentencing decisions may fail to uncover what is often a complex web of legal and political decision making.

Official and other measures of crime

We can see that the path from the commission of a crime to the punishing of an offender is a long, complex and tortuous one. Barclay (1993) and Ashworth (1997) have suggested that only two per cent of crimes actually result in an offender being convicted and sentenced in court. There are, however, differences between different types of crime. For example, Barclay notes that in the case of woundings, fourteen per cent of offences result in a caution or conviction, whereas in the case of vandalism, only one in a hundred offences reach this stage. The statistics contained within annual reports can only hint at the actual level of crime experienced by victims. For this reason, researchers have often looked at alternative methods of discovering the true level of crime. Such methods include the *British Crime Survey* highlighted above. As was noted earlier, such surveys suggest consistently that the actual level of crime in any community is significantly higher than that which official figures would lead us to believe. There is a large so-called 'dark figure' of unreported or unrecorded crime which is missed by official crime statistics.

Household surveys such as the *BCS* can be extremely useful, though they are not without their own problems. For example, they are not very good at identifying crimes where there is no obvious victim. In addition, by concentrating mainly on domestic households, they fail to pick up much corporate fraud and business crime. A further criticism of such surveys is that they tend to have a predominantly 'events' orientation (Skogan, 1981). This begs the question as to whether all crimes are so easily quantified. A householder may have little difficulty in recalling that his car was vandalised twice and his house broken into once over the previous twelve months. However, it may not be quite so easy to obtain an accurate picture of, for example, the number of domestic assaults within a household over a year. In some cases, such assaults may be part of a regular and routine pattern which makes quantification difficult (Genn, 1988; Dobash *et al.*, 1999). It might also be the case that domestic assaults are not reported to researchers for another reason – the perpetrator may be in the same room as the victim and his threatening presence may intimidate the interviewee.

A related problem concerns the meaning which the 'crime' has for the individual. A heavy drinker who gets into, but loses, a fight every Saturday night may not report having been the victim of an assault 52 times over the previous year. Rather, the 'victim' may perceive this as normal and an almost essential element of a 'good night out'. Similarly, a victim's perception of a crime may be 'Oh well, it was my own stupid fault; I really should have been more careful'. Such a victim may choose not to report a crime perhaps partly through a fear of embarrassment.

Although we must acknowledge that household victim surveys have their own problems and limitations, for certain types of crime they are likely to give a more accurate and realistic picture than official figures. The danger is that politicians, the public and the police may respond to the official figures (with all their in-built inaccuracies) rather than relying upon more appropriate and locally relevant information (Crawford, 1998: 167).

Both sets of figures, especially when taken together, may be useful when considering trends and changes in crime rates. Throughout the 1980s, both the official figures and the *BCS* figures showed a yearly rise in crime in England and Wales. However, from 1991 to 1996, there was a divergence between the two measures. Specifically, the *BCS* showed crime still rising, while the official figures showed a yearly fall in recorded crime. In 1997 both measures coincided in showing a fall in the overall level of crime. For the *BCS* this was the first time that an overall fall had been recorded. Although the decrease in recorded crime was fairly consistent across different offence types there was one notable exception. In the case of woundings, the official figures showed an eighteen per cent increase in such offences while the *BCS* recorded a seventeen per cent decrease. This curious finding has two possible explanations. Firstly, the fact that wounding is a fairly uncommon crime means that possible sampling errors may be magnified. Secondly, it is suggested that the eighteen per cent increase in official statistics may be in part due to a change in the police's attitude to domestic violence and to a change in crime categorisation (Mirrlees-Black *et al.*, 1998: 25).

A closer look at crime categories

We have highlighted a number of areas in which a simple glance at official crime figures may be somewhat misleading in presenting a picture of the true level of crime. However, it is also worth looking at some categories of crime in a little more detail. Let us consider the official recorded levels of homicide in recent years (Home Office, 1998). According to Home Office figures, some 739 homicides occurred in England and Wales in 1997. This compares with 726 in 1994, 745 in 1995 and 679 in 1996. Thus, although the numbers of homicides rose by nine per cent in 1997 (when compared to 1996) the figure is very similar to the rates in 1994 and 1995.

Homicide is clearly the most serious of all crimes and the casual observer might presume that the majority of these offences involved attacks by strangers, particularly on females out alone late at night. However, in reality, approximately two-thirds of homicides involve the killing of a victim by a partner, relative, friend or acquaintance. This may partly explain why the clear-up rate for these crimes is particularly high – the police do not need to look very far in order to solve the majority of murders. Of the 739 homicides committed in 1997, two-thirds involved male victims and one-third female. In the case of male victims the attacker was already known to the victim in more than half of the cases but for female victims, the attacker knew the victim in almost 80 per cent of all cases. (These figures are of course based on those crimes for which an assailant had been identified.)

These sex differences are interesting with regard to fear of crime. Females will tend to be the most fearful of suffering an attack at the hands of a stranger and will take precautions to try to minimise the risk. However, the figures suggest that not only are their chances of victimisation less than those of men, but they are twice as likely to die at the hands of someone they know rather than at the hands of a stranger. The other surprising figure concerns the age of homicide victims. If you were asked to guess which age group was most at risk of becoming a homicide victim, you might suggest older people or perhaps teenagers. However, in reality, those most as risk are children under twelve months old with a victimisation rate of 57 per million. A number of these homicides (three in 1997) are officially recorded as infanticide. This refers to cases in which a mother kills her own recently-born child, while perhaps suffering from hormonal disturbance or postnatal depression. Although the killing of a baby by its mother is certainly a horrendous crime, it is a world apart from the more traditional type of homicide which might spring to mind.

Other crimes involving violence also show some interesting and perhaps surprising trends. For example, the 1998 *BCS* records that since 1981 the number of cases of acquaintance violence had risen by 89 per cent and those for domestic violence by 187 per cent. However, over the same period, the reported level of stranger violence has fallen by almost twenty per cent. The authors of the *BCS* do admit that the figures for such crimes are prone to sampling errors and that crime surveys may measure violent crime less accurately than property crime. Further, it is acknowledged that the level of reporting of certain types of incident to the *BCS* researchers may vary over time. Thus, in the late 1990s, the climate is such that victims of domestic violence may be more likely to admit to such victimisation. Nevertheless, the fact that the reporting of acquaintance violence has risen much more sharply than stranger violence since 1981 would not be obvious from a casual glance at the crime figures.

Crimes categorised as 'violence against the person' in the official crime figures contain many crimes which we might expect to find, but some which we might not. For example, along with assaults of varying degrees of severity are crimes such as 'abandoning a child under two years of age'. The category also includes offences such as 'causing death by dangerous driving' and 'causing death by careless driving while over the prescribed blood/alcohol limit'. Any act which results in the killing of another is clearly very serious. However, offences such as these may not be at the front of people's minds when thinking about violence against the person.

It should also be remembered that as society changes its attitudes towards certain crimes they may be more likely to be officially recorded by the police. Earlier we drew attention to the fact that the police are now much more likely to record domestic violence as a crime than was the case only ten years ago. In the past, the police explained their reluctance to prosecute perpetrators of domestic violence by reference to the fact that victims often withdrew their complaint once things had calmed down. However, in an interesting change of tactic, the police (especially in the USA) may today still pursue a prosecution in such cases and rely on photographic and other evidence in order to achieve a conviction.

Crimes such as domestic violence thus achieve a higher profile from time to time and so are more likely to be reported and recorded. In the 1970s it was not domestic violence but muggings which became the focus of a great deal of public attention. However, it has been argued that this 'crisis' was in fact grossly exaggerated and led to an over-reaction or 'moral panic' by the police and other agencies (Hall *et al.*, 1978). In the late 1990s attention was being focused on cruelty towards animals. In the past, such incidents were often investigated and occasionally prosecuted by organisations such as the RSPCA. However, as society becomes more concerned about cruelty to animals, so more prosecutions are likely to follow. The fact that some believe that youths who injure or even kill animals today will injure or kill humans tomorrow may also increase the likelihood of early intervention and prosecution.

Levels of crime and fear of crime

If asked, most members of the public might well claim to have a fairly accurate picture of the current crime rate in their area. However, one might wish to question whether these estimates are likely to be accurate. There is certainly evidence to suggest that, in many cases, fear of crime does not necessarily correlate with the actual risk. For example, one survey in Japan found that over 50 per cent of residents expressed a fear of being the victim of burglary, despite the fact that the likelihood of them actually becoming a victim was less than one per cent (Ito, 1993).

One curious, but often reported, finding is that those who are the least likely to become victims of crime appear to be the most fearful. Conversely, those who express the least fear of being victimised may actually be the most vulnerable. Thus, in relation to personal assault, elderly women are often reported to be the most fearful, yet least vulnerable, members of society. Paradoxically, young men, who are statistically much more likely to become victims of violence, often express the least fear. The 1998 *BCS* found that although men aged 16–24 made up only five per cent of the sample, they experienced 25 per cent of the total amount of reported violence. Thus, twenty per cent (or one in five) of those in this age group reported being a victim of violence on at least one occasion over the previous year. By comparison, for women over 75, the reported level of victimisation was 0.2 per cent or one in 500.

The finding in relation to older people's fears may, however, be more likely to be found in Western cultures. For example, Ito (1993) cites some studies which show that in Japan the fear of victimisation actually declines with increasing age. Further, it is reported that, unlike in many Western cultures, the level of fear is much more in line with the actual risk of victimisation.

In the UK, the fear of being attacked by a stranger, especially when out late at night, means that many people may simply avoid exposing themselves to such a perceived danger. However, this notion of the majority of people being 'prisoners in their own homes' may be more of a media construction than a reflection of reality. It is interesting to note that in the 1996 *BCS* some eleven per cent of women and five per cent of men said that they never went out after dark. However, this reluctance to venture out was only partly explained by a fear of crime victimisation.

Further, people tend to presume that the risk to themselves is now greater than was the case a decade or so earlier (Mayhew *et al.*, 1994). As Mirrlees-Black *et al.* (1996) note:

> The BCS has always indicated that a majority feel that crime has increased in their area when asked to consider 'the last two years'. They are more likely to be making a value judgement than one based on firm facts and it would not be surprising if they had got used to the dominant media message of 'ever rising crime'.
>
> (1996: 49).

Despite the fact that recorded crime levels between 1994 and 1996 had fallen, 55 per cent of those surveyed in the 1996 *BCS* thought that crime **in their area** had increased 'a little' or 'a lot' during this time. Only ten per cent thought that it had fallen during this period. This may point to actual differences between local and national trends, or, perhaps more likely, be a result of biased media reporting.

Despite the fact that the national recorded crime rate actually fell between 1994 and 1996, three-quarters of those interviewed for the 1996 *British Crime Survey* said that they thought that the rate had actually increased. Among these, the majority thought that the increase had been a large one. Only four per cent correctly reported that the crime rate had actually fallen (Mirrlees-Black *et al.*, 1996: 57).

As has been highlighted elsewhere, it is not easy to calm crime fears once an expectation or anxiety has been built up (Ainsworth, 1995a: ch. 11). It would be a brave police officer who went on television and announced that 'as a result of the recent drop in crime figures I am here to tell you that it is now safe to walk the streets at night'. Far more likely is the standard police advice following a crime that 'members of the public should take extra care until this dangerous villain is apprehended'.

One problem with the public's perception of crime rates is that most people do not read official crime statistics, nor victim surveys carried out by academics. Most people's assessment of the level of threat to their own well-being or their property is gathered not from a careful sifting of all available evidence, but rather from the mass media and from rumour, gossip, embellished stories or urban myths. If the media merely reported crime trends accurately and objectively, the public's assessment of their vulnerability might be more accurate. However, the media tend not to highlight trends or levels of risk, but rather to focus on the exceptional, the bizarre and the horrific (Sparks, 1992; Howitt, 1998). One is unlikely ever to read the following in a newspaper: 'Of the 56 million people resident in Great Britain last year, 55.999m were NOT murdered'. The reality is that serious crimes such as murder are still extremely uncommon in Britain. Further, as was noted above, the vast majority of murders are not attacks by strangers, but rather result from arguments between people who are already acquainted. However, for obvious reasons, the media will tend to highlight those more sensational crimes which do stand out and grab the public's attention (Howitt, 1998).

The killing of the toddler James Bulger by two young boys in Liverpool was a despicable crime which shocked the public. It was the lead story on television news reports and in national newspapers for many days. Large numbers of parents became ever more vigilant in the days following the killing, understandably trying to ensure that the same thing could not happen again. However, the James Bulger murder was highly unusual, if not unique. The abduction and murder of a toddler by young boys is (thankfully) extremely rare in Britain. The reason that the media maintained such a high level of interest in the story was that it was so unusual and thus shocking. One high profile case can produce a massive amount of fear and result in an increase in protective (and hopefully preventive) behaviour by a large number of people (Ainsworth, 1995a: 207). By contrast, a slight fall in the annual level of recorded crime will receive scant attention from the media and result in little change in people's behaviour.

Crimes portrayed in television dramas do not tend to reflect reality, but rather concentrate on infrequent crimes such as random attacks on strangers (Gerbner *et al.*, 1977). By coincidence, the April 1997 to March 1998 crime figures were released on the day that the current author was writing this chapter. The lunchtime edition of *Sky News* (13 October 1998) chose to report on the crime figures and did mention briefly the fact that the figures showed a fall overall. However, their subsequent story concentrated on the supposed increase in the amount of violent crime. The report focused on one unfortunate individual who had been robbed a number of times in the last few years and who now 'was scared to go out after dark'. Such stories and images may make powerful television, but they will do little to reinforce the message that overall crime rates were actually falling as we approached the millennium.

Sparks (1992) notes that although the public's anxiety about crime is not a new phenomenon, the media's current preoccupation with criminal matters appeals to many people's fears. There is a well-rehearsed argument which the media tend to use when challenged about such often sensational coverage. The media's defence is that they are merely 'giving the public what they want'. It is argued that people are already very interested in crime and the media are merely reflecting this interest in their coverage. However, there is little doubt that crime stories are often used as a way of capturing television audiences and newspaper readers. Cumberbatch (1989) estimated that although the majority of people living in low crime areas will not become victims of crime, in any one year each will be exposed to some 7,000 crimes via the media. Howitt (1998) expresses this point eloquently when he says:

> Television, newspapers, cinema and radio teach us to fear things alien – crime,
> drugs, violence – which our culture normatively rejects. Crime threatens our
> culture and ways of living, so the media ought to encourage our fear of crime.
>
> (1998: 45)

Gunter (1987) makes an interesting point with respect to television and fear of crime. He notes that those who fear crime might be encouraged to avoid potential victimisation by staying at home and locking themselves in. However, in doing so, they are likely to watch more television which shows more crime stories. The fear of crime is thus reinforced and the likelihood of their venturing out in future is reduced still further. It should also be borne in mind that, despite what the media tell us, the home is not the safe haven which might be presumed. In most years, far more killings occur within the home than in dark, deserted streets. As was noted earlier, one is far more likely to fall victim to an assault at the hands of a relative, partner or close friend than at the hands of a complete stranger. If one looks at the figures for rape it is perhaps surprising to learn that, according to official figures, only about one-third of such crimes are committed by men who did not already know their victim. Further, almost 40 per cent of such attacks were carried out by men described by their victims as 'intimate friends' (Barclay, 1993).

If we accept that the media is to some extent responsible for cultivating the fear of crime, then it might be reasonable to expect that those who watch the most television will be the most fearful. However, as Howitt (1998) notes, the relationship is by no means as straightforward as might be presumed. Howitt notes that although Gerbner's research (Gerbner, *et al.*, 1977, 1980) did find some association between heavy viewing and fear of victimisation, the size of the effect was very small. After controlling for relevant variables, Howitt suggests that less than half of one per cent of the variance in people's tendency to see the world as 'mean and violent' was accounted for by their viewing habits.

It would, therefore, appear that the so-called cultivation hypothesis is not as clearcut an explanation for crime fear as might have been supposed. One obvious consideration is whether those who watch more television overall do actually watch more crime programmes. Some research has tended to presume that an increase in overall viewing time will lead to an automatic increase in the number of hours spent watching crime-related programmes. However, this is not necessarily the case. The advent of the remote control has made it now much less likely that people will switch on one channel and watch its entire evening's programmes. The increase in satellite, cable and now digital television has added considerably to viewer choice. Those who do not wish to watch any crime-related programmes can achieve this relatively easily. Conversely, those who do wish to view a steady diet of such material will have little difficulty in finding a full evening's entertainment.

Howitt draws attention to a further important intervening variable, i.e.

locus of control. This is a personality dimension along which people vary. At one extreme are those who believe that they have almost complete control of their own destiny, while at the other are those who believe that the outcome of their lives is completely controlled by other people, or by fate. Between these two extremes will be those who believe that they have some degree of control. It has been found that the locus of control dimension is a crucial intervening variable between the viewing of crime programmes on television and subsequent fear of crime. If this personality variable is controlled for statistically, then the correlation identified by Gerbner *et al.* disappears. We will say more about locus of control in the next chapter.

There is little doubt that the media will in the future continue to focus on crime and have an effect on crime fears. The debate about the apparent paradox between actual levels of crime and the fear of victimisation will also no doubt continue to fascinate academic criminologists for the foreseeable future. Although for many years, governments and police forces have seen crime reduction as a major goal, it is now acknowledged that a reduction in the public's fear of crime should also be an important priority. How this might be achieved in the light of the power of the media and its apparent preoccupation with serious crime is, however, not always clear.

We have seen in this chapter that crime fear is not directly proportional to local or national levels of crime. Reducing the public's fear of crime is thus seen as a related, but not identical, task to reducing actual levels of crime (Home Office, 1989a). We will see in the next chapter that although the experience of victimisation can have serious psychological consequences, there is not necessarily a simple or direct correlation between victimisation experience and fear of future victimisation.

Summary

Crime is a subject of great fascination for many members of society, and will no doubt remain so for the foreseeable future. However, this chapter has shown that measuring crime levels in society is no simple task. There are a large number of important variables which will affect the figures which are published each year. As we have seen in this chapter there are many stages at which 'crimes' can fall out of the official figures. Although annual changes in recorded crime tell us something about the rise and fall of crime rates, they may also be telling us something about alterations in reporting and recording practices. While acknowledging that victim surveys such as the *BCS* are far from perfect, they do offer some valuable additional insights into crime levels and crime reporting.

We have also seen in this chapter that the media play an important role in determining the public's perception of crime. The fear of victimisation produces very real anxieties for many people and can affect their whole life. However, most people's fear is not based upon a careful assessment of the actual level of risk, but rather on impressions gleaned from the media – a media which invariably concentrates on the sensational and more unusual crimes.

Chapter 2

The psychology of victimisation

It was suggested in the previous chapter that society appears to be pre-occupied with crime and punishment. However, much of the media's coverage tends to concentrate on the more 'glamorous' aspects of crime including the police investigation and the trial. Many recent commentators have remarked on the fact that victims appear to be the forgotten party in the criminal justice process (for example Zedner, 1997). While many resources are directed towards to the police, the courts, and the offender, hardly any are set aside to deal with the victim's needs. Although Victim Support Schemes are now fairly widespread, they operate with very small budgets and rely heavily on work done by unpaid volunteers. Nevertheless, almost every crime has a victim and in this chapter we will start to consider some aspects of victimisation. We will discuss why some sections of society appear to be victimised more than others and consider why repeat victimisation occurs with such alarming frequency. We will also look at the psychological effects of victimisation and consider whether reactions can be seen as a form of post traumatic stress disorder.

Levels of victimisation

In Chapter one we considered crime fears and suggested that people's anxiety is not necessarily directly proportional to the actual level of risk. According to the 1998 *British Crime Survey* (which reports on victimisation in 1997) 34 per cent of the population would have been the victim of one or more crimes over the previous year. Thus, in 1997 one-third of residents would have been victims while two-thirds would not. A naïve interpretation of such figures might be that once every three years, everyone in the country could expect to become a victim. However, such a simplistic suggestion would be misleading. It is essential that we bear in mind two important points.

Firstly, although the figures suggest that the chances of some form of crime victimisation are quite high, the majority of the crimes to which people do fall victim will not be of a serious nature. Thus, as we saw in Chapter one, one reason why the *BCS* consistently reports higher levels of crime than do the official statistics is that many trivial crimes are either not reported or not recorded.

Secondly, we should be aware at the outset that victimisation is not distributed equally among the population – some people experience considerably more than the average, while others suffer much less. One study (Farrell, 1995) suggested that the most victimised two or three per cent of the population report between a quarter and a third of all crime incidents. We will deal firstly with crime seriousness.

The fact that in Britain in the late 1990s, one in three people became a crime victim each year may appear worrying. However, as we saw in the previous chapter, we need to look further to make sense of such figures. Many people's fear of crime will be centred around a dread of becoming a victim of violence, especially at the hands of a stranger. However, recent *BCS* figures suggest that there is approximately four times as much crime against private property as violent crime. While some crimes against property will be distressing, many will have a less severe impact on the individual than will the experience of personal violence. In 1997 in England and Wales, the average chance of experiencing violence was less than five per cent. But even this average can be misleading for, as we will see later, some groups are much less at risk than this average might suggest. We should also bear in mind that 'violence' covers a wide range of behaviour – almost two-thirds of the recorded incidents of violence were 'common assaults' in which there was no serious physical injury.

If we consider crimes against property, then again we may be surprised by a breakdown of the figures. For many people, burglary is the most feared property crime. Not only is the theft of property from one's home distressing, but the invasion of one's own secure base by an unknown burglar can lead to quite severe psychological consequences. It might then be somewhat comforting to learn that in England and Wales in 1997 only 5.6 per cent of residential households experienced a burglary or attempted burglary. This compares with the average chance of experiencing a vehicle-related theft which was 15.7 per cent. It would thus appear that although there is a one in three chance of victimisation in a given year, the average chance of becoming a victim of the more serious type of crime is nearer one in twenty.

Such averages may however tell us relatively little about a given individual's actual level of risk. As was noted earlier, while some people appear to go through life almost completely untroubled by crime, others are much less fortunate. The naïve might assume that whether or not one becomes a crime victim is almost entirely a matter of chance. Alternatively, one might believe that, providing one takes reasonable precautions, one will never become a victim. The evidence would suggest that both of these beliefs may be myths.

It is important to make one distinction in relation to victimisation statistics, i.e. that between the *incidence* of victimisation and the *prevalence* of victimisation. Incidence refers to the average crime rate across the whole population, while prevalence refers to the percentage of the population who actually experience one or more crimes. Figures which concentrate on incidence may not be particularly helpful, as many people are not 'average'. As we will see below, victimisation tends to be concentrated among relatively small sub-groups of the population, meaning that those outside these groups have a considerably lower risk of victimisation. The 'average' figure is thus an average drawn from quite wide extremes – many individuals' risk is much greater than the average while many others' is significantly lower.

Factors in victimisation

Surveys such as the *BCS* have been able to identify which individuals are most likely to be victimised. Further, it has been possible to show that there are differences in the type of crime to which different individuals are likely to fall victim.

Perhaps the most obvious risk factor is geographical location. Certain districts have established reputations for being dangerous places in which to live. When insurance companies are assessing the level of risk (and thus what premium to charge) one of the first considerations will be the postcode of the address where the person lives. Some applicants may find that their premiums are so high, or the exclusions so extensive, that it is hardly worth insuring their property. In extreme cases, people may find it all but impossible to get any kind of insurance cover.

Although location is an important risk factor, it actually covers a number of dimensions. For example the 1998 *BCS* established that the following were important location variables associated with increased risk:

- if the address was in an inner city area;
- if it was on a council estate;
- if it was in an area with more physical disorder;
- if it was on a main or side road (as opposed to a cul-de-sac);
- if it was in the north of England.

But area and type of residence is only one factor which affects victimisation rates. A number of others have also been identified, some of which may be quite obvious, but some of which may not. Thus for crimes such as burglary, other significant variables include:

- the age of the head of the household;
- whether it is a single parent household;

- whether the head of the household is unemployed or on a low income;
- whether the home is rented;
- the type of property (flats and end-terraced are the most vulnerable);
- whether the home is left empty for long periods during the day.

Although these factors are identified individually, it must be acknowledged that many of them overlap. Thus, younger people may be more likely to be unemployed or to be on a low income and to live in rented accommodation in an inner city area. However if we combine two of the more important risk factors, then some large differences in the risk of victimisation are found. For young households in inner city areas the risk of burglary victimisation is almost twenty per cent. However, for older households in rural areas, the risk is only 2.3 per cent.

If we consider vehicle-related thefts, then almost all of the same risk factors identified in respect of burglary appear to be important, with one exception. In the case of burglary risk, the chances of victimisation are highest for those on the lowest incomes. When we look at vehicle related thefts, the reverse is true, i.e. higher income households are more likely to become victims. The *BCS*'s authors suggest that there are a number of possible explanations for this apparent anomaly.

Firstly, higher income households are more likely to possess more than one vehicle and so the chances of being victimised are increased. Secondly, the affluent may own more expensive vehicles which may be more attractive targets for thieves. A third explanation is that affluent vehicle owners tend to be more mobile and so are more likely to leave their vehicles in high risk locations such as public car parks. As we saw with burglary, the chances of any household suffering a vehicle related theft are much higher when certain risk factors are combined. Thus, for older households in rural areas the chances of victimisation are just under six per cent. However, for young households in an inner city area the chances are almost five times as high at 27.3 per cent.

When we start to consider violent crimes, some interesting trends emerge. Earlier we noted that the average risk of becoming a victim of violence in Britain in the 1990s was just under five per cent but that this figure hides large variations in vulnerability. Some of the relevant factors are similar to those identified in respect of burglary and vehicle-related crime, while others are new. Personal factors which increased the risk of becoming a victim of violence were:

- if the person was young and/or single;
- if the person was a single parent;
- if the person was unemployed or on a low income;
- if the person lived in rented accommodation;
- if the person lived in a flat or terraced property;
- if the person went out quite often.

Although younger people in general were more likely to become victims than were the elderly, young men were almost twice as likely to suffer violence as were young women.

We should again be aware of the fact that many of the risk factors are interrelated. Nevertheless there are some very large differences in risk especially when the more important risk factors are combined. Thus, for older adults living in rural areas, the chances of victimisation are less than one per cent. However for younger adults living in inner cities, the chances of becoming a victim of violence were over twenty per cent. Other large differences emerge when we compare owner-occupiers living in rural areas with private renters in inner cities. For the former, the chances of victimisation were less than two per cent whereas for the latter they were almost nineteen per cent.

We must again stress that the risk of victimisation is by no means spread evenly among the population. Many people may believe that whether or not they personally become a victim is largely down to luck, but this appears not to be the case. The fact that a large proportion of recorded crime happens to a fairly small percentage of the population would suggest that luck has little to do with it.

Feelings of control and belief in a just world

While some people may believe that victimisation may be simply a question of bad luck, others may take the opposite view. Some will believe that, providing they take reasonable precautions, they can avoid ever becoming a victim. A relevant factor here is a personality dimension called *locus of control* (Rotter, 1966). This refers to the extent to which an individual feels in control of his or her own destiny. Some people may believe that they are completely in control, while others may feel that they are always pushed or pulled by forces outside their control. Many people will of course fall in between these two extremes and some groups (e.g. children and the mentally ill) will have virtually no control.

We will say more about this later in the chapter, but for now we should bear in mind that victimisation will not affect everyone in the same way – a person who believes that becoming a victim is 'almost inevitable' may be less traumatised by victimisation than will a person who believes that they did everything possible to avoid it happening to them. The reality is that while we can reduce the likelihood of becoming a victim by taking reasonable precautions, it may be all but impossible to eliminate completely the possibility of some form of victimisation.

A related point concerns how other people come to view victims. Although many people will feel sympathy for a victim, there may be a tendency to believe that the victim was at least partly responsible for their own victimisation. This is an interesting psychological phenomenon partly explained by reference to the so-called *just-world hypothesis* (Lerner

1970; Lerner and Meindl, 1981). This hypothesis is concerned with the extent to which people see the world as a just and fair place in which individuals 'get what they deserve' and in which general equity prevails. Those who strongly believe that the world is a just place will find it hard to accept that a victim became a victim for no good reason (Lupfer *et al.*, 1998). There will be a tendency to look for factors within the victim which may have contributed to their victimisation.

One reason why people may adopt this stance is that by doing so they feel less vulnerable themselves. If people believe that the world is generally fair and just, then that means that they can, to some extent, control the outcome of events. They may be heard to say 'If I am good all my life, nothing bad will befall me'. If people can convince themselves that another person became a victim because they behaved carelessly or stupidly, then they may not feel vulnerable themselves – providing that they do not behave in the same way of course. This inclination can be seen in many areas but is perhaps best illustrated by the tendency for some jurors to believe that, in certain circumstances, a rape victim should bear some responsibility for what happened to her (Howard, 1984). It might be suggested that some aspects of her behaviour contributed to her victimisation and that to some extent she should accept some responsibility for what happened (Stephenson, 1992, ch. 6). Rubin and Peplau (1975) found that the strength of belief in a just world varies between individuals. It tends to be strongest in those with little formal education and among those who have strong attachments to institutionalised religion.

Attributions about victimisation

Attribution theory may also offer some insights into this victim-blaming tendency. Attribution theory is concerned with the explanations which people offer for others' (and their own) behaviour (Heider, 1958). Among other findings, attribution theory has demonstrated that, when viewing others' behaviour, people tend to over-emphasise the role of internal (or so-called dispositional) factors and to under-emphasise the role of external (or situational) factors (Schneider, 1995). Thus, if we observe a man tripping in the street, we will tend to blame the person himself for the behaviour – he must just be a clumsy person. So pervasive is this tendency to assign inappropriately others' behaviour to internal factors that it was labelled the *fundamental attribution error* by Ross (1977). Thus, in terms of viewing the victimisation of others, attribution theory would predict that people would tend to assume that the blame lies (at least partially) with the individual. 'Well what do you expect if you walk home on your own late at night' might be a typical response when hearing of a person having been mugged. Such a response will of course do little to comfort the unfortunate victim.

Contrasting with this inclination to look for internal factors to explain others' behaviour is a tendency to look for external factors in explaining our own misfortune. While we may tend to put some of the blame onto other victims themselves, this may not be the case with our own victimisation. If we became the unfortunate victim of the late night mugger, we would seek to explain our misfortune by reference to external factors. A typical response might be 'Well I was just unlucky that night – if only the taxi had turned up, or my friends hadn't left me, or the police had been in the area, it wouldn't have happened'.

Repeat victimisation

Many of the figures quoted from the *BCS* relate to the percentage of people who have experienced one or more crimes over the previous years. However, for some people, victimisation is not a one-off event but rather indicative of an ongoing problem. Of all the findings reported by criminologists in recent years, those relating to repeat victimisation have been perhaps the most illuminating. Before proceeding any further, the reader may wish to consider the following question. If you were asked to identify the variable(s) which would best predict an individual's possible future victimisation, which would you name? Having seen already in this chapter some of the factors associated with victimisation, the answer may come as a surprise. Professor Ken Pease from the University of Huddersfield has been at the forefront of research on repeat victimisation. He states:

> Victimisation tends to recur to such an extent that prior victimisation is usable
> as a predictor for later crime … It is arguably the best single variable predictor
> routinely available to the police in the absence of specific intelligence. Even if
> sophisticated analysis of more extensive demographic and other information
> is available, prior victimisation has so far been found to survive as the best
> predictor.

> (1996: 3)

Repeat victimisation is thus such a well-established phenomenon that in many cases it is the most reliable indicator of whether or not a person will become a victim in the future. Although, as we saw earlier, there are a large number of geographical, demographic and personal factors which make victimisation more (or less) likely, previous victimisation often emerges as the best single predictor.

Figures suggest that a mere four per cent of the population suffer approximately 44 per cent of all the crime recorded (Farrell and Pease, 1993). We should however note that this does vary by offence type and location. It should also be borne in mind that repeat victimisation tends to be concentrated around similar types of crime. In other words burglary victims may have a significantly increased risk of becoming burglary victims for a second time, but may run only a slightly increased risk of being personally assaulted (Ellingworth, Tseloni and Pease, 1997).

Burglary and repeat victimisation

If we think about repeat victimisation carefully then we may be able to see why it occurs. Taking burglary as an example, it is certainly not the case that all homes are equally vulnerable. If one particular house appears to be an easy and attractive target to a burglar, then it may well be selected on more than one occasion. Some writers have referred to this as the *flag* explanation for repeat victimisation. Flag accounts argue that repeat victimisation results from an enduring level of risk – the same house is selected simply because it appears to be a 'soft' target and this vulnerability is enduring.

In some cases, the same burglar may return, or in others a second perpetrator may label the house as a suitable target and break in. Interviews conducted with convicted burglars suggest that there are certain common features which make some houses more attractive to burglars than others (Bennett and Wright, 1984; Bennett, 1995). However, it is also likely that burglars will select a certain target simply because it is a 'known quantity', i.e. they have been in there before.

There are then at least three possible explanations for why repeat domestic burglaries might occur. Firstly, the same offender may simply return to the victimised house at a future date in order to steal more property from what was perceived to be an easy target. Secondly, the burglar may talk about his crime to other criminal associates, who may then select the same 'easy' target. Thirdly, repeats may be unconnected in that they are committed by different perpetrators who are unaware of previous victimisations. This was referred to earlier as the flag explanation – repeat offences take place simply because of the house's obvious and continuing vulnerability.

It would be useful to know which of these three explanations is the most accurate, not least because it would help in planning crime prevention strategies. Unfortunately, it is not yet possible to give definitive answers (Pease, 1998a: 12). The evidence that has been accumulated suggests that the first explanation carries most weight.

Pease (1998a) points out that:

> ... at least some rv occurs because the first offence against a target educates an offender in ways which *boost* the risk of rv, by making it easier, more attractive or more profitable ... a first offence alters offender perceptions of the target ... Thus crime *boosts* the probability of repetition.
>
> (1998a: 12)

Thus if a burglar finds that his selected target is very easy to enter, or that the house has a great deal of valuable property, then he is likely to return. The fact that he was not caught while committing the original burglary may also lead him to believe that he is safer to re-enter this house rather than select a new target which may present unanticipated difficulties. On the first visit a burglar may steal only those items which can be concealed on his person. However, having had a good look around, a burglar may then return with a vehicle at a later date and steal a large number of bulkier items.

Burglars will also be aware that householders will be likely to make an insurance claim and replace many stolen items with new products. Thus the second visit may allow him to steal newer (and thus more valuable) items (Ashton *et al.*, 1998). When one considers these factors it is easier to understand why this type of repeat victimisation occurs. However, we cannot be absolutely certain as to the exact proportion of repeat victimisations which are attributable to the same perpetrator. Reviewing a small amount of recent research, Pease estimates that about half of all crimes which are repeat victimisations appear to form part of a series. He states:

> Taken literally, this means that most victimisation by the same crime type involves a set of similar circumstances and characteristics and 'probably' the same offender.
>
> (1998a: 13–14)

Pease cites some interesting, but as yet unpublished, work which has looked specifically at repeat domestic burglary cases that have been cleared up by the police. Preliminary data from this work suggests that in 80 per cent of cases where more than one crime is cleared up, the perpetrator is found to be the same person. In the remaining 20 per cent of cases (where burglaries were committed by two different people) there were very few instances in which the two burglars were known associates. Drawing on such evidence, Pease concludes that the so-called *boost* account is the most likely explanation for the majority of repeat victimisation.

Other crimes

Repeat victimisation also appears to occur in a range of other crimes. For example, a woman who is attacked by her violent partner may run a continued risk of future victimisation as long as she stays in the violent home. One study which analysed some 500 reports of domestic assault in America found that on average women had experienced 7.2 separate assaults per year from their husband or partner (Straus and Gelles, 1990).

Similarly a child who is sexually assaulted by her own father, may run an increased risk of future victimisation if the home circumstances remain the same. In such cases, repeat victimisation is largely explained by reference to the circumstances of the original offence. If the circumstances remain the same as when the first offence took place, then it is likely to recur. We must also bear in mind that a perpetrator who sees that he has got away with a crime, may be more likely to repeat the offence. Thus the violent man who suffers no adverse consequences as a result of the attack on his wife may have few qualms about repeating the offence (Dobash and Dobash, 1979; 1999).

Repeat victimisation appears to occur across a very wide range of crimes. Although we have concentrated on domestic crimes, figures suggest that some businesses are much more likely to be repeatedly victimised than are others (Mirrlees-Black and Ross, 1995). One recent study (Wood *et al.*, 1997) looking at small businesses in Leicester found that 69 per cent of burglaries were suffered by just seventeen per cent of the businesses surveyed. The same study showed that just three per cent of the businesses suffered 81 per cent of the violent attacks reported. Even offences such as obscene phone calls show high levels of repeat victimisation. Tseloni and Pease (1997) note that prior victimisation distinguishes those who will receive future obscene phone calls three times as well as the best combination of age, parity and marital status. It may be little comfort to learn that the only crime which shows no evidence of repeat victimisation is homicide.

Is knowledge about repeat victimisation useful?

The outlook for victims would appear to be a depressing one. The evidence reviewed so far suggests that those who suffer the indignity of one crime are significantly more likely to become a victim of further crime. However, knowing that this is the case may paradoxically make it easier to prevent future victimisation. One of the most successful recent British crime prevention initiatives took place on the Kirkholt estate in Greater Manchester. Those involved in this project quickly recognised that repeat victimisation was very common on the estate and so directed crime prevention strategies at those houses which were seen as being the most likely to be targeted for future attacks. This proved to be a very successful strategy and was partly responsible for a dramatic fall in the number of domestic burglaries on the estate (Forrester *et al.*, 1990). We will say more about this initiative in Chapter three.

Another point to make about repeat offences is that the repeats are much more likely to occur if the perpetrator believes that the circumstances which led to the original selection of a target remain the same. Thus, if a house was originally selected because it had poor door locks, no burglar alarm and was left unattended for most of the day, the offender may not think twice about a repeat attack, at least if nothing has changed. However, if the householder has now made the premises much more secure and is at home all day, the burglar may well reconsider. In these circumstances the 'advantage' which the burglar gained from his first visit may be nullified (Pease, 1998a: 6). This may be one explanation for another robust finding from the repeat victimisation research, i.e. that when repeat victimisation does occur, it does so fairly soon after the original offence (Polvi *et al.*, 1991).

A further interesting point made by Pease is that those offenders who do carry out repeat attacks on the same target tend to be the more prolific type of offenders. Thus, both burglars and robbers who carry out repeat attacks have been found to be more likely to be career criminals when compared to those who do not repeat their attacks on the same target (Ashton *et al.*, 1998; Gill and Pease, 1998). For this reason, Pease points out that a focus on repeat offences is likely to result in the arrest of the most active criminals in society.

The impact of the research on repeat victimisation should not be underestimated. By identifying likely future victims of crime, the police and other agencies can now target their resources more appropriately and effectively. Knowledge of repeat victimisation research can also be one of the most useful aids to crime prevention. Knowing where a criminal is likely to strike next allows a better focus upon vulnerable people and property. We will return to this point in the next chapter, however, we should bear in mind that by concentrating on repeat victimisation, the roles of victim support and crime prevention become very much interlinked (Pease, 1998a: v). We should also note that by focusing on repeat offences, efforts are concentrated on the highest crime areas, and thus are likely to have the best results. Pease points out that by concentrating on repeat offenders, more crime is likely to be solved and more property recovered. Furthermore, as was noted above, by concentrating on repeat offences the most prolific offenders are likely to be caught, or at least prevented from committing repeat crimes.

Psychological effects of victimisation

There can be few people who would welcome the prospect of becoming a victim of crime. Indeed as we saw earlier, the fear of becoming a victim, especially of violent crime, can lead to people substantially altering their own behaviour. However, if and when a person does become a victim, there will be a number of possible reactions. At least part of the reaction to crime victimisation can be explained by reference to post traumatic stress disorder or PTSD. We will say much more about this later in the chapter.

Research in America (Kahn, 1984) suggested that crime victims can suffer any number of the following reactions:

- depression;
- anxiety;
- paranoia;

- loss of control;
- shame;
- embarrassment;
- vulnerability;
- helplessness;
- humiliation;
- anger;
- shock;
- feelings of inequity;
- increased awareness of mortality;
- tension;
- malaise;
- fear.

Other studies have also pointed out that large numbers of people are affected psychologically by victimisation and subsequently experience a deterioration in their mental health (for example Resnick *et al.*, 1993; Sorenson and Golding, 1990). In one study (Davis and Friedman, 1985) some 75 per cent of victims of burglary, robbery and assault were found to be experiencing distress or sleeping disorders up to three weeks after the event. Although we are focusing on victims, we should also bear in mind that many people who merely witness the more serious type of crime may themselves suffer PTSD. For example, following a shooting in a Texas restaurant in which 24 people were killed, almost all those who survived the shooting showed some signs of PTSD up to two months later (North, Smith and Spitznagel, 1994).

Although almost all victims will find the event stressful, the actual level of distress felt may vary considerably from person to person. This will obviously be affected by the seriousness of the crime but, as we will see later, there are many other important variables. Following the initial feelings of shock, victims are perhaps most likely to feel anger. However, some victims will be better able to deal with their angry feelings than will others (Chapter 8). Recent research suggests that anger may be perhaps the most predominant feeling which victims will experience and that we should perhaps be focusing more upon this important aspect of victimisation (Ditton *et al.*, 1999).

The victim's perception of the crime will be very important in determining his or her reaction to it. If a victim believes that the reason why they were selected as a target was purely random or was entirely the result of external factors, then the crime may be easier to come to terms with. However, if the victim believes that he or she should carry some responsibility for what happened, then it may be more difficult to accept. It is interesting to note that when victims are allowed to meet their attacker and discuss the crime (for example under victim-offender mediation or reparation schemes) one of the most helpful aspects is learning why they had been selected as a target. Discovering that they carry little or no responsibility for their own victimisation often makes it somewhat easier to adjust to life post-victimisation.

Personality as a mediating influence

Earlier, we introduced the notion of *locus of control*, and discussed how this might affect a victim's reaction to a crime. It may appear paradoxical, but the victim who believes that he or she has little control over events in life (i.e. those who score highest in terms of external locus of control) may view the crime as 'just one of those things'. While it may be disturbing, the person might well accept that there is little he or she could have done to prevent the crime happening.

Conversely, people who believe that they have a great deal of control over events (i.e. those who score highest in terms of internal locus of control) may find it much harder to come to terms with their victimisation. Their perception may well be 'I did everything possible to prevent myself becoming a victim, yet I was still victimised'. This will obviously shake the (psychological) foundations of a person who believes that they do have the power to control events in their life. Such victims may well be in need of some form of counselling or therapy, part of which may involve getting the person to accept that the world is not necessarily the ordered and controllable place which they have always believed it to be (see Dryden and Gordon, 1990 for some interesting examples).

We might also wish to speculate about the behaviour of different victims following their victimisation. Those who still cling to their internal focus may do a great deal to try to prevent the crime recurring. However, those who continue to believe that they are at the mercy of others may take little action to try to prevent a repeat crime. It is interesting to note that in the Kirkholt project (see above) researchers tried to convince householders that they could do something about their chances of future victimisation, i.e. they played up the 'internal locus of control' dimension.

There are a number of other personality dimensions which may be relevant to an understanding of how victims react to crime. One obvious dimension is neuroticism which is partly a measure of the extent to which people worry about events in their life (Eysenck, 1970). Those with comparatively stable personalities will tend to be affected less by victimisation than will those who are at the high end of the neuroticism scale. The latter group of people are perhaps also the ones most likely to be fearful of repeat victimisation.

Why victimisation causes distress

It may be obvious that people are adversely affected by victimisation, but it is worth considering some of the psychological factors which may come into play. One reason that has already been identified is that becoming a victim threatens people's feeling of control – they may have to admit that they were powerless to prevent a crime occurring. A feeling of safety and security has been identified as one of the most basic foundations for human self-fulfilment (Maslow, 1954). Thus, if an individual no longer feels safe in their own home, or when walking down the street, much of their fundamental feeling of well-being will be threatened. It is interesting to note that many women's groups now prefer to use the term 'survivor' rather than 'victim' when describing those affected by, for example, domestic violence. This is more than a semantic shift as the term survivor appears to have a much less negative connotation than the word victim – the latter implies helplessness, while the former suggests that the person affected has more in the way of control.

Losing one's personal possessions to a burglar or robber can also be distressing, especially if the items have a great deal of personal significance. Loss covers far more than simply material goods – victims often talk of feeling as if a part of themselves has been taken away. A stolen video recorder might be easily replaced, whereas letters from a now-deceased parent can never be restored. Such losses often assume a far greater significance than any financial loss and in some ways have similar characteristics to the grief felt following a bereavement (Nicolson, 1994). Although we have tended to make a distinction between property crime and crimes involving personal violence, such a distinction may not be so meaningful for an individual victim. Burglary is felt by many to be the most serious form of property crime because it represents a violation of, and an intrusion into, the home. As such its psychological effects can be more severe than all other property crimes. When the burglary also involves the ransacking of the home, then the sense of invasion and disorientation will be particularly severe (Nicolson, 1994: 11).

If the violation of one's own home causes distress, then the violation of one's body will tend to be even more disturbing. Rape is understandably viewed as an extremely serious crime for which any person convicted can expect to receive quite a lengthy prison sentence. According to recent figures (Home Office, 1998: 149) 99 per cent of those convicted of rape at Crown Court are given an immediate custodial sentence, the average length of which is over six years.

Not only does rape represent a physical assault, but the act of forced penetration can understandably cause extreme distress (for example Steketee and Foa, 1987). Reactions to such violation can range from severe anxiety and nightmares to depression and attempted suicide. Indeed it is difficult to imagine how victims can come to terms with such assaults and carry on with their lives. One study (Resnick *et al.*, 1989) found that three-quarters of rape victims could have been diagnosed as suffering from PTSD at some point in the year following their assault. Shipherd and Beck (1999) found that many women suffer from PTSD because they are unable to control intrusive or recurrent thoughts about the rape. Although time does help the rebuilding process, recovery can be a long and distressing process, with some women never completely coming to terms with their ordeal (Rothbaum *et al.*, 1992). One study (Kilpatrick *et al.*, 1987) showed that even after seventeen years almost a fifth of sexual assault victims showed symptoms of PTSD.

Post traumatic stress disorder (PTSD)

As we noted earlier, reactions to serious victimisation can often be understood by reference to the notion of post traumatic stress disorder or PTSD (Joseph, Williams and Yule, 1997). The diagnosis of PTSD has increased significantly in recent years and the condition is now much more widely recognised than was the case only two decades ago. Although post traumatic stress had been recognised in the past (for example when combat soldiers in the First and Second World Wars were diagnosed as suffering from 'shell shock') the disorder was brought to the public's attention more fully following the Vietnam War. Significant numbers of American servicemen returned from combat showing signs of having been severely traumatised by their experience. They found readjustment difficult and many showed signs of mental disorder, including some severe depression.

A focus on the effects of many different types of traumatic experience has allowed researchers to understand the condition more fully and to improve treatment methods. Recognising that victimisation can bring on symptoms such as those often found in other forms of PTSD allows professionals to offer appropriate counselling. Providing that this is introduced at an early stage, the prospects of recovery are much greater (for example Burgess and Holmstrom, 1974). There have been a number of recent promising developments with regard to the treatment of PTSD. For example, Gerbode (1993) has developed a therapy known as Traumatic Incident Reduction (TIR) which is a directive, person-focused method of examining specific traumas. A good review of this method and advice on its use is provided by Bisbey and Bisbey (1998).

The problem for many victims is that the police's need for information to help solve the crime may take priority over any counselling. Although many police officers now recognise that victims have needs of their own, there will still tend to be a focus on the obtaining of evidential information (Ainsworth, 1995a).

Life events

It has been recognised for some time that significant events in one's life can affect both physical and psychological well-being. Holmes and Rahe (1967) developed their Life Events Scale as a way of trying to measure the effects of important events in a person's life. The scale is a useful way of understanding which events in life can cause the most distress. Top of the list is 'death of a spouse' in which those closest to the deceased person experience the greatest difficulty in adjusting to the loss. Being a victim of crime does not appear at the very top of the Holmes and Rahe scale, though obviously those who experience the most severe crimes will suffer greatest distress. Thus, relatives of a murder victim will be likely to experience the most severe trauma. Bereavement is always going to be distressing, though the fact that the death was unexpected and the result of a criminal act will make it even more difficult to accept. 'Death of a spouse', 'death of close family member' and 'personal injury', all of which may be the result of a criminal act, are three of the top six items on the Holmes and Rahe scale. The fact that other possible forms of crime victimisation do not assume prominence may be partially explained by the (comparatively) low crime rate at the time when Holmes and Rahe developed their scale over thirty years ago.

Grieving relatives whose loved one has been murdered appear to get a particularly raw deal from the criminal justice system (Rock, 1998). They may also receive little effective help from the local Victim Support office. Although most victims may be routinely referred to their local Victim Support Scheme, such schemes will be of less value to victims of the rarer forms of crime. Thus while the burglary victim may be comforted by a fellow sufferer, the male rape victim may find it much more difficult to share his experience with someone who really does 'know what he's going through'.

As was noted earlier, Victim Support Schemes have done a great deal to alleviate the suffering of many crime victims, yet their work receives very little in the way of official recognition or government funding. Such schemes rely very heavily on the work of volunteers, most of whom have themselves been victims in the past. Part of the reason why the schemes are successful is that victims often have a need to talk to someone with whom they can share their feelings. Learning that reactions such as anger, anxiety and depression are quite normal will help the person to start the readjustment process. It has long been recognised that many people who are experiencing stress, will tend to look to others for comfort and support. In these circumstances sharing anxieties and comparing feelings with others who are in the same predicament can be particularly helpful (Schachter, 1959).

Before moving on from the consideration of life events, we must consider one important point concerning the perception of criminal events. While Holmes and Rahe made a valuable contribution to our understanding of the effects of stressful life events, their scale was rather simplistic. By assigning numerical values to different life stressors, they implied that similar events would have a very similar impact on each and every individual. However, this may be rather naïve. For example, while the death of a spouse may be distressing for all, it may be more severe for some than others. The death of a cherished lifelong friend and partner will understandably be hard to take. However, the death of a bullying and violent spouse may be greeted partly with a feeling of relief.

For this reason, it is not always easy to predict which individuals will be the most severely affected by crime victimisation and which might cope comparatively well. The theft of one's car might be extremely annoying and cause a great deal of inconvenience. The victim whose unique vintage car is stolen may be particularly distressed as the vehicle is literally irreplaceable. However, the victim who has been trying for some time to sell an unwanted car may be almost grateful to find that it has been taken and torched – providing they have adequate insurance cover of course.

Earlier in this chapter we talked about how common repeat victimisation appears to be. We should bear in mind that repeat victimisation may have its own psychological consequences – having to come to terms with being a victim once may be bad enough, but to suffer again when one is just starting to come to terms with the original offence may be even harder to handle. Indeed, Shaw (1999) suggests that chronic victimisation can have such a devastating emotional impact that it can produce many of the symptoms normally associated with bereavement.

On the other hand, if victimisation becomes very common, each new episode may have less impact than the first. People may eventually show evidence of habituation and adaptation, although secondary consequences (e.g. high insurance bills and an inability to sell their home) may add further distress.

We started this chapter by noting that victims are often referred to as the forgotten party in the criminal justice process. Although this is generally true, there are some signs that things are starting to change. In a recent comprehensive review of the literature on victims, Zedner has noted that:

> Victims now attract an unprecedented level of interest, both as a subject of criminological enquiry and focus of criminal justice policy. Far from being a compartmentalised topic, victim research has impacted upon every aspect of criminological thinking and profoundly altered our picture of crime …
>
> (1997: 607).

While this positive note is to be welcomed, Zedner cautions that a focus on the victim may not improve victim services, but may serve simply to justify an ever more punitive approach to offenders. Having said that, the increased use by courts of powers to compel an offender to make reparation to a victim is a positive sign.

Summary

We have seen in this chapter that victimisation is rarely a random act, but rather is associated with a number of identifiable variables. Despite the rise in crime rates over the last 40 years, many people will go through life suffering little victimisation, at least of a serious nature. It may be comforting to note the words of Hough and Mayhew who, when writing in 1983, estimated that the 'statistically average' person over sixteen years of age could expect to be burgled once every 40 years and to be robbed once every 500 years! That may however be of little comfort to the statistically abnormal victim who experiences the effects of crime on a regular basis.

Although there are a large number of predisposing variables that affect the risk of victimisation, the best predictor of future victimisation appears to be past victimisation. Knowing this fact can help the police to better target resources.

Learning that the more serious types of crime are comparatively rare may be of little comfort to those who become victims of such attacks. Readjustment following such victimisation will be a long and painful process, and in some cases never be fully achieved. Knowing the reactions which people are likely to experience following victimisation can however help those who counsel the severely traumatised victim.

Chapter 3

Preventing crime and offending

We have seen in Chapters 1 and 2 that crime is a cause of great concern for a large number of people. Even though the risk of serious victimisation is thankfully quite low, many people still fear crime and will do what they can to reduce their own chances of victimisation. We have seen that victimisation often has its most serious effects on those people who felt that they were powerless to prevent the crime. For this reason, people will generally be motivated to take measures which will prevent them from becoming a victim. Installing a burglar alarm may well have a deterrent effect but may also serve to make the householder feel more secure. However, the belief that we can remove completely the risk of any form of victimisation may well be a myth. One can think of many famous thefts in which valuable property has been stolen despite the best efforts of eminent security consultants and the police. One can also think of initiatives brought in by governments (e.g. the compulsory fitting of steering locks to cars) which were hailed at the time as important breakthroughs but which sadly did not always produce the amount of crime reduction anticipated.

Stemming the tide of crime

If we consider the rate at which crime has increased over the last 50 years (see Chapter 1) then it might be fair to say that the majority of crime prevention strategies have been spectacularly unsuccessful. A tenfold increase in the amount of officially recorded crime since 1950 would hardly lead one to believe that most crime prevention initiatives have worked. If we think about the amount of time, effort and money spent on crime and its prevention then we may well be left feeling discouraged. Successive governments have responded to the public's fears, promised that they will be 'tough on crime' and that they will devote the necessary resources to tackling the problem. The criminal justice system is said to cost the UK treasury over £10 billion per annum, yet many members of the public remain fearful of victimisation (see Chapter 2). Members of the public have also contributed to the crime prevention effort by spending more and more money on burglar alarms, CCTV, car immobilisers, tracker systems etc. Yet only in the last few years of the twentieth century did we start to see a reduction in crime in the UK. The cynic may be forgiven for suggesting that if all this effort has produced such discouraging results, then perhaps we should simply accept that we cannot win the battle against crime. Crawford (1998) has noted that:

> The traditional institutions of policing, prosecution and punishment appear powerless to make a significant impact. Against this background, concerns about personal security have become an increasingly powerful dynamic in social life influencing what people do, where they live, as well as whether, where and when they go out ... we are becoming more, rather then less fearful of criminal victimisation.
>
> (1998: 1)

In this situation it would be understandable for the public to look for someone to blame. The question is to whom should they direct their frustration? Hearing that 'social inequality' or 'the breakdown of the family' may be partly to blame for the amount of crime in society does not offer an obvious target upon which members of the public might direct their anger. In these circumstances, it would be understandable if the public looked for a scapegoat. Scapegoating can be extremely unfair and irrational, yet serves an important psychological function by allowing people to focus their anger, frustration and dissatisfaction on someone or on some institution (Aronson, 1988: 258–60).

The public may well round on law enforcement agencies and direct their frustration and anger towards their local police force. However, if there is anything to be learned from the failures of many crime prevention initiatives it is that they can only be successful if they adopt a joint approach to the problem. Far too many initiatives appear to have failed because one agency or another has tried to go it alone and not consulted with others. Despite 'the prevention of crime' being one of the police's primary roles, most police officers do accept that they can do little to stem the flow of crime if they act alone. The traditional sight of a uniformed police officer patrolling the streets may make the public feel more secure, but may actually prevent or deter very little crime (Hough, 1996).

The need for the police to work with local authorities and agencies has recently been formalised. The police in the UK are now obliged to work in partnership with others in identifying joint strategies aimed at tackling the most pressing local crime concerns (Hough and Tilley, 1998). These concerns will have been identified by carrying out crime audits, usually inviting local people to comment on their own crime concerns. This allows the police better to identify their priorities. It is however disappointing to note that surveys of residents about crime concerns typically have a response rate of less than ten per cent – a surprising figure considering that most members of the public are apparently so concerned about crime (see Chapter 2).

In a recent Home Office publication it is recognised that while the police can play a major role in preventing crime many other agencies also have an important part to play. Hough and Tilley (1998) note that:

> The police are ... not the only agency with a preventive role to play. The local authority, probation, health authorities, the private and voluntary sectors, as well as members of the general public can all act in ways that can make crime more or less likely. The police cannot bear sole responsibility for crime prevention, and local prevention will normally require effective partnerships with other agencies.
>
> (1998: ii)

It remains to be seen how successful such partnerships will be, although it should be noted that the police have not always found it easy to work with other agencies (Ainsworth, 1995a: ch. 12). Indeed Hough and Tilley acknowledge that 'it has often proved difficult to establish robust, routine, trusting, and open-minded multi-agency groups' (1988: ii). However, these same authors suggest that the best crime prevention initiatives adopt a problem-solving approach. They propose a four stage model, i.e. the routine scanning of relevant data; strategy formulation; implementation of attempted solutions and monitoring and evaluation.

It has also become obvious that members of the public stand a better chance of protecting themselves successfully if they adopt a common approach to the problem rather than each relying on individual strategies. As Newman (1972) noted: 'When people begin to protect themselves as individuals and not as a community, the battle against crime is effectively lost' (1972: 4).

When we think of crime prevention we may well envisage traditional methods such as the fitting of better door locks or an alarm, or the installation of security cameras. However, this form of prevention (traditionally known as target hardening) is only one of a large number of approaches which might all be subsumed under the general heading of crime prevention. Other less obvious forms might include such things as anger management courses for those who may be prone to violence, 'parenting skills' courses which might prevent parents from abusing their children, setting up of youth clubs so that youngsters will spend less time roaming the streets, providing free late night buses for female students, persuading electricity companies to remove cash payment meters from homes, serving beer in plastic rather than glass containers in order to reduce the opportunities for woundings in pubs, drug education programmes which reduce the likelihood of addiction, giving longer prison sentences to persistent offenders (McCord, 1999). While all these initiatives may serve to reduce or prevent offending, some may not be seen by many as the most appropriate use of resources in the battle against crime.

Pease (1997) makes a number of important points with regard to crime prevention. Firstly, he points out that 'crime' covers such a wide range of different behaviours that it would be inappropriate to look for universality in techniques of prevention. Secondly, he notes that the best way to control crime may not necessarily be through the police and the courts. He suggests that 'the behaviour itself must be understood, to determine where change could best be brought about' (1997: 964). His third point is that, although crime prevention is a laudable goal, a society in which more crime is prevented is not necessarily a more pleasant society. Imposing a curfew on all citizens, insisting that all new homes should be devoid of windows, banning motor cars, or prohibiting the consumption of alcohol, would all undoubtedly reduce the amount of crime in society but at a considerable 'cost' to its citizens.

A useful distinction between different forms of crime prevention was made by Brantingham and Faust (1976). (Their categorisation was later amended by Van Dijk and De Waard (1991)). Drawing on terms used in public health and mental health literature they make a distinction between **primary prevention**, which seeks to reduce the opportunities for crime with no reference to criminals themselves; **secondary prevention**, which seeks to prevent those who may be tempted into a criminal career from doing so; and **tertiary prevention**, which aims to prevent known criminals from committing further crime. Although it must be acknowledged that all three approaches may lead to a reduction in crime, this chapter will focus largely on the more traditional forms of crime prevention contained within what Brantingham and Faust refer to as primary prevention. However, the reader should be aware that many topics covered elsewhere in this book may have the effect of reducing the amount of crime in society. For example, programmes which target and educate vulnerable youngsters at an early age may prevent a large amount of crime later on (Farrington, 1997). And, of course, sentencing an offender to a long prison term will prevent that individual from committing further crime in the community for the duration of the sentence (see Chapter 7).

Situational and environmental crime prevention

In the UK at least there has tended to be quite a heavy focus on situational or environmental strategies to reduce crime. As Crawford (1998) notes:

> Situational crime prevention has become a major force in policy and research since the early 1980s. Primarily focused around the work of the Home Office, it has enjoyed a period of considerable political success and influence in the UK.
>
> (1998: 65)

The approach in some way mirrors the change in emphasis which has taken place in psychology over the last 30 years. For much of its early history, psychology focused almost exclusively on the individual as a way of understanding and explaining human behaviour. Thus a large number of psychometric tests were devised in an effort to measure and categorise humans. These tests covered many aspects of personality and intelligence. However, through the development of social and environmental psychology, there came a growing recognition of the importance of the social and physical environment in determining human behaviour. Writers such as Kurt Lewin (1943) and Rudolf Moos (1976) suggested that if we are to understand fully why a person behaved in the way they did, we must take account of the total 'field' that existed at the time the behaviour was exhibited. Thus, studying only the personality of a young male student will be unlikely to provide the whole explanation for why he behaved the way he did when watching a rock concert, viewing a football match, sitting his final year exams, or attending a friend's funeral. In these cases, an understanding of the situational and environmental forces which were present on each occasion is crucial if we are to make sense of any particular behaviour.

This is not to say that the environment should be seen as **more** important than personality; only that situational forces should be acknowledged and, if possible, measured before we reach a conclusion as to why people behave the way they do. Most psychologists today would accept that it is inappropriate to try to explain behaviour solely by reference to either personality variables or to environmental forces. Rather, there is an acceptance that any behaviour is a result of an interaction between the individual and their environment. Having said that, it is all too easy to focus upon the individual while disregarding the environment. Thus, in trying to explain why a person committed a certain crime it is often tempting to focus largely on their underlying personality. The apparently heartless burglar who steals property from the blind pensioner may well be labelled by the Press as 'evil'. Yet such a simplistic and perhaps naïve explanation will not explain why this particular pensioner was attacked while another was ignored.

In the same way that psychology now acknowledges that it is unhelpful to consider behaviour only in terms of individual variables, so attempts at crime prevention have tended to move away from an exclusive focus on the individual criminal and towards a consideration of the role of the environment. Early writers such as Newman (1972) and Jeffery (1971) stressed the role which the environment can play in encouraging or discouraging criminal activity. Newman was one of the first to draw attention to the fact that the modern architectural environment may provide far more crime opportunities than did the more traditional forms of housing. In fact, Newman went so far as to argue that '... the new physical form of the urban environment is possibly the most cogent ally the criminal has in his victimisation of society' (1972: 2).

Newman drew on the work of writers such as Jacobs (1961) and developed the notion of *defensible space*. Defensible space was seen firstly as a way in which territoriality among residents might be encouraged. Thus, by demarcating zones within the immediate environment, residents might be more likely to defend their territory while outsiders would be discouraged from entering. Newman also stressed the importance of surveillance; not in the sense of CCTV cameras, but rather as a form of natural activity which residents would exhibit while going about their everyday activities. The siting of kitchen windows to overlook building entrances might allow residents to see who was coming and going and would also make any potential burglar feel vulnerable when entering the building. In addition to territoriality and surveillance, Newman saw the image of buildings themselves and the planning of the whole area as important.

Newman's work has been criticised on a number of grounds ranging from questions over his methodology to doubts about his assumptions of human nature (for example Mawby, 1977; Mayhew, 1979; Merry, 1981). Much of the criticism suggested that his notion of defensible space was far too simplistic an explanation for a great deal of criminal activity. To be fair, in his later writings, Newman did come to acknowledge that many factors other than the physical environment had an effect on criminal activity and that the architectural environment might not after all be the most important variable (Newman, 1976).

Nevertheless, as we will see below, the notion that the architectural environment can be relevant in determining crime levels appears to live on in the work of more modern researchers examining situational crime prevention. We should also note that although most writers have criticised and challenged Newman's hypothesis, there has been a small amount of empirical support for his views. For example, Sommer (1987) found that university halls of residence which appeared to have good defensible space properties suffered much less crime and vandalism than did those which lacked these features. It is also interesting to note that many British police forces have appointed architectural liaison officers to advise on ways of designing out crime. In the case of Greater Manchester Police, the liaison officer's role is reported to be to 'persuade architects and developers to see commonsense and design out crime' (Stephenson, 1992b).

Some of the criticism of Newman's work stemmed from the fact that his theory was seen as an example of *architectural (or environmental) determinism*. In its most extreme form, architectural determinism suggests that all behaviour is determined by the environment and that the environment is the only, or at least the primary, cause of behaviour. Thus, if we change the environment we can in theory change the behaviour. According to Newman's original work, a reversion to more traditional forms of housing with good defensible space properties would reverse the ever increasing crime rate and result in a large reduction in criminal activity. As we saw earlier, most psychologists would take issue with the notion that any behaviour can be explained entirely by focusing on either the individual or the environment. For this reason many have criticised architectural determinism and pointed out that such an extreme position fails to acknowledge the importance of social and cultural factors. In addition, it has been argued that people are not simply passive and thus shaped entirely by the environment – rather they interact with the environment, and in some cases might modify it to suit their needs better. Although design may well influence behaviour, people's needs and activities might then modify these effects.

Opponents of the notion of architectural determinism have suggested different ways of conceptualising the physical environment. One such approach is the idea of *environmental (or architectural) possibilism* (Porteus, 1977). This is the view that many different forms of behaviour are made possible by any given environment. The environment is thus seen as presenting people with many behavioural opportunities, though the setting of some rather broad limits is acknowledged. As such, environmental possibilism envisages a much less deterministic role for the environment and rather sees it merely as a context in which behaviour occurs. This view has been seen by some as unhelpful as it allows one to make few predictions as to the likely behaviour which would be exhibited in any particular environment – literally almost anything is possible.

As a middle ground between the two extremes of architectural determinism and environmental possibilism was the notion of *environmental probabilism* (Porteus, 1977). As the name implies, this view argues that although a wide range of behaviours might be possible in any given environment, some are more probable than others. Thus we might want to argue that although we cannot eliminate crime completely by modifying the environment, by making changes we can perhaps make it less (or more) likely that criminal activity will occur. Better, more 'defensible' housing design or the installation of CCTV cameras may not completely eliminate all criminal activity in a given area, but it may make some crimes less probable.

Newman's work was focused almost entirely on residential locations, though some of the concepts have been extended to other locations through the notion of Crime Prevention Through Environmental Design (CPTED). Many of the ideas were developed by Jeffery (1971) who sought to introduce notions of territoriality to many different environments including schools and commercial premises. Extensive research funding was granted by the US federal government in the 1970s in an attempt to develop the notion of crime prevention through better environmental design. Unfortunately, almost all of the projects which implemented the ideas of CPTED appeared to be unsuccessful and did not result in a reduction of crime. Clarke (1995) has suggested that this may be partly explained by the fact that while territorial behaviour might well be displayed in residential environments, it is much less likely to occur in non-residential environments.

The importance of the physical environment as a factor in crime was further highlighted by the work of Coleman (1985). Coleman spent a great deal of time examining public sector housing estates in Britain. She noted that many local authority developments, especially high rise blocks, had a number of design features which put them at a disadvantage when compared with more traditional forms of housing. For example, a large number of storeys, overhead walkways, the lack of physical boundaries within the blocks and multiple entry points all conspired to constitute what Coleman called a 'design disadvantage'. Taking various measures of crime and antisocial behaviour (e.g. the amount of graffiti) she suggested that there was a correlation between the physical design of the buildings and the amount of crime. Furthermore, she suggested that it was the physical environment itself which produced the criminal activity. Coleman argued that children growing up in such poor environments may be encouraged (rather than discouraged) to commit crime. She went so far as to argue that bad design can cause social breakdown by destroying communities and thus preventing them from defending their territory against criminal elements.

Coleman's views certainly have great intuitive appeal. Someone who moves onto an estate which gives off all the wrong signals may be unlikely to take a pride in their home nor to challenge those who are further damaging an already poor environment. In such conditions norms of behaviour can quickly become established and are then difficult to change. Previous work in the USA (Yancey, 1971) had also highlighted the way in which physical design can serve to all but destroy communities. For example, the notorious Pruitt Igoe complex in St Louis (Missouri, USA) had been a spectacular failure as its design did not allow residents to form the informal social networks which were considered necessary to make life more bearable. In the case of Pruitt Igoe, the architect had been praised for the way in which he had been able to reduce the amount of 'wasted' space in the buildings, yet this design feature was partly responsible for the large amount of resident dissatisfaction and the premature demolition of the housing complex (Yancey, 1971). Many housing estates in Britain (e.g. The Crescents in Hulme, Manchester) suffered similar fates and were eventually demolished to make room for what was considered to be more suitable (and more desirable) housing.

The problem for a psychologist studying such estates is that it is often difficult to separate out the relative contribution of the environment and that of other factors. Although some housing estates are poorly designed and quickly gain undesirable reputations, it may be inappropriate to see the problem as entirely environmental. As an estate's reputation starts to decline there will be a tendency for those who can leave to do so. Councils may then be tempted to put the most disadvantaged families onto the unloved estate, thus perhaps adding to the problem (Power, 1989). We must also bear in mind a point made earlier with regard to the interaction between personality and environment. In some cases it is not that housing designs are in themselves bad, or that certain types of people are 'the problem'. Rather, the difficulty arises because of the fact that the design simply does not meet the needs of the majority of residents. Thus, although a design such as that used in Pruitt Igoe was suitable for young, mobile and largely single households, it was totally unsuited to the needs of many working class families with young children.

One reason why Newman's original premise was greeted so warmly at the time was that it offered practical advice to those who wished to try to reduce crime. Unlike many theorists of crime causation, Newman spelled out concrete and practical steps which could be taken to reduce the level of crime in society. According to Rubenstein *et al.* (1980) these might include such things as improving external lighting, reducing opportunities for criminals to conceal themselves, reducing the amount of unassigned open space, locating outdoor activities (e.g. children playing) in sight of windows, increasing designated walkways and increasing pedestrian activity. Such practical, and in some cases inexpensive, changes may well serve to reduce crime opportunities and thus to reduce the level of victimisation.

Despite the difficulties encountered when trying to disentangle the effects of the physical environment from other variables, the work of writers such as Coleman has had some impact on crime prevention strategies in Britain. For example, the Department of the Environment recently published its Circular 5/94 which set out some suggestions for the way in which crime-free environments might be created. Other writers have also recently stressed the fact that good design can only help in the fight against crime (for example, Ekblom, 1995; Poyner and Webb, 1992). Against this, however, we must recall that Newman's, and indeed Coleman's, theories remain largely unproven and that it would be naïve to presume that better design will eradicate all crime. Having said that, the emphasis on situational crime prevention does appear to have some success, as we will see below.

Situational crime prevention

In the UK it was the Home Office's Research and Planning Unit which developed the situational approach to crime prevention in the 1970s and early 1980s (Clarke, 1983). Situational crime prevention emphasises the control of crime through practical measures. It has an emphasis on modifications to the physical environment which might discourage criminal activity and also emphasises the importance of informal social control of environments. Perhaps its most important feature is the emphasis on the offence itself, rather than on the offender. It tends thus to look at the relationship between certain crimes and the areas in which they occur, rather than studying offenders themselves. Unlike some early American work (e.g. Shaw and McKay, 1942) situational crime prevention points out that the areas with the highest crime rates are not necessarily those which contain the largest number of offenders. Thus an out-of-town cinema complex which suffers a large amount of vehicle-related crime might be targeted for action despite the fact that there are very few criminals living within the immediate area.

Hough, Clarke and Mayhew (1980) defined situational crime prevention as follows:

(i)   measures directed at highly specific forms of crime;
(ii) which involve the management, design, or manipulation of the immediate environment in which these crimes occur;
(iii) in as systematic and permanent a way as possible;
(iv) so as to reduce the opportunities for these crimes;
(v)   as perceived by a broad range of potential offenders.

(1980: 1)

Clarke (1992) suggests that these objectives might be achieved in one of three ways, i.e.:

1. Increasing the amount of effort involved in committing a crime

This could take the form of target hardening by, for example, fitting extra locks, erecting a fence around vulnerable properties or fitting bollards outside retail premises to prevent ram-raids.

2. Increasing the perceived level of risk involved in committing a crime

This might be achieved by increasing the perceived likelihood of detection and apprehension of the offender. The fitting of CCTV is the most obvious example of this strategy, as would be the introduction of alarms to houses or the fitting of security tags to expensive clothing in retail premises. Some of the ideas suggested by Newman (see above) might also fit into this category. Designing buildings in such a way that potential burglars feel that they are likely to be observed will tend to have a deterrent effect.

3. Reducing the likely rewards of crime

Examples of this approach might include the marking of a householder's property with their postcode so as to reduce the property's resale value. Signs informing potential thieves that petrol station cashiers do not have access to the safe might also reduce the likelihood of robberies. Replacing coin-operated public telephones with those requiring phonecards would also serve to reduce the amount of damage in the form of attempted theft.

Ultimately situational crime prevention seeks to increase the possible costs of offending and to decrease the likely benefits. 'Costs' include both the ease with which the offence can be committed and also the risk of possible detection. If the 'cost' increases significantly, and the likely rewards are reduced, then it is possible that the crime will not be attempted. Thus the potential robber who sees that the bank clerk is sitting behind a bulletproof screen, that the premises have CCTV cameras prominently cited, and that the bank does not carry a great deal of cash, may choose not to target those particular premises.

Of course, one down side of this approach is that, rather than being deterred permanently, the criminal may simply choose an alternative target where the costs are lower and the rewards higher (Heal and Laycock, 1986: 123). This so called *displacement* may be of little concern to the householder whose actions have prevented them becoming a victim personally, but will obviously be a cause for concern in society at large. The possible displacement of crime from one target to another or from one point in time to another is obviously worrying and is a concern which must be addressed by any crime prevention initiative, especially those utilising situational measures. For this reason we will return to the notion of displacement later in the chapter.

To some extent, situational crime prevention assumes that a great deal of crime is opportunistic. Indeed Mayhew *et al.*'s (1976) pioneering writing on the subject was entitled 'Crime as Opportunity'. Their research stemmed from a somewhat unlikely source, i.e. data on the number of suicides due to gas poisoning. Following the introduction of (non-poisonous) natural gas to British homes, it was noted that the number of suicides actually fell. Mayhew *et al.* reasoned that if the number of suicides could be reduced by such a form of opportunity reduction, then similar attempts at opportunity reduction in the area of crime might also be effective.

Situational crime prevention assumes that the criminal elements in society are attracted by easy targets and the prospect of easy pickings. There is certainly some evidence to support this view. For example, Bennett and Wright (1984) conducted some interesting research in which they asked convicted burglars about how they came to select their targets. Most of those questioned confirmed that they tended not to select as targets those homes which had an alarm fitted, or where there was a dog in the house, or where people appeared to be at home. Other relevant factors in their target selection included whether or not there was a way of gaining access without being observed by neighbours, and whether there appeared to be valuable property in the home. The three factors which affected choice of targets could be classified as **risk**, **reward**, and **ease of entry**, with risk being by far the most important.

These views support the reasoning behind many situational crime prevention initiatives. There were however some other rather more surprising results from Bennett and Wright's work which challenge some presumptions. For example, most burglars (69 per cent) said that the presence of locks on windows would not deter them. In fact some said that window locks might even encourage them to break in, as the locks would signify that there was valuable property within. Another rather surprising finding concerned the presence of dogs in homes. Many burglars (76 per cent) said that a dog's presence would deter them. However the burglars' fear was not so much that the dog might attack them but rather that it would bark and alert people to their presence. Some burglars said that in this case they would feel bad about having perhaps to hurt the dog in order to stop it barking. It seems as though the same burglars who had few qualms about breaking into homes and stealing property balked at the thought of having to harm an animal!

One reason why situational crime prevention initiatives may have been so popular in Britain is that they allow people to address very immediate and real problems in a practical way. In particular, they allow the police and victims to do something to reduce the likelihood that a particular person or particular premises will be victimised. As Crawford (1998) says:

> One of the central attractions of situational measures is their apparent simplicity and their capacity to provide what appear to be realistic solutions to specific kinds of offending in a variety of different contexts ... Situational crime prevention is a pragmatic response to crime in that it focuses on what can most easily be achieved.
>
> (1998: 69)

Crawford is making an important point here. Situational crime prevention gives people a sense that something practical can be done. As he notes, most people can do little to alter the social forces which may be contributing to the level of crime in society, nor can they do anything about the way in which most offenders think or behave. However, what they can do, at least to some extent, is to make things more difficult, or to make themselves or their property a less attractive proposition for the criminal. As such it is less likely that people will feel helpless and may instead feel that they can have some control over their own fate.

It has been recognised for some time that a feeling of helplessness can be damaging psychologically and can result in the onset of depression

(Seligman, 1975). If people feel that they are able to do something to prevent their own victimisation, the psychological benefits can be significant. Perhaps this is why there is often great enthusiasm, at least initially, when Neighbourhood Watch schemes are launched. As was noted earlier, most people who are fearful of crime will be motivated to do something to try to reduce their own risk. Providing that this does not involve too much time, effort or money, and that there might be tangible results, people may well do something. However, to return to an earlier analogy, if the 'costs' appear to outweigh the likely rewards, then action is perhaps less likely.

As we have seen, situational crime prevention rests on a number of assumptions about criminal activity. These include the belief that much crime is opportunistic; that increasing the perceived risk of detection will reduce offending; that situational crime prevention strategies are easily introduced; and that offenders have a 'rational choice' in deciding whether or not to commit crime. This latter point is an interesting one and will be discussed below.

Rational choice theory

Rational choice theory presupposes that offenders do not pick targets at random, but rather exercise a judgement as to whether the perceived level of risk outweighs the anticipated reward. Thus, according to this view, the perceived risk of detection will be seen as a more powerful motivating factor than the length of sentence that the person might receive if they are arrested.

Rational choice theory has some appeal, but it may not apply in all cases. It would also appear to be more applicable to some types of crime than others. While research such as that by Bennett and Wright (see above) suggests that burglars do make mental calculations when contemplating offending, many of the burglars interviewed by Bennett and Wright admitted that they did not always follow their own rules and sometimes just decided to break into a particular property regardless. We must also bear in mind that interviews with convicted burglars in prison may not offer a representative sample of offenders. For example, the burglar who is never caught will not have been interviewed. In addition, young offenders just embarking upon a criminal career will tend not to be found in prisons, and so their voices will not be heard.

It would also appear that much crime is not planned and the idea of weighing up the costs and benefits before deciding whether or not to act may be unrealistic. The young man in a pub who finds his girlfriend being molested by a stranger may simply lash out rather than carefully considering the costs and benefits of his actions. As Crawford says:

> The image of the self-maximising decision maker, who carefully calculates the net advantages and disadvantages of certain activities, does not fit the impul-

sive, reckless, opportunistic and ill-considered nature of much criminality, particularly that associated with young offenders.

(1998: 73)

As such, rational choice theory should perhaps be seen not as a general theory of crime, but rather as an organising perspective from which theories might be developed (Cornish and Clarke, 1986; 1990). Thus while rational choice theory may well explain target selection for certain types of acquisitive crime, it is perhaps less relevant as an explanation of other forms of criminal activity. It should also be acknowledged that not all offenders will go through the careful decision-making process which the theory presumes. Indeed, one might want to argue that if offenders were actually any good at weighing up risks they would be unlikely ever to be caught. Despite these provisos, we must acknowledge that interviews with offenders have been extremely useful in understanding why some types of offenders choose to commit some types of crime. Armed with such knowledge, it is possible to introduce crime prevention initiatives which will be likely to deter some offending behaviour by increasing costs and reducing potential benefits.

Routine activity theory

Sharing some similarities with rational choice theory is routine activity theory (Cohen and Felson, 1979). According to this view, if a crime is to occur there must be a combination of three elements, i.e. a motivated offender, a suitable victim, and the absence of a capable guardian. The theory was originally developed as an explanation of personal-contact predatory crimes such as muggings, but was later extended to cover a wider range of offences.

According to this view, the reason why cities harbour so much crime is not to do with the architectural environment (see above) but rather the fact that cities bring together the three elements, i.e. motivated offenders, vulnerable targets and a lack of suitable guardians. The theory does not consider the motivations for offending, but rather simply assumes that there are within society a number of likely offenders. Similarly, 'suitable victims' are not defined but might include anyone whom the offender may choose to attack. The reader may however wish to note that some writers (e.g. Hindelang et al., 1978) have suggested that a victim's lifestyle may contribute significantly to their chances of victimisation. For example, the people with whom an individual associates, the number of times they choose to go out at night alone and the area in which they live may all contribute to a person's chances of victimisation.

The term 'guardian' is used in the traditional sense of anyone whose presence deters crime. However, Felson (1995) also talks about others who may influence an offender. These include 'handlers' who supervise potential offenders and 'managers' who monitor the places where crime might occur.

Felson (1993) suggests that it is elements of our modern Western lifestyle which contribute to the high level of crime in society. For example, most homes will possess fairly high value and desirable electrical goods such as video recorders and, increasingly, computers. Many homes are also left unoccupied for much of the day while owners are out at work. Furthermore, many of today's young, mobile householders are unlikely to spend time building up good relations with their neighbours or potential guardians. These three elements in combination may make victimisation of certain targets more likely.

Some writers have recently sought to bring together the ideas incorporated in rational choice theory and routine activity theory (for example Clarke and Felson, 1993). When the two views are combined this tends to lead to an increased focus on the relationship between certain places and crime. The fundamental question is whether certain locations actually generate crime, or whether they simply provide a suitable environment in which an almost inevitable crime just happens to occur (Sherman *et al.*, 1989). Writers such as Newman (see above) have assumed that the former is the case, while others have argued that the environment does not so much cause crime as merely provide an appropriate setting for its occurrence. Perhaps the truth lies somewhere in between these two positions with certain environments more likely to encourage or harbour criminal activity and certain environments less likely to do so.

Before moving on we should perhaps note the shift in emphasis which both rational choice theory and routine activity theory suggest. Unlike many early sociological theories of crime, both views see crime not so much as a pathological activity requiring explanation, but rather as an almost normal everyday activity in today's society (Garland, 1996). As such, crime is seen as a risk which can be calculated and, hopefully, avoided or at least managed.

Although there have been some failures in initiatives which utilised situational prevention methods, many more schemes have met with success (see Pease, 1997: 970 for a brief review). Many of these initiatives are of the type which might be expected. For example, a great deal of the British Home Office's crime prevention budget is now taken up with the installation of CCTV in public places (Koch, 1996). While schemes utilising CCTV have often met with success (Horne, 1996) a number of writers have expressed concern about CCTV's widespread adoption. One reservation is that the quality of images generated, especially by the less expensive type of equipment, means that the 'evidence' provided by the cameras is not particularly useful. Research currently being carried out by Vicki Bruce in Edinburgh suggests that mistaken identifications can occur even when apparently good CCTV images are obtained.

There are other concerns over the expertise and training of the staff who monitor the images provided by the cameras. Personnel may be untrained or inefficient, or may choose to use the equipment inappropriately. In addition, some have argued that CCTV is an invasion of privacy, a concern heightened when some tapes are sold to television companies for the purposes of entertainment.

CCTV is an obvious example of primary prevention, but other measures are perhaps less obvious. For example the introduction of technology which enabled telephones to display the calling number on a potential victim's phone served to reduce the number of obscene phone calls (Clarke, 1991). Smith and Burrows (1986) showed how simple changes in a hospital's management procedures could reduce the amount of fraud. Another study established that certain bus seats are more prone to vandalism than others, and this enabled the bus company to use vandal-resistant materials in the most vulnerable seats (Sturman, 1980). The latter study is an example of risk analysis, which allows levels of risk to be calculated and crime prevention initiatives to be targeted appropriately (Pease, 1997: 972).

Crime displacement

One potential problem in all the discussions of situational prevention is the thorny issue of displacement. The concern is that by introducing measures which make some targets less vulnerable, the determined criminal will not be deterred but will simply switch their attention to a slightly easier target. Thus, if all new BMWs are fitted with sophisticated alarm and immobilisation systems, the thief may simply target older cars with less sophisticated protection. The bank robber who is deterred by the installation of a state-of-the-art security and surveillance system in the local branch of Barclays may switch his attentions to the local building society instead. The mugger who is deterred by a large police presence may simply wait until the officers are occupied elsewhere before striking. A rapist may wait until his victim is out of range of the CCTV cameras before attacking. Perhaps even more worrying are cases of displacement in which an offender switches not so much the place or time of an attack, but rather the type of offence. A burglar who is deterred by the increasing number of domestic alarms may instead satisfy his need for money by switching to muggings.

As Heal and Laycock (1986) have noted, if offending is merely displaced, then situational crime prevention measures are worth little in the long term. The problem is that it is often difficult to prove or disprove whether displacement has occurred. If a crime prevention initiative in one small geographical area proves to be successful, it might be thought a simple matter to measure whether the reduction is mirrored by a corresponding increase in adjoining areas. However, this is far too simplistic, and, one might argue, naïve. For example, the burglar may shift attention not to the adjoining area, but to one in a different police district or county. In this case, the increase may go unrecorded by any researcher trying to prove or disprove the existence of displacement. Similar problems may well be encountered if the offender switches from one type of crime to another. Thus a domestic burglary prevention scheme may lead to a reduction in the number of domestic burglaries, but to an increase in the number of commercial premises targeted. The police may fail to acknowledge this when reporting on the success of their original initiative.

Those who believe that displacement is likely or perhaps even inevitable are basing their beliefs on a number of assumptions. For example, it is assumed that most if not all offenders are highly motivated and will eventually overcome the initial attempts to prevent their criminal behaviour. Such an assumption seems to suggest that criminals are addicted to their criminal lifestyle (Hodge *et al.*, 1997) and will find some way of victimising society no matter what is done. This may however be a rather simplistic assumption.

Supporters of the displacement theory also seem to presume that offenders are almost infinitely adaptable and they can turn their hand to almost anything. Thus, if the acquisition of money is seen as the primary motivating factor, then it may be immaterial whether this is obtained through robbery, burglary or extortion. However, one must question whether this is actually true. Although some offenders do have convictions for a wide range of offences, the vast majority tend to concentrate on a rather restricted range of crimes (see Chapter 4). In any case, if a criminal does switch the type of crime they commit then this change might be for the better or for worse. Barr and Pease (1992) make an important distinction between malign and benign displacements. The former involves situations in which an offender switches to a more serious type of offence, while the latter refers to a scenario in which an offender changes to a less serious type of crime. Although both would technically be classified as displacement, one would obviously be seen as less worrying than the other.

A final assumption made by advocates of the displacement hypothesis is that there is an almost unlimited number of alternative (and equally attractive) targets available in society. This would appear to be a presumption with little empirical foundation. Not all criminals continue to offend irrespective of what is tried, as the success of some crime prevention initiatives confirms. If it were possible to prevent totally the unauthorised taking of cars, what crime would we expect the joyrider to turn to as an 'equivalent alternative'?

We can thus see that it is all but impossible to prove whether displacement will or will not occur in any given situation. A number of the assumptions made by advocates of displacement theory appear to be questionable. While there is some evidence of displacement following the introduction of certain initiatives, displacement is by no means inevitable (for example Hesseling, 1994). It is surely unrealistic to assume that *every* crime prevented will be displaced. If half of the crime initially prevented by an intervention is displaced, then it could still be argued that the initiative was worthwhile.

Pease (1997) suggests that a fundamental flaw in the displacement argument is a failure to consider how crime patterns arise (see Chapter 2). Rather than talking about crime displacement, Barr and Pease (1990) prefer to use the term crime deflection when discussing prevention initiatives. Such a term simply acknowledges that a crime has been prevented, without an over-concern for its possible displacement. Barr and Pease argue that even if some crime is displaced, this fact can be addressed by crime prevention strategists, and the original initiative should not be simply abandoned. Barr and Pease (1990) suggest further that whereas crime displacement is always seen as a failure of the initiative, crime deflection is not necessarily so. As was noted above, if one particular crime is deflected, and instead a much less serious crime committed, then this might reasonably be labelled a success.

If, as has been argued above, many primary prevention strategies have been successful, then the cynical reader may well be asking why there is still so much crime in society. This question will be addressed throughout this volume, but for present purposes we should perhaps note that in terms of policy, intentions and actions are not always equivalent (Crawford, 1998). For example, although the British government sees crime prevention as an important priority, Barclay (1995) notes that only three per cent of crime and criminal justice expenditure is spent on crime prevention. Pease (1997) notes that because over three-quarters of Home Office crime prevention expenditure is devoted to CCTV schemes, local authorities quickly learn that the way to get money is to apply for funding for local CCTV schemes. Thus, although a CCTV scheme may not necessarily be the best solution to a local problem, the authority is more likely to be successful in its bid for funding if it goes down this path. There is a fallacy in this approach, for as Pease notes:

> ... *good* primary prevention requires a clear crime focus, an objective analysis of the presenting problem, and a choice of means from among those available. What is *actually* happening is that, by its patterns of expenditure, the Home Office demonstrates the marginality of crime prevention; by the way it makes money available, it by-passes the necessary analysis, and once the money hits the maelstrom of local politics, expenditure is a matter more of need and expedience than crime control.
>
> (1997: 980)

Pease goes on to argue that while situational crime prevention is a good way to prevent certain types of crime, it is less adaptable to certain other forms. Thus, such initiatives may well deter a proportion of property crimes, but will probably have less success in deterring crimes such as personal assaults. He also notes that situational crime prevention strategies may be more likely to be adopted by commercial organisations than by public authorities. A company whose financial survival is being threatened by a large amount of theft will tend to be highly motivated to take measures to reduce the level of loss. However, local authorities and national governments, while acknowledging the very real concerns of its citizens, may be less motivated to bring in situational crime prevention strategies. Pease (1997) notes that in recent years there has been something of a switch away from primary prevention initiatives and towards secondary and tertiary prevention. However, he notes that this has not been done as a result of a failure of the former, nor a demonstrated success of the latter. Given Pease's own important work on repeat victimisation (see Chapter 2) this is perhaps surprising.

Summary

We have seen in this chapter that 'crime prevention' can cover a very wide range of strategies and initiatives, some of which have met with more success than others. The chapter has concentrated on what is known as primary prevention and in particular on situational and environmental strategies. We have seen that crime prevention strategies are inextricably linked with assumptions about human behaviour, and in particular about the behaviour of those who may be tempted to commit crime. It does appear that situational crime prevention still has a great deal to offer at least in the reduction of property crime. It should be noted that although this chapter has necessarily had a restricted focus, many theories of criminal behaviour (see Chapter 4) can be readily converted into crime prevention strategies. Similarly, strategies which persuade offenders to change their behaviour can be good crime prevention initiatives (see Chapter 8). We should also bear in mind that a better understanding of the true level of crime and of victimisation can lead to more successful crime prevention work.

Chapter 4

Psychology and criminal behaviour

Among the questions most often asked in relation to crime is 'What makes someone a criminal?' Given that psychology's main goals are to understand, explain and predict human behaviour, it would be natural to expect that psychologists would have a ready answer to this perennial question. The reader may however be disappointed to learn that it has not proven easy to provide a simple answer. While there are a large number of theories which have added greatly to our understanding, there is often disagreement among academics as to the most important factors which might lead to criminality. The trap which some researchers and lay persons have fallen into is to search for **one** cause of criminal behaviour. If the massive amount of research on criminality has taught us anything, it is that it would be naïve and perhaps dangerous to expect to find just one explanation for all criminal behaviour. As with almost all behaviour, it is not possible to identify one simple explanation for criminal behaviour. Any piece of behaviour is the result of a complex interaction between genetic, social, and environmental factors. Despite this, as we will see below, many theorists have tried to develop single and often simplistic explanations. In this chapter we will examine a small number of representative theories which have added to our knowledge and understanding. For a more comprehensive review, the reader may wish to consult the excellent coverage provided by Blackburn (1993a).

In order to understand the difficulty encountered when trying to explain criminality, we should perhaps first consider what 'criminal behaviour' actually is. At its simplest, criminal behaviour might be defined as the performance of any action which is prohibited by law. While we may all have stereotypes of what we mean when we use the word 'criminal', categorisation of this form of behaviour can vary enormously. What one country defines as unlawful, may not be so defined in another. What is prohibited by law at one point in time may be considered legal at another. Let us take a few examples to illustrate the problem. At the present time it is unlawful in Britain to assist in the suicide of another person. However, in Holland such behaviour is no longer classed as unlawful, providing that it falls within certain boundaries. Thirty years ago, homosexual acts were prohibited by law in Britain. Today, providing that the acts take place in private, are between consenting adults and do not involve physical harm, such acts are considered lawful. Twenty years ago, a man who assaulted his wife would be unlikely to face prosecution, providing that the injuries were not particularly serious. Today, such acts are much more likely to lead to prosecution as society has become less willing to tolerate violence in the home. If we were to search naïvely for an explanation of 'criminal behaviour', such anomalies would cause great difficulty. Was the man who assaulted his wife 20 years ago any less a 'criminal' than one who did so today?

Much as we may wish to be able to draw a neat dividing line between criminals and non-criminals, it is not always possible to do so. While it might be relatively straightforward to divide the population into those who have a criminal record and those who do not, this might be rather misleading. By definition, the former group would include only those who have been prosecuted and convicted of a criminal offence. Within this group may well be some individuals who have been wrongfully convicted (see Chapter 9). The 'non-criminals' would include both those who have never committed a crime and those who have simply never been convicted. As we saw in Chapters 1 and 2, the number of people who are convicted of a criminal offence appears to be only a small proportion of those who actually commit a crime at some point in their lives. For this reason, a simple comparison of 'criminals' and 'non-criminals' may not reveal a large number of psychological differences between these two groups.

There can be few people who have never committed any form of criminal behaviour. The worker who uses the office phone to make a private call, or takes home a few envelopes for personal use, exaggerates his expenses, or gives misleading information on his tax return may be guilty of a crime. Yet most who commit or observe such behaviours would tend not to label the person a criminal. Nor would one be likely to go rushing off to find some explanation for this 'criminal behaviour'. The point is that most people are guilty of committing some crime or other during their day-to-day lives. Taking a few envelopes from work and robbing a disabled old woman are poles apart, yet both are defined as unlawful acts which could result in a criminal conviction.

It is important to bear these points in mind in what follows. While society considers that distinguishing between criminals and non-criminals is a fairly straightforward process, this is certainly not the case. It should also be remembered that there is such a vast array of acts which are prohibited by law, that it is unhelpful to lump all such acts together and expect to find one all-embracing explanation for why people break the law. The young person on her way to a rave who happens to be in possession of an Ecstasy tablet is hardly likely to be motivated by the same factors as a fire-raiser or an armed robber. Yet once again, each of these three people are committing unlawful acts which could lead to a criminal conviction.

Despite these provisos, there have been numerous attempts to explain criminal behaviour by reference to single variables. We will consider some of these attempts, focusing in particular on the notion that criminality might be caused either by genetic or environmental factors.

Genetic factors, family influence and simplistic theories

The attempt to make distinctions between criminals and non-criminals is perhaps best epitomised by the writings of the Italian Cesare Lombroso (1876). After studying the physiological make-up of a number of convicts, Lombroso reached the conclusion that criminals were in fact of a different genetic 'type' from non-criminals. He believed that one could literally see the difference in the physical characteristics of criminals. In Lombroso's view, criminals were a throwback to more primitive times (he used the word atavistic) and this explained their physical difference. He suggested that, typically, criminals had smaller brains, heavy jaws, abnormal and asymmetrical skulls, projecting ears, and a crooked or flat nose. Furthermore, they were often colour-blind, left-handed and physically weak.

Lombroso even went so far as to suggest that different types of criminals had different physiologies. Thus, murderers were said typically to have cold, glassy, bloodshot eyes, abundant curly hair, strong jaws, long ears and thin lips. By comparison, sex offenders were said to have glinting eyes, strong jaws, thick lips, an abundance of hair and projecting ears. Lombroso's suggestions were partially mirrored by the work of Sheldon (1942) and Glueck and Glueck (1956) who suggested that certain body types (mesomorphs) were associated with criminality while others (ectomorphs and endomorphs) were not.

It is easy to scoff at Lombroso's ideas today, yet the notion that criminals may be physically different, at least in appearance, has persisted. For example, Bull and McAlpine (1998) suggest that people often have stereotypes of the facial appearance of criminals and that such stereotypes might even affect judgements of guilt and innocence in court. Television and film producers know how to harness such stereotypes and the same actors are often selected to play the part of 'the baddie' in different films, simply because their face (literally) fits the stereotype. However, to return to the ideas of Lombroso, it is interesting to note that, despite the lack of good scientific evidence to support his theories, many people were quick to adopt his ideas. Garland (1997) comments on the enormous amount of attention which Lombroso's views attracted:

In the twenty years following the appearance of *L'Uomo Delinquente* in 1876 this strange new science came to form the basis of a major international movement, manifesting itself in an outpouring of texts, the formation of new associations, international congresses, specialist journals, national schools of thought, and interested officials in virtually every European and American state.

(1997: 31)

As Garland and others have noted, such enthusiasm appeared partly to reflect a desire to adopt a scientific methodology to the study of 'criminals'. Despite the fact that Lombroso's methods and theories were fundamentally flawed, the approach did at least attempt to use observation and measurement, rather than mere speculation about human behaviour. As such, it was seen by many as the foundation of criminology as a discipline (Garland, 1985). Sennett (1977) suggests that part of the reason for the enthusiasm with which Lombroso's work was greeted was the fact that it confirmed some deeply rooted middle-class prejudices about the 'criminal classes'. The fact that Lombroso did not use adequate control groups, that his sample of 'criminals' actually contained a large proportion of the mentally disturbed and that he assumed that correlation proved causality, were all ignored in the rush to adopt his basic ideas. As we will see below, enthusiasm for biological explanations of criminal behaviour has been repeated in a number of more recent theories.

Genetic abnormalities and crime

During research by biologists in the 1960s, a number of genetic abnormalities were found in the cells of humans. Among these was a condition labelled XYY. The designation stems from the fact that a person's sex is determined by a pair of chromosomes – females normally have 2 X chromosomes (hence XX) while males normally have one X and one Y (hence XY). However, researchers discovered that a small proportion of the male population had an identifiable genetic abnormality and were in fact XYY. The fact that such individuals had double the male chromosomes normally found in men led to the abnormality acquiring the unfortunate label of 'the supermale syndrome'. The condition appeared to be associated with above average height and below average intelligence. However, the condition achieved notoriety when it was claimed by some researchers that it was associated with violent crime (Price *et al.*, 1966; Jarvik *et al.*, 1973). One can see how the reasoning might have gone. Given that males tend to be more aggressive than females anyway, if some people had double the normal number of male chromosomes, they may be twice as violent and aggressive as the average male.

Early work suggested that XYY males were over-represented in the population of prisons and special hospitals and that these men appeared to have a propensity towards high levels of violence. The potential impact of such a finding should not be underestimated. If the theory was true then it could be argued that such individuals are likely to be dangerous all their lives – their genetic abnormality will stay with them, and perhaps propel them towards violence. For this reason, some researchers advocated screening for the abnormality at an early age, in order that preventive measures might be taken. Others argued that these individuals may not be fully responsible for their actions – they behaved the way they did because of their genetic abnormality and not because they had 'chosen' to commit violent crime. In some murder trials, defendants tried to use their genetic abnormality as a defence against conviction.

The XYY story is interesting, not because it was true, but because of the way in which the media and members of the public reacted to it. In much the same way as the public greeted news of Lombroso's findings 80 years earlier, people seized upon the suggestion that criminals were genetically different from non-criminals and ran with the story. In reality, later, more comprehensive research established that although XYY males were more likely to be involved in crime, they were no more likely to be involved in violent crime (Witken *et al.*, 1976). It was also suggested that as their condition was associated with low intelligence, it may be this fact, rather than their genetic abnormality *per se*, which contributed to their levels of conviction.

Why do people want to believe in such theories?

The implication of both Lombroso's work and the XYY syndrome is that criminals are born and not made. While current research suggests that this is largely untrue, the public's reaction to such suggestions is interesting from a psychological point of view. It appears that the public would like to think that criminals are somehow a 'different breed' from the rest of law-abiding society. If it is possible to identify such people (e.g. by studying their facial features or their genetic make-up) then it can provide some feelings of comfort. Labelling and stereotyping those so identified makes it easier for others who are not included in this category to feel superior. In such circumstances, the public's calls to 'lock them up and throw away the key' are perhaps understandable. The wish to draw a line between criminals and non-criminals can be psychologically comforting – provided of course that one includes oneself in the latter category. This has partly been explained by social identity theory (Tajfel, 1981).

Social identity, labelling and stereotyping

Social identity theory has established just how important group membership can be in enhancing self-esteem. Membership of a group tends to increase in-group pride as we feel good about ourselves and those who appear to be similar to us. (It should be noted that we are talking here about groups which have a mainly positive image.) However, it has also been established that an increase in in-group pride tends to correspond with an escalation in out-group hostility. Thus, members of a local Home Watch scheme may band together partly to feel more secure, but also to try to fight the 'enemy' outside. The easier it is to identify or even name the enemy, the better people will feel. Those who find that 'the enemy' may actually come from within their own ranks will tend to feel much more uncomfortable.

The labelling and stereotyping of criminals has parallels in the field of mental illness. Although mental illness is increasingly common, most people like to feel that it is easy to draw a dividing line between those who suffer from this condition and those who do not. Making such a distinction allows people to feel less vulnerable to the condition themselves. To assist in this out-group stereotyping and hostility, society has come up with a vast array of slang words to describe those who suffer from mental illness. One need look no further than the tabloid press for many worrying examples. The media also tend to perpetuate some of the myths about mental illness through subjective, and at times inaccurate, reporting (see Philo, 1996 for some fascinating examples).

Does crime run in families?

The desire to identify, label and stereotype those who we fear (be they 'criminals' or 'the mentally ill') may be an understandable if disconcerting human trait. Perhaps then we should not be surprised to learn that the search for some way of differentiating criminals from non-criminals did not stop with the disproving of the XYY theory. While accepting that it is far too simplistic to suggest that a single gene can somehow 'cause' all criminal behaviour it may be that genetics still has some part to play.

Those who support such a position point to the fact that criminality does appear to run in families. For example, Osborn and West (1979) found that 40 per cent of the sons born to fathers with a criminal record went on to have a criminal record themselves. While such figures are interesting, we should make two important points. Firstly, the fact that criminal fathers are more likely to have criminal sons does not prove that the tendency is transmitted genetically. Socialisation into a criminal lifestyle may have as much, or possibly more, to do with the level of criminality in families than does genetic transmission. We will return to the notion of genetics and criminal behaviour shortly. The second point to make about figures such as those produced by Osborn and West is that if 40 per cent of criminal fathers' sons do become criminals, this means that 60 per cent do not. If genetic transmission was the simple and total answer, we would expect the figure to be up at the 100 per cent level. We should also note that according to Osborn and West's own figures, thirteen per cent of the sons of non-criminal fathers also develop criminal careers. This fact is not adequately explained by a simple genetic transmission theory.

Twin studies

If there is a genetic link in criminality, then one way of examining the topic is through the study of twins. Twins are of great interest to psychologists, as they can often help to unravel the mystery as to whether behaviour can be explained predominantly by genetic factors or environmental factors. Twins can be of two types, monozygotic (MZ or identical) and dizygotic (DZ or non-identical/fraternal). Identical twins are of great interest for, as the name implies, they are genetically identical. The way in which the human reproduction system works ensures that there are never two genetically identical people in the world – with the exception of identical twins. Identical twins are formed when the zygote splits and each individual embryo then contains an exact match in terms of chromosomes. By comparison, non-identical twins are formed when two different eggs are fertilised by two different sperm at the same time. These twins are thus more like brothers or sisters who happen to be born on the same day.

Because of these differences between the two types, psychologists have been very eager to study sets of twins and to establish whether one type are more similar to each other than the other type. If it is found that identical twins are more similar than non-identical, then this suggests that genetics is playing some part. Conversely, if identical and non-identical twins are equally similar, then this suggests that genetics is less important. Let us take an example. If we wish to establish whether criminality might be inherited, we could study sets of identical twins and compare them with sets of non-identical twins. We would be particularly interested in what is known as the concordance rate between pairs of twins. Concordance measures the extent to which one twin's possession of some characteristic, is mirrored in their twin. Thus, a concordance rate of 100 per cent would mean that in every case, if one twin possessed a characteristic, the other also did.

For present purposes we would want to establish whether, if one twin had a criminal record, their twin also possessed a criminal record. We might then compare the concordance rate between the two different types of twins to establish whether there were differences. A number of studies have done exactly this and produced some interesting, though not always identical, findings. So, for example, Lange (1931) found that for MZ twins the concordance rate for criminality was 77, while for DZ twins it was only twelve. Christiansen (1977) found that the concordance rate for MZ twins was 60, while that for DZ was only 30. Compared to these large differences, Kranz (1936) found that the concordance rates were rather less different, at 65 and 53 respectively.

A casual glance at these figures suggests that criminality does appear to have a genetic component – otherwise why would we find such differences between concordance rates in MZ and DZ twins? Indeed some writers have used such figures to argue that criminality (along with other things like intelligence and personality) does have a large genetic component. However, before accepting these suggestions we must consider a number of important facts with regard to twin studies. Firstly, most of the twins who have been studied will have been raised in the same home and thus been subject to the same environmental conditions. If they behave similarly in later life, it may therefore be impossible to disentangle the genetic effects from the environmental.

One way to try to address this problem would be to study identical twins who are raised in different environments. If such twins still show a high concordance rate, then it might be argued that it must be down to genetics. Unfortunately (at least for research purposes!) identical twins are not often reared in different environments and there are no good studies which have looked at criminality concordance rates among large samples of MZ twins reared apart. In any case, even if such studies had been carried out, they would not necessarily prove that it was genetics which were causing the effect. Some geneticists have argued that if identical twins reared in different environments end up being very similar then this **must** be down to genetics. However, such an argument implies that there is absolutely no similarity between the environments in which each was raised. Surely this is unlikely. For example, it may be that one twin is raised by the mother and the other by an aunt. As such there will probably be many similarities in each twin's home environment. Even if MZ twins are put up for separate adoption, the chances are that the homes in which they are raised will share some common characteristics. Screening by local authorities and adoption agencies will have narrowed down the field of possible adoptive parents to the point where each will have a number of similar attributes. It is therefore obvious that even twins reared in separate environments would share some similar experiences, each of which might affect their later behaviour.

The difference between MZ and DZ twins' concordance rates may be at least partly explained by the fact the parents are more likely to treat identical twins identically. Parents will tend, for example, to dress them the same and be more inclined to treat them as a pair, rather than as two completely different individuals. As such the twins are likely to share very similar social experiences. We should also bear in mind that while MZ twins will always be of the same sex, DZ twins can be of different sexes. We know that men are much more likely to have a criminal record than are women and the apparently lower concordance rate between DZ twins might be partly accounted for by this factor. We should also bear in mind that MZ twins are more likely to develop a very close relationship with each other, in some cases even developing their own language so that they can communicate with each other secretly. In situations where such a close relationship does exist, it seems likely that one twin may follow the other into a criminal (or indeed non-criminal) career. We should also bear in mind that in the case of identical twins, mistaken identifications are perhaps more likely to occur and miscarriages of justice to ensue (see Chapter 9).

Studies of adoption

Another way of addressing the question of genetics and criminality is to look at adoption studies. If a child of criminal parents is subsequently adopted by non-criminal parents it would be interesting to see whether this child does subsequently follow a life of crime. One recent meta-analysis of some thirteen adoption studies (Walters, 1992) suggested that there was some association between the criminal history of biological parents and the subsequent criminality of the child. Having said that, Bohman (1995) suggested that while genetic transmission may have a part to play, the interaction between genes and the environment is vitally important. Bohman found that if the biological parents and the adoptive parents both had criminal records, there was a 40 per cent chance that the child would go on to develop a criminal record. However, in cases where the adoptive parents had no criminal record, the offspring of criminal parents had only a twelve per cent chance of developing a criminal record.

Adoption studies suffer from some of the same methodological difficulties highlighted earlier in respect of twin studies. In particular, we would draw attention to the fact that children put up for adoption may each end up in very similar family circumstances and as such share similar social experiences. It should also be borne in mind that not all children are adopted at birth. In some cases, a child may only be put up for adoption after a period of very poor care by the natural mother and/or father. In some cases, a child's future criminality may in part be explained by these early pathological experiences, rather than by genetics.

Reconsidering genetics and criminality

In the absence of good data, the question of whether criminality does have a genetic component is difficult to answer conclusively. Some authors (e.g. Raine, 1993; Mednick et al., 1987) have argued strongly that genetics plays an important role in understanding why some people appear drawn to a criminal lifestyle. The few studies which have been carried out have often used fairly small samples and few if any have been able to look at twins or adoptees reared in completely different environments. It would also appear that some early twin studies were not particularly rigorous in deciding which twins were identical and which were not. Today, it is fairly easy to carry out genetic testing, but when some of the studies were carried out 60 years ago it was not so straight-forward a task. There is a suspicion that some twins may have been misclassified, making it difficult to be sure of the accuracy of the subsequent data.

If one thinks about genetics and criminality, it is hard to imagine how genetic transmission might actually take place. Would we really expect to find some day a gene which propels certain people into a criminal lifestyle? The rich variety of offences prohibited by law, and the fact that different acts are declared illegal at different points in time, makes such an idea seem unlikely. We should also bear in mind that, as noted earlier, convicted criminals make up only a small proportion of the total number of people who commit unlawful acts. Would we want to argue that genetics leads people to commit the more serious kinds of crime, but not the more trivial ones? Might it be that some people's genes lead them to commit crimes badly and thus be more likely to be arrested and convicted? The genetic position would also have difficulty explaining why many men start offending in their early teens, and stop, or at least change their offending, in their mid-twenties (Newburn, 1997). If their genes are propelling these people into criminality, how does the effect come and go?

If there is even a small genetic link with criminality, the effect may in any case be an indirect rather a direct one. The children of criminal parents may not so much inherit a 'bad' gene but rather certain predispositions or potential disadvantages when it comes to being able to deal with the world. We know that a great many aspects of human functioning have some genetic component (for example Bouchard *et al.*, 1990). In some cases, these inherited predispositions may interact with relevant environmental conditions to produce one form of behaviour or another. However, it is important to emphasise that any inherited predisposition may only reveal itself if the relevant environmental conditions are met. One can make comparisons with mental illnesses such as schizophrenia. It would appear that this form of mental illness has a genetic component in that the offspring of schizophrenic parents run a heightened risk of developing the condition themselves. We should note, however, that by no means all the children of schizophrenic parents do develop the illness. Rather, such children appear to inherit a predisposition towards the development of the condition, and this may or may not be realised in each particular case. In some environmental conditions the illness may manifest itself, but in others it will not.

One reason why some writers have refused to accept the idea of a genetic component in criminality is that such a position can, if taken to extremes, give rise to a number of politically difficult questions. For example, if it were possible to test young babies for possession of a 'criminal gene', what would we then do with those who appeared to possess it?

Would we want to go back a stage and test all prospective parents and insist that those who might give birth to criminal offspring be banned from having children? Thankfully, such questions are never likely to arise for, as was pointed out earlier, criminal behaviour appears always to result from a complex interplay between genetic, social and environmental factors. The research by Bohman (1995) also suggests that many of those who may be slightly more predisposed towards criminal behaviour may never realise this potential if they are raised in an appropriate environment. Genetics may play some part in defining the limits within which a person will develop, but it is the environment which will ultimately shape the behaviour within such broadly defined limits.

Perhaps we should accept that genetics plays at least some part in almost all behaviour, but never in isolation. Genetic predispositions interact with the environment in complex and, at times, unpredictable ways such that it is all but impossible to make absolute predictions based on genetic information alone. If there is a link between genetics and criminal behaviour it is perhaps that some aspects of personality have a genetic component. Thus, what is inherited is not a tendency to commit criminal acts as such, but rather a predisposition to develop certain aspects of personality, some of which may be linked to criminal behaviour. We will consider this suggestion when we review the work of Eysenck below.

Family influences

If genetics does not provide the answer to the question of why some people commit crime while others do not, this should not be taken to mean that the family is irrelevant. Indeed we noted earlier that what appear to be genetic influences may instead be more to do with the environment in which a child is raised. Thus, a boy who sees his father regularly threaten and hit his mother may eventually become a wife-beater himself. Should we treat this as evidence that violent tendencies can be passed on genetically or as evidence of social learning? Parenting styles, the quality of the home environment and the atmosphere within the home can all have significant influences on the developing child. Some psychologists (including Freud) believe that events in the first few years of life can have dramatic and long-lasting effects on children.

Bowlby (1953) achieved considerable notoriety in the 1950s and 1960s by suggesting that young children need their mothers as ever present companions if they are not to suffer the effects of maternal deprivation. Bowlby suggested that children who are deprived of maternal care will suffer psychological damage, resulting in a number of difficulties in later life. These might include an inability to form close and trusting relationships and, in some cases, the development of juvenile delinquency. To be fair to Bowlby, he did not claim (as some have suggested) that maternal deprivation would always lead to delinquency, merely that it was one of the possible consequences.

It now appears that many of Bowlby's basic premises were in fact false (see for example Rutter, 1971). In particular, Bowlby's notion that the child needs the mother as an ever present companion has been challenged. It has been shown for example that children are capable of forming multiple attachments during their development and that the biological mother certainly does not need to be at the baby's side constantly. The other important point to make concerns the quality of care. By focusing on the physical presence of the mother, Bowlby did not appear to attach sufficient importance to the quality of care which the child received. Thus, a mother may be constantly present but fail to nurture her child properly. Faulty child rearing practices could lead to many of the psychological problems which Bowlby associated with maternal deprivation. Rutter (1971) suggested that a number of factors were relevant in producing antisocial behaviour, including parental criminality, ineffective and inconsistent discipline in the home, family discord and a deviant peer group.

Despite the criticisms of much of Bowlby's work, the idea has persisted that the quality of care in early life can have an effect on the individual. However, it would now appear that Bowlby was wrong to follow Freud's lead in emphasising the permanence of events in early life. With advances in therapy it is now possible to reverse some of the damage caused by faulty or ineffective child rearing. Nevertheless, as we will see below, a focus on the home environment has revealed other interesting findings.

Farrington's longitudinal study

One of the most interesting contributions to our understanding of the development of delinquency has been provided by David Farrington and his colleagues (Farrington, 1991; Farrington 1997). At a time when most psychological studies take a brief snapshot of behaviour, Farrington and colleagues have carried out a longitudinal study of some 411 working-class boys born in London's East End in 1953. At the time of writing, the follow-up period is 30 years. Farrington found that of his sample, twenty per cent had acquired criminal convictions by the time they were seventeen and a further thirteen per cent by the time they were 25. Having said that, half of the total number of convictions were accounted for by just 23 boys who made up just over five per cent of the sample. Among the more important factors which Farrington identified as relevant to the development of delinquency were low income, a large family, parental criminality and poor child rearing practices.

Of the chronic offenders (i.e. those who had a large number of convictions) Farrington found that there were warning signs of their possible future lifestyle at an early age. For example, they were invariably identified as troublesome and/or dishonest while still at primary school. At age ten they were often described as hyperactive, impulsive, unpopular and of low intelligence. By the age of fourteen they were invariably identified as aggressive and they tended to have friends who were delinquents. By the age of eighteen, the delinquent group were found on average to drink, smoke and gamble more, be more likely to have tattoos, to bite their nails, to have a slow pulse rate and to be associated with gangs. The nature of Farrington's study meant that the same boys have been followed into their early thirties (to date) where they were typically found to be living in poorer housing, to have suffered a marital breakdown, to be suffering from psychiatric disorders and to be experiencing problems with their own children.

Farrington's contribution to our understanding of the development of criminal behaviour should not be underestimated. He suggests that if we wish to reduce the amount of criminality in society, we need to improve achievement in schools, improve child rearing methods, reduce impulsivity and reduce poverty in society. While all these are laudable aims, society seems unable or unwilling to tackle some of these issues in a constructive way.

Personality theories

Psychologists have developed a large number of psychometric tests in an effort to identify the many aspects of human personality. Given this fact it might be reasonable to expect that the different 'types' of personality which are most likely to become involved in criminal activity could be identified. The best known example of this approach is that of the English psychologist Hans Eysenck (Eysenck, 1977; Eysenck and Gudjonsson, 1989). Although often regarded as a general theory of criminal behaviour, Eysenck focuses in particular on the antisocial, psychopathic type of criminal and on why such people appear not to learn to behave in appropriate ways.

Eysenck originally believed that there were just two major personality dimensions along which humans varied. These were *neuroticism (N)* and *extraversion (E)*. Neuroticism runs from the high extreme (neurotic) to the low extreme (stable). It includes such characteristics as proneness to anxiety and depression, poor self-esteem and negative affectivity. Extraversion runs from the high extreme (extravert) to the low extreme (introvert). In fact, Eysenck later suggested extraversion appears to contain two slightly different elements, i.e. sociability and impulsiveness.

Eysenck devised fairly simple paper and pencil tests which could assess where individuals fell on these two dimensions. It is important to stress that Eysenck did not seek to categorise people as either extrovert or introvert, but rather to say where their scores lay in relation to the general population. Thus, most people would fall around the mid-point of his scale, and only a few people would be near the extremes. Nevertheless, Eysenck suggested that neuroticism and extraversion were two of the most important dimensions along which people's personalities varied. Eysenck came to believe that individuals who scored highly on both the extraversion and neuroticism scales were the ones most likely to become involved in criminal activity.

Eysenck believed that a large proportion of a person's personality derived from their genetic make-up. He hypothesised that some individuals are born with cortical and autonomic nervous systems which affect the way in which they deal with, and learn from, environmental stimuli. According to Eysenck, the extravert, because of their genetic make-up, is generally under-aroused and so constantly seeks stimulation. Such a person is, therefore, likely to be impulsive and to be constantly seeking excitement. Eysenck also believed that it was more difficult to condition extraverts and as a result they were less likely to react appropriately to reward and punishment. In terms of neuroticism, Eysenck suggested that those who score highly on this dimension have an autonomic nervous system which is labile and that these individuals react strongly to unpleasant stimuli. He believed that such individuals often display moody and anxious behaviour. Eysenck argued that those with the highest neuroticism scores are the most difficult to condition due to their high levels of anxiety.

Eysenck believed that high extraversion and high neuroticism, when combined, produce an individual who is constantly seeking excitement and stimulation, but who is not easily controlled (or conditioned) and does not appear to learn from their mistakes. Thus, the neurotic extravert will not have learned appropriate rules of behaviour through the normal process of socialisation.

There is perhaps a certain intuitive appeal to this notion. The male adolescent joyrider who takes cars and appears to enjoy chases with the police, fits the picture in terms of seeking excitement. The same person who continues to offend, despite the threat to his own (and others') life would also seem to fit into Eysenck's typology.

In his later writings, Eysenck identified a third personality dimension, *psychoticism (P)*. This was not so much a measure of susceptibility to psychosis, but more a measure of what we might today see as psychopathy (Blackburn, 1993a: 118). We will discuss psychopathy more fully in Chapter 5. Psychoticism was not so well researched as the other dimensions, though Eysenck believed that people who scored highly on this scale would be more likely to engage in criminal activity. High psychoticism scores were, according to Eysenck, typified by individuals who were uncaring, solitary, tough minded, aggressive, cruel, cold and impersonal. As with the other major dimensions of personality, Eysenck believed that there was a large genetic component to scores on his psychoticism scale. According to Eysenck, the neurotic extravert who also scored highly in terms of psychoticism would, largely as a result of genetic factors, be the most likely to become a criminal. In the case of psychoticism, the person might also be more likely to engage in violent and aggressive crimes in which a victim was made to suffer.

Eysenck conducted a number of studies in an effort to prove his theory. As with much of Eysenck's writing, it is easy to be convinced by his arguments, but a more careful analysis of his findings suggests that the theory may not have been proven. A number of writers have questioned some of the methodology used in Eysenck's work (for example Trasler, 1987). If we take one of the main components of the theory (that extraverts are more likely to be found among the criminal population than are introverts) there are contradictory findings. Eysenck's own work claimed to show quite a high correlation, but other researchers failed to find such a connection and in some cases found the opposite of what Eysenck had claimed (Hollin, 1989: 56; Blackburn, 1993a: 124). It was suggested that one possible reason for these contradictions is the fact that extraversion contains two possibly distinct elements, i.e. impulsiveness and sociability. Eysenck and McGurk (1980) found that samples of offenders did typically have higher impulsiveness scores than did non-offenders, but that there was no difference in terms of their sociability scores. It is, therefore, claimed that it is impulsiveness rather than extraversion in general which might be associated with criminality.

The balance of research carried out since Eysenck's views were first published suggests that there is little correlation between extraversion and criminality in general. Blackburn (1993a) concludes:

> ... Eysenck's theory of criminality is not well supported. While attempts to test it have produced a number of significant findings, these are not for the most part related to the central components of the theory ... the crucial prediction that the ranks of criminals are swelled by extraverts has not been upheld with sufficient consistency to justify confidence in the theory.
>
> (1993a: 127)

The studies most likely to show consistency between extraversion and offending are self-report studies, in which extravert respondents may perhaps be more prone to exaggeration. Indeed, it has been suggested by Feldman (1993) that high E, N, and P scores are all associated with what he terms 'Yea-saying' (1993: 169). Individuals who score highly on these scales may thus be more willing to admit their own delinquency.

Eysenck's predictions with regard to neuroticism scores have also shown some inconsistency, although Hollin (1989) claims that 'the majority of studies show that offender samples score highly on N' (1989: 56). The findings with regard to psychoticism have produced rather more consistent results, with many studies showing a positive correlation between high P scores and offending. This relationship is found in both official and self-reported delinquency and high P scores are often found among the most serious and persistent offenders. However, Blackburn

(1993a) and others have taken issue with the whole notion of psychoticism as a personality dimension and suggest that it is unclear as to what exactly the dimension represents. Blackburn suggests that some of the elements contained within the psychoticism dimension are more akin to a measure of impulse control. Blackburn also suggests that, contrary to what Eysenck had predicted, high P scores were more likely to be found in secondary (as opposed to primary) psychopaths (Chapter 5).

Thus while there appears to be some evidence linking P with offending, Blackburn concludes that:

> ... given the ambiguities surrounding the meaning of P, and the lack of a
> theory linking P to socialisation, this association currently has little
> explanatory power. Moreover, cluster analytic studies reveal that high P scores
> form only a small minority of the delinquent population.
>
> (1993a: 127)

It would appear from this brief review that the majority of psychologists who have examined Eysenck's contribution to our understanding of criminal behaviour have been less than fully convinced by his arguments. So should we conclude from this that personality is irrelevant to criminal behaviour? Perhaps not. A more appropriate conclusion might be that personality is one of a number of variables which is linked with criminality, but not in an absolute or directive way. Even if there is a correlation between some aspects of personality and some forms of criminal behaviour, it may be inappropriate to assume that the former somehow causes the latter. It is important to recognise that correlation does not prove causality. It is also important to recognise that individuals do make some choices irrespective of their genetic make-up or personality. Indeed, as we saw in Chapter 3, one of the more interesting recent theories to emerge from the crime prevention literature is rational choice theory. This theory rests on the premise that criminals often make rational (or at least calculated) choices in deciding whether or not to commit a particular criminal act.

Perhaps all that we can say is that some aspects of personality may well interact with some aspects of the environment and result in a number of people committing certain forms of criminal activity. Such an apparently bland statement may not be very helpful in trying to narrow down the causes of crime. However, it does appear that, as with the genetic theories of crime discussed above, the mistake is to assume that personality is **the** reason why people commit crime. It is certainly not the total answer but neither is it completely irrelevant. It is also possible that personality is more relevant to certain types of crime than others (Blackburn, 1995b). We have already drawn attention to the vast array of behaviour subsumed under the heading 'criminal activity'. While some crimes are undoubtedly linked to some aspects of personality, others may be much more situationally determined (see Chapter 3).

A final point concerning personality is the fact that some individuals who do embark upon a criminal lifestyle find it difficult to change their behaviour. As Kohnken (1996: 259) has noted 'the best predictor of offending at one age is offending at a preceding age'. This notion has prompted some writers to suggest that some people might become addicted to crime in the same way that others might become addicted to drugs. Thus Hodge *et al.* (1997) suggest that addiction models may help us to understand why some people grow out of offending as they reach early adulthood, while others persist in criminal activity.

Social learning theories

In contrast to many of the views expressed so far, social learning theories suggest that committing crime has little to do with genes or personality, but is in fact a learned response. Social learning theories of crime have their origins in the work of the sociologist E.H. Sutherland who developed a theory known as *differential association* (Sutherland, 1939; Sutherland and Cressey, 1970). This theory suggested that criminal behaviour is learned through association with other people, usually in the form of close groups. This learning includes both the acquisition of attitudes towards the commission of certain acts and the learning of criminal techniques. The learning experiences (or differential associations) will vary in frequency and importance for each individual, although, according to Sutherland, the learning of criminal behaviour is no different from the learning of any other form of behaviour. For Sutherland, it is the ratio of exposure to criminal norms rather than just criminal associations which is important.

Sutherland's views have some intuitive appeal perhaps best describing the individual who rebels against parental influence, joins a local neighbourhood gang and becomes involved in criminal activities. The theory lays some considerable emphasis on the process of socialisation. In some cases, an individual may have received inadequate or inappropriate socialisation from parents and in others, socialisation will have been at the hands of important friends and role models. As such the theory represents a very different view of the criminal – they are not propelled towards a life of crime by genes or personality, but rather learn inappropriate behaviour during the process of growing up.

More psychological developments of social learning theory are perhaps best epitomised by the writings of the psychologist Albert Bandura (Bandura, 1977). Bandura believed that a great deal of each individual's behavioural repertoire is a result of learning experiences. 'Learning' in this sense would include both observing (and perhaps imitating) others' behaviour and being rewarded (or punished) for exhibiting certain kinds of behaviour through the process of socialisation. Bandura's best known contribution to our understanding of social learning was his early experiments examining aggression.

Bandura hypothesised that people behave in violent and aggressive ways mainly because they see others behaving in this way and, therefore, learn that this form of behaviour is appropriate. His original studies involved allowing groups of children to observe an adult interacting with a large inflatable 'Bobo' doll. Some children watched the adult interacting in a very aggressive way, while others were shown a much less aggressive adult model. Shortly after observing the adult's behaviour, the children were allowed to play with the doll themselves. As Bandura had predicted, those children who had been exposed to the aggressive adult model were much more likely to behave aggressively than were those who were shown the less aggressive model.

Bandura's theory is thus relatively straightforward – people learn aggressive or criminal behaviour by observing others behaving in this way. He argued that social learning can take place in the family, in the individual's prevalent subculture, and through the observation of cultural 'heroes' or role models in the media. Influence on the individual is thus likely to be greatest if the person being observed has high status or prestige. If the person is also shown to benefit from their aggressive acts (what is termed vicarious reinforcement) then the behaviour is also more likely to be imitated. At first glance, social learning theory appears to be modelled on traditional behaviourist beliefs in that behaviour is seen to occur because of reinforcements in the environment. However, as Blackburn (1993a: 98) notes there are a number of identifiable differences between the two approaches (see also Nietzel, 1979).

Screen violence

One aspect of social learning theory which has been seized upon by the media and politicians is that people may become violent or aggressive by observing others on television and in films behaving in such a way. There can be few topics that have generated as much debate and controversy as the suggestion that screen violence leads to violence in society (Howitt, 1998; Petley and Barker, 1997; Reiner, 1997). For this reason we will now consider this issue.

There are at least two ways in which screen violence might affect individuals. Firstly, people may observe those in films or on television behaving in violent ways and simply imitate this behaviour in their normal lives. Secondly, people may observe a great deal of violence and begin to see such behaviour as perfectly normal. The cumulative effect of continued exposure to violence may result in the person becoming desensitised to the effects of such behaviour. In such cases the person may be uninhibited and be less likely to curb any aggressive urges they may feel.

Those who wish to censor television or to control what we may see on film have seized upon the ideas contained within social learning theory. It has been suggested by such groups that the reason that society is apparently becoming more violent is that there is so much violence on television, on video, at the cinema and now in computer games (Griffiths, 1993). Following the school shooting in Denver in April 1999, the state governor suggested that in his view screen violence was a contributory factor to this appalling killing. Some infamous cases (e.g. the murder of James Bulger in Liverpool and the killing of people in Hungerford by Michael Ryan) have also been cited as 'proof' of the view. The desire to point the finger or to blame someone or something is interesting from a psychological viewpoint but the notions are less easily proved. As we saw with many early theories of criminality, it is unrealistic to expect to find one simple explanation for criminal behaviour, even that of a violent nature.

In the James Bulger murder trial, the judge (Mr Justice Morland) drew attention to the fact that at least one of the young boys involved in the killing had access to violent videos (specifically, *Child's Play*) and that this might explain the awful crime (Young, 1996). The judge said: 'It is not for me to pass judgement on their upbringing but I suspect that exposure to violent video films may in part be an explanation.'

Such speculation was seized upon by an eager media desperate to explain the horrendous crime committed by two young boys. However, one obvious question is why the other 99.999 per cent of people who had also watched the same video did not choose to go out and abduct and then kill a toddler. A similar question can be asked in the case of Michael Ryan who reportedly dressed up in 'Rambo' style clothes and set about imitating his screen hero by killing a number of people in Hungerford (Canter, 1994: 191–3). Once again, we must ask how many people also watched the Rambo film and chose not to go on a killing spree? It would appear that almost every year some new film is targeted as an example of the great danger which is contained within this medium. In the 1960s it was films such as *Clockwork Orange*. In the 1970s it was television series such as *Starsky and Hutch* and *The Sweeney*. More recently it has been film releases such as *Reservoir Dogs*, and *Natural Born Killers*. Howitt (1998: ch. 6) provides a number of other interesting examples.

There is a massive amount of research data accumulated on the subject of media violence. It has been reported that over 5,000 articles on the subject have been published to date (Wallbott, 1996: 335). In the vast majority of these research studies it has not been possible to prove a causal link between the watching of screen violence and the commission of violent acts (see Petley and Barker, 1997 for a good up-to-date review). Those readers who would prefer not to accept this view may wish to ask themselves two questions. Firstly, was there aggression and violence in society before the advent of film and television? Secondly, are the vast majority of people who choose to watch such material affected by it? The answers are affirmative in the first case and negative in the second.

Some early studies did appear to show a correlation between the watching of screen violence and the commission of violent acts. However, as was noted earlier, correlation does not prove causality. In some cases, the presumed causal relationship appeared not to be in the direction assumed, i.e. people who already had violent tendencies appeared simply to enjoy watching violent material. Although there was a correlation, the watching of violent material was not the primary cause of such a person's violent acts. Having said that, some research suggests that young offenders might learn novel forms of violence from the screen and wish to try out such techniques in real life (Ainsworth and Armitage, 1989). Even here though it was not suggested that the watching of violent acts initiated violent conduct.

What does emerge from the literature is that children are more likely to be affected by screen violence than are adults (for example Belson, 1979; Snyder, 1995). This however should not be taken to mean that all children will be so affected. In addition it would appear that violence committed by 'respectable' authority figures may have more of an effect than violence committed by those already labelled as criminal. There is also a danger that films which show an aggressor being rewarded for their aggression may be more likely to be emulated than are actions for which an aggressor is punished.

In his excellent review of crime and the media Howitt (1998) makes an interesting point in respect of copycat crimes, especially those involving violence. He says:

> Copycat crime may occur, but the evidence in its favour is more than occasionally flawed. Copycating is a largely unpredictable phenomenon and many real-life crimes which have been held to be copycat incidents have only tentative links with the media.
>
> (1998: 90)

The same author suggests that claims that up to half of violent crime in the USA is the result of television is a gross exaggeration and may be completely unfounded. This has not, however, prevented some campaigners from demanding greater restrictions on what can be seen. One question that arises in respect of copycat crimes is the generality of any such imitation. If a film is watched by 20 million people, only one of whom imitates actions seen on screen, should this be grounds for banning such a film from public viewing? The fact that only one person chose to exhibit such imitative behaviour suggests that this one individual is unusual or perhaps disturbed. If the person had never seen the film in question is it not possible that their disturbance may have sought expression in some other form of violent outburst, unconnected to a film? The problem with such a debate is that there must be a line drawn somewhere. Supposing ten out of twenty million choose to imitate a screen action, or 100? At what point should we decide that the film is having an unacceptable level of influence? There are also some films and videos (e.g. so called 'snuff movies' or those involving sexual assaults on children) which invoke such revulsion that almost all in society would wish to see them banned, irrespective of their possible influence.

We should also bear in mind a point made earlier with regard to the possible cumulative effects of media violence. Although the evidence for 'copycat' crimes is sparse, there remains a concern that increasing levels of violence will have an uninhibiting effect on the general population. There is a danger that violence will become normalised to the point where it no longer arouses concern in those watching. Normalisation also means that each individual may be less constrained when contemplating using violence themselves.

We can see that while social learning theory has much to say about some forms of imitative behaviour, it cannot explain a great deal of crime, especially that of a violent nature. Because society is apparently obsessed with understanding why people behave violently, it should come as no surprise to learn that there are a very large number of theories which have been proposed to account for such behaviour (Geen, 1998, provides an excellent recent overview). At various points in time, all of the following have been put forward as psychological explanations for why people commit violent acts:

- brain damage;
- genetics;
- inbuilt urges or instinct;
- early child rearing practices;
- personality;
- mental illness;
- peer group pressure;
- deindividuation;
- presence of aggressive cues (e.g. guns);
- frustration;
- provocation;
- alcohol and other drugs;
- social learning;
- violent television/films/videos;
- computer games;
- heat;
- pollution;
- noise;
- overcrowding.

This list is by no means complete, but does show the wide range of explanations available. Acknowledging that so many factors may be at least partly responsible for violent behaviour also illustrates the futility of trying to find the **one** reason why people commit crime, even violent crime.

Violence and aggression appear to have been part of most societies for much of their history. The level of violence may change from time to time and the form which the violence takes also alters. In the early 1990s the concern was with so-called 'road rage' attacks. As we approach the millennium concern has switched to 'air rage' attacks in which some airline passengers are reported to have behaved aggressively and endangered the lives of others. One can only speculate as to what the next cause for concern might be, but some early reports have identified 'pool rage' as a possible contender. (This is the tendency for those swimming in overcrowded swimming pools to bump into each other and then to behave violently!)

An interesting final point is made by Farrington (1997: 398). He points out that in trying to understand why people commit crime it might actually be helpful to consider three questions, i.e. why the person started offending, why they continue to offend (and perhaps to escalate the offending), and why the person stops offending. Interestingly, Farrington suggests that there may be three different reasons – the person may start offending because of poor child rearing practices, continue to offend because of parental criminality and delinquent peers and stop offending because they settle down and have family responsibilities. Farrington's own contribution to our understanding of criminal careers can also help to identify, and hopefully prevent, some of the conditions that lead to offending.

Summary

This chapter has suggested that it is unhelpful to try to identify one specific factor which can account for criminal behaviour. The diversity of actions subsumed under the heading of 'illegal acts' means that a single causative factor is unlikely to be found for criminal behaviour. There has, however, been some interesting research which has identified some of the more important variables. Although no single theory can provide all the answers, when some of the variables are combined a clearer picture emerges. Genetic predisposition, personality variables, the home environment, and peer and media pressure may all combine to the point where a criminal career may be much more likely. So long as people recognise the multicausal nature of almost all criminal behaviour, psychology can offer a number of valuable insights. Such insights are helpful as explanations but, as we will see in Chapter 8, they may also allow us to change the behaviour of some offenders.

Chapter 5

Crime, intention and mental illness

In Chapter 4 we highlighted some of the difficulties encountered when trying to make a clearcut distinction between criminals and non-criminals. We also identified some of the psychological factors which are associated with offending behaviour, with explanations ranging from genetics and personality to upbringing, the media and peer pressure. In this chapter we will start to consider the extent to which an individual's mental state might have some effect on their behaviour. We will consider whether some forms of mental illness might lead to criminal behaviour and assess the extent to which a mental disorder might render an individual not fully responsible for their actions to the point where they might be found not guilty in court. Although we may like to imagine that all criminals are 'bad' and should be punished, it appears that significant numbers of those accused of criminal offences might equally be labelled 'sad' or 'mad'. As with many topics covered in the book so far, there are many myths and misunderstandings surrounding mental illness and crime. Some of these misconceptions will be challenged in what follows.

Intent and responsibility

It is a fundamental principle of law in almost all countries that, in order to be found guilty of a crime, the person must not only have committed the act (*actus reus*) but must also have intended to commit the act, i.e. they were in such a state of mind as to have a guilty intention or *mens rea*. (There are however a small number of 'absolute' offences where it is not necessary to prove guilty intent.) In other words, in most cases it must be shown that the person had criminal intent, was exercising free will and can, therefore, be held fully responsible for their actions while committing the crime in question. One immediate problem is that intentions cannot be observed directly but must be inferred from other observations. Owens (1995) notes that in cases where a defendant argues that they did not intend to do harm, the prosecution will need to submit further evidence to challenge this suggestion. He notes:

> From a psychological viewpoint, the prosecution needs to show that circumstances were such that it would be reasonable to infer that the defendant had intent. In practice this may be extremely complicated.
>
> (1995: 318–19)

Owens makes a very interesting point with regard to Freudian theories of human behaviour. Freud believed that whatever people do, they do it for a reason. However, Freud suggested that such reasons are not always obvious to the individual and may be contained within the individual's unconscious. Freud firmly believed that an individual never does anything 'accidentally'. Thus, slips of the tongue were seen not as simple errors but as the unconscious trying to express itself verbally. According to Freud, events which appear to be simple accidents may instead be viewed as deliberate acts. An example might make this notion clearer.

Suppose a man is accused of killing his partner by reversing over her with his car in the couple's driveway. He claims that the act was in no way intentional, but was simply a tragic accident. However, a Freudian interpretation might suggest that this was not simply a freak accident. Rather, it might be suggested that the man had previously wished his partner harm, but had suppressed such feelings and repressed them into the unconscious. The feelings might then remain in the unconscious, but seek expression at some other point in time. It might be argued that the man's actions were in fact not accidental, but rather were motivated, albeit by unconscious forces. Owens makes the point that while today almost all psychologists have rejected such Freudian notions, any determinist psychology (including radical behaviourism) could open up a similar debate with regard to intention and motivation.

One immediate question is thus whether mentally ill offenders can be held to be responsible for their crimes. This is an issue which has taxed English law for many years (Walker, 1968). The problem is well illustrated by the case of Peter Sutcliffe, who acquired the label of The 'Yorkshire Ripper'.

In the 1970s in the north of England, Peter Sutcliffe carried out a number of horrendous attacks on women, including thirteen murders. The police experienced great difficulty in identifying the perpetrator of the crimes and whole communities felt threatened by his continuing presence on the streets. The nature of the offences caused many to suggest that the attacks must be the work of a 'madman'. It was argued that the attacks were so bizarre and horrendous that they could not have been carried out by anyone 'in their right mind'. When Peter Sutcliffe was eventually caught in 1980, he (or rather his defence counsel) claimed that he was in fact suffering from a mental disorder and could, therefore, not be held fully responsible for his actions. It was claimed specifically that he was suffering from paranoid schizophrenia and that he had heard voices telling him to commit the crimes in question. However, many of those who had earlier been all too ready to describe his actions as 'those of a madman' now saw his claims of mental illness as a deliberate attempt somehow to 'get away with it' and not to admit his crimes.

At Peter Sutcliffe's trial, defence counsel introduced expert testimony by psychiatrists in an attempt to prove his mental illness (Jones, 1992). However, the prosecution did not accept his plea of diminished responsibility and argued that he should be convicted of murder. Peter Sutcliffe was in fact found guilty of thirteen murders and sentenced to life imprisonment. In finding him guilty, the jury appeared to decide that he was not mentally ill, or at least not to the extent that would negate his responsibility for the crime. However, arguments over Sutcliffe's mental state persisted, and three years after his conviction he was transferred to a special hospital because of his mental illness (Hollin, 1989: 125).

In the Peter Sutcliffe case we can see the difficulty in trying to establish whether, at the time of the offence, a person was sufficiently mentally competent to possess the necessary *mens rea*. There have been many legal rulings about these matters and we will consider some of the more important decisions below. However, debate over the mental state of some offenders will continue to raise concerns. In the USA, there was a great deal of debate on this matter following the trial of John Hinckley. Hinckley shot President Reagan, allegedly as a love offering to Jodie Foster with whom he had become obsessed. Hinckley had been pursuing Jodie Foster for some time and, frustrated by his inability to get her attention, plotted a number of bizarre stunts. In court Hinckley claimed that he was suffering from a mental disorder. Franzini and Grossberg suggest that 'Hinckley's trial resembled a psychiatric circus in which opposing psychiatrists took turns declaring Hinckley's mental illness and denying it' (1995: 12). Hinckley was in fact found 'not guilty by reason of insanity'. This verdict produced a public outcry and led to calls for changes in the way in which psychiatric evidence might be considered (Stone, 1984).

The insanity defence

A review of the insanity defence was provided by Jacobs (1971). Jacobs suggests that the defence can be traced back to an English jurist, Matthew Hale, who as long ago as 1736 argued that the insane should not be punished because they do not understand the consequences of their actions. In 1800 one Jonas Hadfield was acquitted of shooting at George III. Although he was deemed not to be insane, his counsel argued that he was suffering from a delusion and so should not be punished.

The most famous case in the history of the insanity defence is that of

Daniel McNaghten whose trial took place in 1843. McNaghten was accused of murdering the secretary to the then British Prime Minister, Sir Robert Peel. (His intended target had been the Prime Minister himself.) McNaghten claimed that he was suffering from paranoid delusions, one of which involved persecution by Peel. His defence claimed that at the time of the crime, McNaghten had lost control and been unable to resist his delusions. This defence proved to be successful and led to a verdict of 'not guilty by reason of insanity'. Such a verdict did however lead to considerable public outcry (and indignation from Queen Victoria). The fifteen most senior English judges were commanded to appear before the House of Lords and eventually gave a ruling on the insanity defence. This led to the establishment of the so-called McNaghten rules which incorporated two main principles. These were, firstly, that every man (*sic*) is presumed sane until the contrary is proved. Secondly, that it must be clearly proved that, at the time of committing the act, the accused was labouring under such a defect of reason, from disease of the mind, as not to know the nature of the act, or not to know that he was doing wrong. Interestingly, McNaghten himself was transferred to Broadmoor hospital where he eventually died. Blackburn (1993a) notes that:

> The McNaughtan (*sic*) rules survive in Anglo-American law, but they provide a very strict standard, which McNaughtan (*sic*) himself would not have satisfied and have been a continual source of controversy.
>
> (1993a: 256)

One difficulty with this defence is that it is necessary to prove that the accused was suffering from a 'disease of the mind' over which he/she had no control and that the 'defect of reason' was the result of such a disease.

Though posing considerable difficulty, the McNaghten rules did at least try to make a distinction between those who were 'bad' (and who were thus responsible for their actions) and those who were 'mad' (and not responsible for their actions). Over the years, verdicts of 'not guilty by reason of insanity' have sometimes been replaced by verdicts of 'guilty but insane' (Blackburn, 1993a: 257). This is more than a semantic shift as the former assumes that the defendant should not be viewed as guilty, while the latter does. Feldman (1993: 132) notes that the McNaghten rules provided the main test of insanity for over a century in both the British and American courts. However some jurisdictions introduced the notion of 'irresistible impulse'. This allowed a jury to acquit a defendant if his or her actions appeared to stem from a sudden and overpowering impulse. The insanity defence was modified in the USA in 1962 by the American Law Institute (ALI). The new rules made it easier to show that a defendant lacked the necessary criminal responsibility. However, the rules were attacked by a large number of professionals, including many lawyers and psychiatrists and eventually the provisions were challenged by the Insanity Reform Act 1984 (Feldman, 1993: 134).

Blau (1998) notes that the ALI Code introduced a volitional element into the equation and permitted consideration of a wide range of mental impairments. However, writing in 1998 he notes that 26 US states use a version of the ALI 'substantial capacity' rule, 22 states still adhere to the McNaghten rule while three have abolished the insanity plea.

Owens (1995) makes an interesting point with regard to the defence of insanity. He suggests that it will not generally be sufficient simply to show that the defendant was suffering from a mental disorder. Rather it will be necessary to demonstrate that the condition in some way led to the commission of the act in question. Thus, Owens suggests that an individual who suffers from non-specific auditory hallucinations may not successfully use insanity as a defence. However, a defendant who claims that his auditory hallucinations directed him to attack the person in question, or told him that society would not punish him if he did so, may be successful in this defence. Owens notes that:

> ... an understanding of normal psychological processes may be essential in determining whether or not an abnormal mental state may or may not be implicated in a particular criminal episode.
>
> (1995: 325)

Blau (1998) and many other writers have pointed to the fact that there are no valid, scientific diagnostic tests of insanity. The main problem stems from an apparent inability to distinguish between a defendant who is genuinely unable to control unacceptable impulses and one who is simply unwilling to do so. However, Blau notes that:

> Neuropsychological assessments may, in the future, provide objective more valid data to help the courts decide on the merits of an insanity defence ... expert neuropsychological testimony stating that minimal brain dysfunction destroyed a defendant's capability to choose right and refrain from wrong does establish a connection between defect and behavior.
>
> (1998: 70)

However, for present purposes we should be aware of the fact that sanity and insanity are not easily defined. Psychologists and psychiatrists use tools such as the *Diagnostic and Statistical Manual (DSM IV)* in order to identify individuals who suffer from different forms of mental illness. However, the vast majority of those who may be diagnosed as suffering from some form of mental illness would certainly not be considered 'insane'. In fact, insanity tends to be defined in legal, rather than psychological, terms.

Part of the problem stems from the way in which mental illness is classified and defined. Although manuals such as *DSM IV* help professionals to identify those who are suffering from particular forms of mental illness, there is a degree of subjectivity in such decisions. Many diagnoses are based upon the extent to which an individual's behaviour is statistically abnormal. Thus to experience hallucinations is statistically abnormal and a person who suffers in this way may (providing that certain other criteria are met) be diagnosed as schizophrenic. However, an individual with an exceptionally high IQ is also statistically abnormal yet is unlikely to be defined as mentally ill.

An individual who engages in sexual activity with a dead body is certainly statistically abnormal and such behaviour would be viewed by most observers as 'sick' (Jaffe, 1998). Yet if a man was charged with a crime involving necrophilia would we expect him to escape conviction because he was, almost by definition, mentally ill? Members of a jury who had to decide on such a question would undoubtedly be torn between a desire to punish a person who engaged in such an unacceptable sexual perversion and a need to recognise that the person was 'sick'. (Perhaps unsurprisingly there is little empirical research on the subject of necrophilia, though the interested reader may wish to consult Rosman and Resnick, 1989.)

Franzini and Grossberg (1995) have produced a fascinating book dealing with some of the more eccentric and bizarre forms of human behaviour. These include necrophilia, but also cover such things as erotomania (or obsessive loving) and the Capgras delusion (in which an individual believes that those around him/her have been replaced by imposters). In all of the cases cited by Franzini and Grossberg, the behaviour is certainly statistically abnormal. However, in some cases the person performing such acts might be convicted of a crime, but in others might be recommended for psychiatric treatment. Interestingly, some types of behaviour (e.g. erotomania which often leads to what we now refer to as 'stalking') have only recently been defined as criminal offences. Franzini and Grossberg ask whether ardent pursuit and persistence in the love quest is a form of mental illness. They answer the question by reference to the fact that the obsession may become a cause for concern when the individual uses methods which threaten the object of their obsession. They also note however that courts are unable to deal with such issues in a consistent manner.

Competence to stand trial

A concept related to questions of an accused's mental state is that of competence to stand trial (see Nicholson and Krugler, 1991 for an overview). In some cases, defence counsel may claim that while an accused was not actually insane (in the McNaghten sense) when they committed the crime, they are unfit to be tried because of their current mental state. This would apply to those cases where an individual cannot understand the trial procedures or evidence or where they cannot make a proper defence. This form of defence does not necessarily lead to an accused being released, but can lead to indefinite detention in a special hospital. Recently there has been a tendency for such cases to be adjourned in the hope that the defendant's mental state will improve (in some cases following treatment). Feldman (1993: 135) also suggests that defence counsel may introduce the competency issue in an attempt to avoid a defendant receiving a lengthy prison sentence, particularly in cases of violence. Roesch *et al.* (1999) suggest that issues of competency to stand trial are now much more common than is the insanity defence. They point out that in the USA there are between 25,000 and 39,000 competency evaluations carried out each year. Put another way, this suggests that questions of competency are raised in between two and eight per cent of all felony trials. However, as Roesch *et al.* note, the issues surrounding competency determinations are highly complex.

Diminished responsibility

Defences of insanity became much less common in England following the introduction of the Homicide Act 1957, the introduction of hospital orders under the Mental Health Act 1959 and the abolition of capital punishment in 1965. The Homicide Act 1957 introduced for the first time the defence of *diminished responsibility*. The Act spelled out the circumstances under which such a defence could be made. The main criterion was that there must be proof of 'substantially impaired mental responsibility'. Unfortunately, 'substantial impairment' was not clearly defined although it appeared to be a less rigid rule than the total impairment implied in the McNaghten rules (Griew, 1986).

The significance of the introduction of the defence of diminished responsibility was substantial. A person who puts forward such a defence will, if found guilty, be convicted of manslaughter rather than murder. Whereas in the UK the sentence for murder is always life imprisonment, that for manslaughter can vary enormously, depending on the circumstances of the case. Diminished responsibility defences have been used where defendants were suffering from serious disorders such as psychosis or reactive depression, but have also been attempted where a defendant was suffering from premenstrual tension or was said to have a psychopathic personality.

Mentally disordered offenders

Linked to these notions of responsibility for criminal acts is the question of what should happen to mentally disordered offenders who appear in court. The Reed Report (1991) stated that: 'Mentally disordered offenders, should, wherever appropriate, receive care and treatment from health and personal social services rather than in custodial care' (1991:

para. 2.1). This ruling was in line with an earlier recommendation in the Butler Report (1975) which had introduced the idea that an accused with a mental disorder could be placed in the hands of doctors rather than be sent to prison. Peay (1997) suggests that in the case of mentally disordered offenders, diversion and treatment should take precedence over punishment and protection. However, she argues that this is by no means always the case. She cites the *Report on Mentally Disturbed Offenders in the Prison System* (Home Office/DHSS, 1987) in which it is noted that:

> ... the response to the needs of individual mentally disturbed offenders has to take account of the legitimate expectation of the public that government agencies will take appropriate measures for its protection.
>
> (1987: para. 3.6)

This would suggest that in some cases the needs of the offender will be seen as less important than the need to 'protect the public' (see Chapter 8).

Peay also argues that recent legislation which makes life sentences mandatory for a second serious offence further serve to reduce the discretion which courts might otherwise have in the sentencing of mentally disordered offenders (see also Ashworth, 1997). Peay expresses great concern over such provisions noting that they will:

> ... trump the court's discretion to impose certain kinds of therapeutic disposals on offenders found to be disordered at the point of sentence, thereby challenging at one stroke forty years of consistent jurisprudential thinking.
>
> (1997: 662)

As we saw in the case of Peter Sutcliffe (see above) there remains a paradox within the criminal justice system when it comes to dealing with those who appear to be mentally disordered. While it is accepted by many that the mentally disordered should receive treatment rather than punishment, there appears to be a suspicion about what such therapeutic disposals signify. The criminal justice system seems reluctant to give up its powers both to control and punish those who offend, even when such defendants' mental condition would make punishment inappropriate. This reluctance appears part of a growing trend towards the politicisation of sentencing policy (Ashworth, 1997).

Peay suggests that problems arise mainly when the ordered-disordered continuum overlaps with the law-abiding law-breaking continuum. She notes that while care and treatment are appropriate for the seriously disordered, problems arise when such people's offending is of a worrying or disturbing nature. Drawing on the work of Gostin (1986) she suggests that the conflict is primarily between notions of legalism (in which a patient is wrapped in a series of legal protections) and welfarism (in which legal safeguards are seen as less important than speedy treatment and care).

We should also be aware that although mentally disordered offenders are often lumped together as an easily identifiable group, in reality individual offenders pose different problems for the courts. As Peay notes:

> The mentally disordered are not a class and the law, practitioners, policy-makers and the caring professions will mix and match philosophies in response to the problems created by *individual* offender-patients.
>
> (1997: 663)

In this respect, the mentally disordered offender may be diverted towards treatment rather than punishment at various stages along the criminal justice process (Hoggett, 1996; Prins, 1995).

Links between mental illness and violence

Peay argues that there appears increasingly to be a desire to maintain penal control over all offenders, including those who are mentally disordered. This desire is partly grounded in the concern over crimes committed by former psychiatric patients. There have been a number of such high profile cases which have generated heated media and public debate. In the public outcry that has followed some notorious crimes, it is easy to lose sight of the fact that reoffending rates for released mentally disordered offenders are approximately equal to those for non-disturbed offenders (Murray, 1989). It should also be recognised that psychiatric patients are far more likely to kill themselves than they are to kill others (Sims, 1996). Of the small number who do commit serious assaults, only a small proportion of these will be upon strangers. Despite these facts, some sections of the media would have the public believe that unprovoked attacks on strangers by former mental patients have reached epidemic proportions. While those with experience of mental illness may quickly reject such media images, those without such personal experience may be more likely to accept this view (Philo, 1996: 98).

Over-reaction by the media is partly explained by Howitt (1998) who suggests that:

> Traits such as dangerousness and unpredictability are common features of the representation of the mentally ill in newspapers ... and television ... The association appears to be highly newsworthy – stories linking mental illness to crime seem to have a good likelihood of being front page news.
>
> (1998: 39)

Howitt suggests that the tendency to think of the mentally ill as dangerous is not a new phenomenon and would appear to have been established in the nineteenth century, partly under the influence of the medical profession. However, the proclivity to think of the mentally ill as dangerous today is perpetuated both by sensationalist media reporting of factual events, and by the portrayal of mental illness in fictional television programmes. Although the vast majority of people who suffer from mental illness pose little threat, up to two-thirds of the characters portrayed as mentally ill in television dramas are shown as being violent (Philo, 1996).

The image of the mentally ill as potentially dangerous may be based upon outdated images of patients in strait-jackets, chains, or padded cells. The fact that modern drugs can control most symptoms in even the most disturbed individuals is not so widely known. A fear persists that an individual whose behaviour is to some extent unpredictable or not readily understood also has the potential to become violent. The vast majority of our interactions with others follow fairly well-rehearsed patterns making such social contact mundane and predictable. When interaction breaks the normal rules and conventions, we are apt to become concerned and fearful. A person whose thought processes appear disturbed, or who displays inappropriate affect (two of the classic symptoms of schizophrenia), will tend to set off alarm bells in the uninformed.

Part of the public's concern about the mentally ill stems from moves towards deinstitutionalisation over the last twenty years. Violence by mental patients upon other mental patients within the same institution may not have been seen as a cause for great concern by the general public – assuming that such incidents were even brought to light. However, once such patients are released into the community, the public is more likely to express concern about the potential threat. Torrey (1994) sounds one note of caution in this regard when he states:

> … the vast majority of individuals with serious mental illness are not violent and are not more dangerous than individuals in the general population. A subgroup of such individuals, however, are more dangerous, and the data suggest that this problem is increasing.
>
> (1994: 658)

This concern over the small percentage of mentally ill people who are dangerous is echoed by Levey and Howells (1994) and Beck (1994) who note that concern often focuses particularly on those diagnosed as schizophrenic. However, in a recent review of a number of studies, Quinsey *et al.* (1998) found that the rates of reported violent recidivism among schizophrenics was usually quite low and rarely exceeded twenty per cent. (This compares with rates of over 75 per cent for some psychopathic offender populations.) Interestingly, Quinsey *et al.* report that the predictors of violent recidivism in the mentally disordered are broadly similar to the predictors in those offenders who are not defined as mentally disordered (1998: 101).

While there is justifiable concern when former psychiatric patients commit serious and violent offences, the reality is that the vast majority of such crimes are committed by those who have no history of psychological disorder (Beck, 1994). In fact there are a number of variables that are more highly correlated with violence than is mental illness. These include male gender, age, socio-economic class and abuse of alcohol. Research in the USA (Monahan, 1992) suggests that mental disorder accounts for less than three per cent of the violence in that society. Monahan (1997) warns against a simplistic presumption that most violence in society is linked with mental disorder. He notes that, compared to alcohol and drug abuse, mental disorders account for a very small proportion of the violence currently found in US society.

Peay (1997: 687) notes that offending rates among the mentally disordered are roughly equivalent to those in the 'normal' population and that in fact the mentally disordered are more likely to commit property offences than offences involving violence. Eschewing obfuscation she suggests that: 'Images of axe-wielding maniacs are based on highly visible and intuitively attractive evidence, but are not statistically replicable' (1997: 688).

In England, Robertson *et al.* (1995) suggest that only about two per cent of those taken into custody by the police show signs of mental illness. While this figure may appear low, it is rather disconcerting to learn that police officers themselves do not always recognise that a prisoner is mentally ill (Palmer and Hart, 1996; Gudjonsson *et al.*, 1993). Although the Police and Criminal Evidence Act 1984 made a number of specific provisions for those suspects who were mentally ill, the provisions will never be enacted if a suspect's illness is not detected.

Despite data such as this, some writers have argued that the majority of criminal activity can be linked with some form of psychiatric illness or other (for example Bluglass and Bowden, 1990). In one recent book (provocatively entitled *The Psychopathology of Crime; Criminal Behavior as a Clinical Disorder*), Raine (1993) argues that it may be appropriate to consider much recidivist criminal behaviour as a disorder. Raine draws upon a large amount of biological data in support of this position. He admits that such a proposition is unlikely to go unchallenged:

> To present-day society, the very notion that crime may be a disorder seems both unreasonable and very unlikely. It is not currently an acceptable view, it has no strong advocates, and it goes against the grain of common sense.
>
> (1993: 318)

Nevertheless, Raine argues that in the same way that our understanding of mental illness has changed dramatically over the last 200 years, so our conception of criminal behaviour may also eventually have to be fundamentally rethought. One reason for this concern is his belief that many offenders are more likely to benefit from some form of treatment than from punishment. As such he believes that far more could be done to prevent reoffending if there was a better understanding of the real reasons why people engage in criminal activity. He asks whether:

... less than 200 years from now a more advanced society will look back aghast at our current conceptualisation of criminal behavior, with its concomitant incarceration and execution of prisoners, with the same incredulity with which today we look back at earlier treatment of mental patients.

(1993: 319)

While we contemplate such a notion, it seems inappropriate today to presume that there is an easily identified link between most mental illness and violence. Equally there is no clearcut link between mental illness and other forms of criminal activity (Prins, 1995). Even where correlations have been identified, it is often difficult to establish cause and effect. Given that most people will commit some form of crime at some time in their lives (see Chapter 1) it would be naïve to presume that those who suffer from mental illness are propelled towards criminal activity solely by their mental state. Having said that there are, as we will see below, some fairly well-established links between some forms of personality disorder and criminal activity.

Personality disorders

Perhaps nowhere is the distinction between those who are labelled 'mad' and those considered 'bad' less distinct than in the case of personality disorders. The *Diagnostic and Statistical Manual (DSM IV)* lists some ten distinct types of personality disorder plus a category of 'not otherwise specified' disorder. For present purposes we will consider perhaps the most controversial type, i.e. *antisocial personality disorder* or APD. The term is often used in the psychiatric literature in preference to labels such as psychopath or sociopath – such labels are often misunderstood and used in pejorative terms. There is considerable overlap between APD and psychopathy, although the two concepts are by no means identical (see Hare *et al.*, 1993: 166 for a discussion of some differences). Kendall and Hammer (1995) suggest the following differentiation:

> *APD* is a personality disorder characterized by social misconduct and antisocial personality traits.
> *Psychopathy* is a personality style that refers to certain affective and interpersonal traits such as selfishness, self-centredness, and a lack of empathy – rather than to specific antisocial behaviors.

(1995: 468)

APD is thought to be quite common. According to Robins *et al.* (1984) five per cent of adult American males and one per cent of adult American females are thought to possess the disorder. However, within the prison population, up to 50 per cent of inmates appear to meet the criteria for APD. This compares with 25–30 per cent who might be defined as psychopathic (Kendall and Hammer, 1995: 468). Some of the most notorious serial killers are said to exhibit classic symptoms of APD, making it a feared condition. For example, Ted Bundy sexually assaulted and killed more than 30 women in the USA before being caught, yet many around him had little idea of his true character. Although many individuals diagnosed as APD do not commit such serious crimes, their lives are invariably characterised by petty offences and an apparent lack of concern for other's feelings.

According to *DSM IV*, to be diagnosed as having this disorder the following criteria must be met.

(1) The individual shows a pervasive disregard for the rights of others. This is indicated by at least three of the following:

    (a) repeated illegal behaviour;
    (b) repeated lying or cheating of others for profit or pleasure;
    (c) impulsivity;
    (d) aggressiveness (indicated by repeated fights or assaults);
    (e) disregard for the safety of the self or others;
    (f) irresponsibility (indicated by poor work performance or failure to honour financial obligations);
    (g) a lack of remorse (indicated by being indifferent to hurting, mistreating or stealing from others).

(2) The individual is at least 18 years of age.
(3) There is evidence of a conduct disorder before the age of 15.

There are two major dimensions to APD, i.e. the antisocial behaviour itself and a lack of anxiety, remorse or guilt feelings which might normally follow the commission of certain antisocial acts. Individuals with APD are often thought of as lacking a conscience and as such they act impulsively and fail to consider or be concerned about the effect that their actions might have upon others. A distinction is sometimes made between primary and secondary APD. Although both types are associated with low levels of anxiety (see below) it is thought that in the case of primary APD, the individual is simply incapable of developing anxiety. By contrast, the secondary APD individual is thought to be capable of experiencing anxiety, but has learned to avoid it. This distinction is important in terms of treatment outcomes – no amount of treatment will be likely to lead the primary APD individual to experience anxiety, whereas treatment may be more successful in the case of a secondary APD individual.

Rather confusingly, Blackburn (1975) also referred to primary and secondary personality patterns in respect of psychopathy, but uses the terms somewhat differently. Blackburn refers to different personality types within the Mental Health Act 1993 definition of psychopathic disorder. He talks of primary psychopaths (impulsive, aggressive, hostile and extroverted); secondary psychopaths (impulsive, aggressive, hostile, socially anxious and withdrawn); controlled or conforming (defensive, sociable, unaggressive); and inhibited (unaggressive, withdrawn, introverted). Of these four types, Blackburn suggests that the first two show classic psychopathic traits. The Mental Health Act 1993 defined a psychopathic disorder as 'a persistent disorder or disability of mind ... which results in abnormally aggressive or seriously irresponsible conduct on the part of the person concerned'. However, as Blackburn (1995a) and others have pointed out, this legal definition is imprecise and at odds with clinical conceptions of a personality disorder.

Patrick *et al.* (1994) provided an interesting illustration of the way in which people with APD appear not to exhibit normal anxiety reactions. In this study, individuals were asked to listen to a number of sentences which were either neutral in content or threatening. The individuals' heart rates were monitored while they were listening to the sentences. Patrick found that when listening to the neutral sentences, both those individuals diagnosed as APD and others not so diagnosed showed only a slight increase in heart rate. However, when listening to the threatening sentences, normal individuals showed a much increased heart rate, while APD individuals showed only a very slight increase. It thus appeared that, when exposed to a threat, APD individuals showed none of the physiological responses normally associated with anxiety.

In a previous study (Patrick *et al.*, 1993) it had also been shown that APD individuals do not appear to have normal physiological responses when shown distressing pictures such as mutilated bodies. These and a number of other studies (e.g. Blair *et al.*, 1997) have convinced some researchers that APD individuals may be physiologically different from those not so diagnosed. Blair (1998) has pointed out that although adult psychopaths have apparently learned to identify and label others' emotions correctly, the fact that they do not show normal autonomic responses to such emotions would suggest a dysfunction in a part of the brain known as the amygdala.

One interesting consequence of this failure to experience anxiety is that people with APD are often able to 'beat' a polygraph test. The polygraph (or lie detector) works on the basis that people will experience anxiety when they lie and that this anxiety will be detectable on the polygraph charts (Gale, 1988; Vrij, 1998c). However, as those with APD experience little anxiety, they may appear not to be lying when in fact they are.

In addition to the characteristics already identified, APD individuals appear to exhibit quite distinctive behavioural patterns. For example, they are self-centred and pleasure seeking and appear unable to defer gratification even if their actions harm others. Their pleasure seeking may take the form of sensation seeking in which they engage in potentially dangerous activities just for the 'buzz'. Although a sub-group of APD individuals do show high levels of violence, many do not engage in overt physical aggression (Hart, 1998). However, their manipulative behaviour can cause other forms of harm to those around them. APD individuals also appear to lack any genuine emotional attachment to others. As such they may have a number of sexual partners but show little genuine commitment to any of them.

One reason why APD individuals' true characteristics are not always immediately obvious is that they are invariably above average in intelligence and possess good social skills. As such they are often able to manipulate others' impressions of them. If challenged about their true motivations, they are able to lie convincingly, or to offer plausible explanations for their more questionable behaviour. However, one of the more worrying aspects of APD is that if such individuals are challenged, they appear not to respond to punishment. Many individuals who are sent to prison reoffend almost immediately following their release, irrespective of what form of treatment has been attempted. Indeed, at least two recent reviews (Hemphill *et al.*, 1998 and Quinsey *et al.*, 1998) have suggested that the diagnosis of APD or psychopathy is one of the best predictors of recidivism. We should however be aware that by no means all practitioners would agree with the notion that those with a psychopathic disorder are untreatable. Blackburn (1993b) argues that some treatment programmes are successful, although he admits that knowledge in this area is still at a relatively rudimentary level.

Lion (1978) suggested that the only way in which APD individuals will change is if they come to believe that their actions are wrong. However, convincing APD types of this fact has not proved to be easy in many cases. One worrying corollary of this is that those with personality disorders might be detained even if they have not actually been convicted of a crime. At the time of writing, the current British Home Secretary is said to be considering introducing such a power. According to *The Guardian* (16 February 1999) Jack Straw has defended plans to lock away indefinitely those with severe personality disorders whether or not they have actually been convicted of a criminal offence. It is admitted that such preventative detention is a controversial step but is to be considered as a 'justified abuse of human rights' in order to protect the public.

The move has come in response to claims by some psychiatrists that, as many personality disorders are untreatable, there is no point in detaining individuals with such a condition in psychiatric hospitals. However, the notion of detaining individuals on the basis of what they **might** do raises many concerns. One may for example ask how a person would ever be able to convince others that they are **not** dangerous? Psychiatric diagnosis has not always been renowned for its accuracy, consistency or reliability (for example Rosenhan, 1963). The prediction of dangerousness has also proved not to be as straightforward as one might hope (Monahan and Steadman, 1994; Webster *et al.*, 1995; Litwack and Schlesinger, 1999). A further problem is that while most APD is diagnosed in the late teens or early twenties, many individuals appear to 'burn out' by the age of 40 and may no longer be dangerous (Weiss, 1973).

While the public may feel reassured by the knowledge that dangerous psychopaths will be locked up, there will remain serious concerns over issues of definition and of dangerousness. Perhaps we are right to be concerned given Blackburn's comment that 'Since psychopathy is a theoretical construct rather than palpable entity, there can be no "true" measure...' (Blackburn, 1993a: 84).

Can APD and psychopathy be identified reliably?

The understanding and diagnosis of APD and psychopathy have advanced enormously in recent years (see for example Cleckley, 1976). There are now quite sophisticated measures by which the traits can be identified (Hare, 1996). Today, the most commonly used instrument in measuring psychopathy is the Hare Psychopathy Checklist-Revised or PCL-R (Hare, 1991). The items on this list are:

(1) glibness/superficial charm;
(2) grandiose sense of self-worth;
(3) need for stimulation/proneness to boredom;
(4) pathological lying;
(5) conning/manipulative;
(6) lack of remorse or guilt;
(7) shallow affect;
(8) callous/lack of empathy;
(9) parasitic lifestyle;
(10) poor behavioural controls;
(11) promiscuous sexual behaviour;
(12) early behaviour problems;
(13) lack of realistic, long-term goals;
(14) impulsivity;
(15) irresponsibility;
(16) failure to accept responsibility for actions;
(17) many short-term marital relationships;
(18) juvenile delinquency;
(19) revocation of conditional release;
(20) criminal versatility.

Despite the widespread adoption of such instruments, there remain some difficulties when attempting to administer the tests (see Hare, 1998 for some worrying examples).

As with many other categories of disorder, there is a blurred line between 'normality' and 'abnormality'. Indeed, individuals with medium scores on Hare's psychopathy checklist are labelled 'partial psychopaths'. Blackburn (1993a) notes:

Given the varying conceptualisations of psychopathy, it is perhaps not surprising that unanimity on appropriate definition has not been achieved, and available measures reflect differing assumptions about psychopathy ...

(1993a: 81)

Hare *et al.* (1993: 166) note that, contrary to popular belief, there are many psychopaths who function within the law. These individuals are labelled adaptive, successful or non-criminal psychopaths. Unfortunately, little information is available on these individuals, for, unlike their criminal counterparts who are already incarcerated, they may be less easy to identify and less willing to participate in research.

One further problem is the fact that, unlike many other forms of disorder, the individual with a personality disorder may not necessarily see themselves as having a problem at all. In the case of antisocial personality disorder, the individual may experience little distress personally, yet cause a great deal of distress in those around them. To this extent APD differs from some other forms of personality disorder.

If one reads the identifying characteristics of many personality disorders, it is possible to identify some traits which a significant proportion of the population might possess. Large numbers of people may well appear egocentric, aggressive, somewhat irresponsible and apparently uncaring (at least to some degree) yet would not be classified as possessing antisocial personality disorder. Similarly, many people show some signs of obsessiveness or compulsiveness yet would not necessarily be defined as having an obsessive-compulsive personality disorder.

Some critics have argued that most forms of personality disorder should not be seen as 'disorders' as such, but simply reflect the extremes of a normal range. With many forms of personality disorder, it is extremely difficult to draw a clear dividing line between individuality/eccentricity and a disorder. Each of us has a distinct personality which combines a whole range of characteristics in a unique way. Some have argued that it is inappropriate to decide that some variations in personality characteristics should be labelled as a disorder, while others should not. A related problem is the fact that many with personality disorders do not show any of what might be considered the classic signs of abnormal behaviour (e.g. acute anxiety or hallucinations). Indeed some who possess personality disorders are able successfully to hide this from most of those around them.

In practice, three factors are used to separate those who are defined as having a disorder from those who are not. These are:

(1) The individual with the disorder will exhibit the behaviour consistently.
(2) The individual with a disorder will generally show a more extreme form of the behaviour than will one not so defined.
(3) The behaviour results in serious and prolonged problems with normal functioning.

Writers may continue to debate the exact relationship between psychopathy and APD. When one reads the literature, many American writers (e.g. Halgin and Whitbourne, 1993) stick to the *DSM IV* classification of APD and assume that most of those who are labelled as psychopaths or sociopaths are included within this category. However, British writers (e.g. Blackburn, 1993a) appear more likely to see psychopathy as a distinct entity. Debates over definition and identification will no doubt continue as society's understanding (or misunderstanding) of personality disorders grows. At the present time the question as to whether psychopathy should be viewed as a separate taxon or merely an extreme personality form continues to produce debate (Quinsey *et al.*, 1998: ch. 11).

Summary

In this chapter we have examined a number of ways in which an individual's mental state might have a bearing on criminal activity. We have seen that some individuals with severe mental disorders are judged not to be responsible for their actions and may, therefore, be more likely to receive treatment than imprisonment. However, we have also seen that the distinction between normality and abnormality is not always easy to establish. Some individuals are deemed to be insane, others unfit to stand trial, while others are judged to have a diminished responsibility for the acts in question. We have also seen that even when a defendant is quite obviously mentally ill, the criminal justice system is reluctant to hand over responsibility to the medical (or indeed psychological) profession.

We have also seen that the presumed link between mental illness and violent crime is something of a myth. While some mentally disturbed individuals do commit horrendous acts, the vast majority do not do so. Further, the vast majority of crime, including violent crime, is committed by those considered not to be mentally ill.

The most controversial area in the mental illness/criminality debate is that of personality disorders. We have seen that there is considerable debate about the exact nature of antisocial personality disorder and psychopathy. A growing body of evidence has suggested that there are some physiological differences between those with APD or psychopathy and others not so diagnosed. Nevertheless understandable concern is expressed at the recent suggestion that some individuals with severe personality disorders might be incarcerated despite the fact that they may have committed no crime and will receive no treatment. If individuals are to be detained on the basis of what they might do (as opposed to what they have done) we should surely be extremely concerned.

Chapter 6

Crime analysis and offender profiling

In Chapter 2 we saw that crimes are rarely completely random events and that victimisation often appears to follow a pattern. In Chapter 3 we also saw that offenders often select their target after a consideration of the risks and possible rewards which a crime might involve. Such information, if used properly, can help in the reduction of crime and in the arrest of offenders. In this chapter we will start to consider how a detailed analysis of crime patterns can reveal a great deal about the offender(s) and how such analysis can help the police better to target their resources and to solve crimes. Offender profiling has become one of the most publicised examples of the way in which psychology might be applied to crime, although as we will see in this chapter, its usefulness may be somewhat limited. To date profiling has been used predominantly in cases such as serial rapes or murders and we will thus focus largely on these two areas.

Analysing and profiling crime

We noted in the introduction to this book that the public's perception of how psychology might help in the detection of crime will probably stem from work on offender or psychological profiling. Films such as *The Silence of the Lambs*, and, in the UK, the television series *Cracker* have done much to (mis)inform the public in this respect. In the film *The Silence of the Lambs* Anthony Hopkins plays the fictional character Hannibal Lecter, a psychiatrist and mass murderer. As the film develops, Lecter helps the FBI to identify a serial killer through his insight and knowledge. In the British television series *Cracker*, Robbie Coltrane plays a maverick psychologist 'Fitz' who solves a number of serious crimes through a combination of psychological insight, deductive reasoning and flashes of inspiration. The solving of crimes such as serial rapes and murders arouses a great deal of public interest despite the fact that, as we saw in Chapter 1, such offences are extremely rare. Despite its popularity in fictional programmes, the reader may be surprised to learn that profiling was used in only 75 cases in the UK in 1994 (Copson, 1995). Having said that, each year appears to witness an increase in profiling usage over the previous twelve months.

There is some debate in psychological circles as to whether psychological profiling should be seen as a scientific endeavour or merely as subjective deduction. As we will see later, the English psychologist David Canter has been particularly critical of the FBI's approach to profiling, as he believes it to be unscientific. Garberth (1983) sees offender profiling as a combination of brainstorming, intuition and educated guesswork. Reisser (1982) suggests that, despite hopes that profiling should be considered to be a scientific endeavour, it is in fact largely an inferential process similar to any other psychological evaluation with a client. One of the foremost attacks on profiling has come from Campbell (1976). He believes that profiles are often too vague to be of value, or rely on little more than common sense. He also suggests rather cynically that police officers might be more seduced by the academic standing and status of the profiler than by the actual usefulness of their material.

Gudjonsson and Copson (1997) suggest that it is easy to understand why there is confusion about what profiling involves as it is 'neither a readily identifiable nor a homogeneous entity' (1997: 76). Indeed these same authors note that surprisingly little has been published in the academic literature on what profilers actually do and how they do it.

Psychology is seen by its practitioners as a science. For this reason, psychologists adopt a scientific methodology in their attempts to understand and explain human behaviour. A great deal of psychological research is carried out in the laboratory where hypotheses can be tested and conditions can be controlled. While the laboratory is an ideal place for exerting control over extraneous variables, some experiments conducted therein have been criticised for lacking what is called external validity (Ainsworth, 1998: 166). The concern is whether the results obtained inside the laboratory also apply outside. When one considers an area such as profiling, it is very difficult to conduct a laboratory experiment in order to test a hypothesis. Even if such experiments could be conducted it would be difficult to generalise the findings. Rather, in the area of profiling, theories have tended to be developed as a result of visits to crime scenes, analysis of evidence and, as in the case of *The Silence of the Lambs*, interviews with serial offenders.

While this latter form of data collection may provide interesting and possibly valuable insights, such a method of gathering information could hardly be said to be scientific. The views of one person may well be unrepresentative and for this reason, psychological research usually tries to use a large number of subjects, ideally selected randomly. Despite the difficulties, systematic controlled research will be seen as preferable to individual, anecdotal stories. In any case, information from known offenders relies on the offenders' accurate and ideally unbiased recall of information. Social psychological research suggests that this ideal is unlikely to be met (see for example Kerby and Rae, 1998).

There were some isolated attempts at psychological profiling throughout the nineteenth and twentieth centuries (see Brussel, 1968) and at least one writer (Tetem, 1989) has suggested that profiling has its roots in the writings of Sir Arthur Conan Doyle and his fictional character Sherlock Holmes. Certainly Doyle's creation paid great attention to the actions of criminals in an attempt to identify who they might be. More systematic and modern offender profiling has its origins in the USA where the FBI's Behavioral Science Unit (now called the Investigative Support Unit) built up considerable expertise in the 1970s and 1980s (Hazelwood, 1983; Reisser, 1982; Horn, 1988). While there is still some debate about what exactly offender profiling is, underlying most definitions is a belief that **offender** characteristics can be deduced from a detailed knowledge of **offence** characteristics. A profile can often generate hypotheses about an offender's most likely demographic and physical characteristics and about his or her behavioural habits and personality. As such it can be a valuable aid to crime detection especially if the crime is part of a series (Adhami and Brown, 1996). Blau (1994) provides a good summary of what is involved:

> The process is basically a method of helping to identify the perpetrator of a crime based on an analysis of the nature of the offense and the manner in which it was committed. The process attempts to determine aspects of a criminal's personality makeup from the criminal's choice of action before, during, and after the criminal act. The personality information is combined with other pertinent details and physical evidence and then compared with characteristics of known personality types and mental abnormalities. From this, a working description of the offender is developed.
>
> (1994: 261)

In Europe, the police define offender profiling as:

> Attempting to produce a description of the perpetrator(s) of a criminal offence on the basis of analysis of characteristics of the incident and other background information.
>
> (Stevens, 1995: 10)

This definition was the one adopted in the UK by the Association of Chief Police Officers' Behavioural Science Investigative Support Sub-committee.

A detailed examination of the crime scene might thus be seen as an essential first step in the gathering of relevant information. While a physical examination is already carried out by forensic scientists searching for fingerprints, clothing fibres, semen samples etc., the scene can also reveal other clues to the profiler. As Blau's description suggests, a detailed examination of the crime scene may well provide clues as to the underlying personality of the offender. For example, the FBI's early work led them to believe that an important distinction could be made between 'organised' and 'disorganised' offences and offenders. It appeared that some offences were carried out with a great deal of forward planning, while others were committed with little planning or preparation. In the latter case, a victim may have been selected at random, whereas in the former, a victim may have been targeted and observed for some time in advance of the offence. While a detailed examination of the crime scene will be helpful to a profiler, such an examination is not always possible. For example, some recent research in the UK (Smith, 1998) has suggested that profilers tend not to be brought in at the earliest opportunity, but rather are contacted when other more traditional forms of police enquiry have failed. By this stage the crime scene will probably have been disturbed and vital clues possibly lost.

If the police are investigating a number of rapes in the same area, they will be keen to establish whether they have been committed by the same person. The police obviously need to know whether they should be looking for one offender or several. In addition, if they can establish that a number of crimes were committed by the same offender, this will allow them to put together evidence from more than one crime scene in order to build up a better picture of the perpetrator. An initial investigation may lead the police to believe that the crimes were committed by the same person, especially if the victim characteristics and the timing and location of the offences is similar. However, a careful examination of the offences may lead a profiler to believe that they may actually have been committed by two completely different 'types' of offender. For example, one crime scene may show clear evidence of a planned and rehearsed attack, while another may suggest that it was an unplanned and impulsive act. Thus, the psychologist may well draw up two very different profiles of the likely perpetrators and advise the police that they should be looking for more than one suspect. In some cases, DNA analysis may also be able to confirm the profiler's hypothesis.

Profiling would appear to be more appropriate for certain types of offence than others (Stevens, 1995). Currently the most common crimes for which it is used are murder and the more serious sexual offences, especially where it appears that there is a series of connected crimes. The FBI believe that property crimes and robberies are not particularly suitable for profiling, as such offences are unlikely to reveal many clues about an offender's underlying personality.

It is important to dispel one myth in relation to offender profiling. Profiling cannot in most cases tell the police who actually committed an offence. What it can do is to suggest to investigators some personality and demographic characteristics which the offender is **likely** to possess. The emphasis on 'likely' is important. Profilers tend to talk in terms of probabilities rather than absolutes. A profiler may suggest that an offender probably lives quite close to the scene of the crime and is unemployed. However, it would be a brave and perhaps unwise profiler who went so far as to suggest that anyone who did not meet these criteria should be completely eliminated from the investigation. While there have been a number of famous cases where psychologists have been able to offer very detailed and accurate profiles (Canter, 1994) there are many less publicised cases where they have been less helpful (Copson, 1995). Because profiling has attracted such widespread public interest, the layperson may have an over-optimistic vision of what can be achieved. A note of caution is sounded by Jackson and Bekerian (1997) in their book on offender profiling. They note that:

> ... the answers that are offered are *not* solutions. Offender profiles do not solve crimes. Instead ... profiles should be viewed as simply one more tool that can be extremely useful in guiding strategy development, supporting information management, and improving case understanding.
>
> (1997: 3)

In many cases, the drawing up of a profile can help investigators to narrow down their pool of suspects and to avoid wasting time on lines of enquiry which are likely to be fruitless. If one of the police's suspects does not match any of the profiler's predictions, then the police might justifiably spend less time pursuing this person. In some cases the profile may well fit someone whom the police already suspect and will thus allow detectives to concentrate their investigations on the most likely suspect. In such cases, a profiler might also offer advice on the way in which an interview with the suspect might best be conducted. In other cases, the profile may help the police at least to know where to start looking for an offender, in terms of their most likely area of residence, previous convictions, etc.

An interesting example of how a profile can be helpful is provided by Ault and Reese (1980). This case involved a woman living in the northeastern United States who was raped and subsequently reported the offence to the local police department. The investigating officer realised that the circumstances of the offence were similar to six previous rapes in the area and that they may well have all been carried out by the same person.

Unfortunately the six previous rapes had yielded few good clues and the police had been unable to identify a suspect. The case files were then sent to the FBI's Behavioral Science Unit and a psychological profile constructed. This investigation concluded that all seven crimes had indeed been committed by the same person. The suspect was predicted to be a white male, probably in his late twenties or early thirties. He was most likely to be divorced or separated and to have a job as a casual labourer or similar. It was also hypothesised that he would have had a high school education and to live in the immediate area of the offences. It was also thought that he would be likely to have a poor self-image, and to have previous convictions for minor sexual offences. The FBI Unit also predicted that the person may have been stopped previously by the police in the area as he would probably have been out on the streets in the early hours of the morning.

Upon receiving this profile, the police narrowed down their list of suspects to some 40 local males who met the age profile. Using other information provided by the profiler, they then focused their investigation on one particular individual. This person was soon arrested and was subsequently convicted of all the offences.

While this is an interesting illustration of what can be achieved, profiling does not always have such dramatic and successful results. When a profile proves to be accurate and leads to the conviction of a perpetrator, the media may well take an interest; but such successes will perhaps be rare. Because psychological profiling is still in its infancy, there have been few scientific and systematic studies to test exactly how useful it is. The fact that profiling can take different forms also serves to make evaluation difficult. It has proved difficult to establish the number of cases in which the information is 'better' than that which detectives working on the case could have deduced for themselves. If only half of the information which a profiler provides turns out to be accurate should we count this as helpful? If profilers tend only to be brought in on those cases in which the police are already experiencing difficulty, is it reasonable to expect that a profiler will have a high success rate? A further problem with regard to evaluation concerns the likely accuracy of information about whether or not a profiler's input really was helpful. It is just possible that a senior detective with a reputation to uphold will seek to play down the usefulness of an input from an 'outsider' such as a profiler (Ainsworth, 2000; Smith, 1998). We will return to the question of evaluation towards the end of this chapter.

Although a number of countries have set up their own profiling units, many are based on the approach adopted by the FBI, stemming in particular from the work of Hazelwood. We will consider this approach next.

The FBI's approach

The FBI's early approach was based on in-depth interviews with some 36 sexually-orientated serial murderers. The technique tried to identify the major personality and behavioural characteristics of serious offenders. This was based on a very detailed analysis of the crimes they had committed. Thus the FBI would consider evidence derived from the crime scene, the nature of the attacks, any forensic evidence, medical examiners' reports and the characteristics of the victim. Such information would then help investigators to classify the offender and to make predictions as to their likely characteristics. Hazelwood and Douglas (1980) define the FBI's approach to profiling as:

> An educated attempt to provide investigative agencies with specific informa-
> tion as to the type of individual who committed a certain crime ... a profile is
> based on the characteristic patterns or factors of uniqueness that distinguish
> certain individuals from the general population.
>
> (1980: 5)

One illustration of the FBI's work is provided by the distinction made
between 'organised' and 'disorganised' murderers (see above and Hazelwood, 1987). Organised offenders tend to commit crimes which have
clearly been planned, where there is an attempt to control, where few
clues are left and where the victim is a targeted stranger. By contrast, the
disorganised offender would be more likely to use a sudden, unrehearsed
style with a minimum use of restraint and little attempt to hide evidence.
Knowledge is built up by studying the crime scene and the exact nature of
the attack. As a result of this, the likely offender would then be classified
and reference made to the characteristics which the offender was presumed to possess. For example, the FBI's research led them to believe
that an organised criminal would typically be of above average intelligence, be sexually and socially competent and to be living with a partner.
He would also be likely to be suffering from depression or experiencing a
great deal of anger around the time of the attack. Following the crime, he
would tend to follow the media coverage of the attack closely and may
even leave the area shortly afterwards. By contrast, a disorganised attacker
was believed to be someone who lived alone (probably close to the scene),
was sexually or socially inadequate, had been mistreated as a child and
was frightened and confused at the time of the attack.

Although this approach appears to be objective, there is inevitably
some degree of subjective interpretation by the individual profiler. While
relying on the same information, each profiler decides what emphasis
should be placed on the various characteristics and thus what type of person the suspect is likely to be. It is this fact that has led some academics
to question whether the approach is scientific or merely personal intuition (for example Rossmo, 1996). The fact that much of the FBI's
approach stemmed from interviews with such a small sample of 'specialist' offenders has also been a cause for concern.

Hazelwood and Burgess (1987) argue that a very careful study of the
exact behaviour of an offender can lead to a better understanding of
the underlying motive for an attack. This in turn provides insight into
the type of person the offender is likely to be. Although this may not be
possible in exact terms, Hazelwood believes that descriptions of an
offender can be built up to a point where they will be recognisable to his
friends and family. The profiler would look for a systematic behaviour
pattern which would then allow the use of a typology. One example of
this is whether a sexual assault or rape can be categorised as predominantly **selfish** or **unselfish**. Although it might reasonably be argued that
all rapes are selfish in that the victim's rights are totally ignored, some

rapists exhibit behaviour which Hazelwood has labelled pseudo-unselfish. In this case the offender's verbal utterances will tend to be reassuring, complimentary, self-demeaning, ego building, concerned, personal, non-profane, inquisitive and apologetic.

This type of rapist will often try to involve the victim in the act. He appears to be seeking intimacy with the victim by, for example, asking her to kiss or fondle him and he will fondle parts of the victim's body before intercourse. Such an attacker would appear not to wish to harm the person physically (other than the rape itself) or to force her into acts when she resists. When force is used it will tend to be in order to intimidate rather than to harm. This offender's style of behaviour is thought to stem from a lack of confidence on his part. If the victim does resist physically the assailant may end the attack or may even attempt some kind of compromise with the victim. The victim's resistance may serve to destroy the rapist's fantasy that she is a willing participant in the act.

By contrast, the so-called selfish rapist appears to be solely interested in self-gratification and shows absolutely no regard for his victim's welfare, wishes or feelings. His verbal behaviour will be characterised as offensive, threatening, profane, abusive, demeaning, humiliating, demanding, impersonal and sexually orientated. Unlike the so-called unselfish rapist, this type of assailant will do whatever he wants, irrespective of the victim's suffering or feelings. Resistance on the part of the victim will tend to have little deterrent effect as sexual domination would appear to be the primary motivation.

Once the rapist's behaviour is classified as broadly selfish or unselfish, further categorisation may be attempted. This is done on the basis of the apparent motivation for the attack. Hazelwood draws on the classification system first used by Groth *et al.* (1977). This typology is based on the assumption that power, anger and sexuality are fundamental components of all rapes. The most common type of behaviour is classified as **power-reassurance**. For such offenders, the primary motivation is an attempt to remove doubts or fears about their own sexual inadequacy and masculinity. Such rapists tend to exhibit pseudo-unselfish behaviour and not to use large amounts of force. Their attacks are usually carefully planned and the victims are often within the same age range as the offender. Following the attack, the rapist may apologise to the victim or ask to be forgiven and he may contact the victim again later on. The behaviour of such offenders is thought to go some way towards reassuring them about their sexual insecurity. However, this effect tends to be short-lived and the offender may strike again in the near future, probably in the same area. Such attackers often take an item of clothing from their victims as a souvenir and they may even keep records of their crimes. It is believed that such attackers are unlikely to grow out of their offending and will continue until caught.

By contrast the **power-assertive** rapist harbours no doubts about his sexuality. Such a person will tend to be very confident of his masculinity and may see his own acts of rape as merely expressions of his masculinity, virility and dominance. Such an attacker will often use a high degree of force, though not necessarily in the early stage of the interaction. He may initially appear friendly and non-threatening, and put his intended victim at her ease. However, his demeanour will then change, and his true intentions become clear. Such a pattern may be typical of assaults now labelled as 'date-rapes'. These are the types of offences which juries often have difficulty accepting, believing that to some extent the victim contributed to her own victimisation by agreeing to accompany an assailant. What jurors may well not realise is that this type of offender may well appear completely innocent and harmless on first meeting an intended victim. Following the rape this person may revert to his former image and appear affable and 'innocent' when in the dock. Because this type of person probably does not fit society's stereotype of a 'typical' rapist, he may well be acquitted. This type of rapist is less common than the power reassurance offender and his crimes will tend to be less frequent or regular.

A third type of rapist identified by the FBI is labelled **anger-retaliatory**. As the name implies, this type of offender commits rape as a way of expressing his own rage and hostility. He will typically have a great deal of anger and animosity towards women and uses rape as a way of expressing this anger and as a way of degrading his victims. His typical pattern will be one of selfishness and he will tend to show very high levels of violence. Because the attack is usually an emotional and impulsive outburst it will tend to be unplanned. This form of attack has been labelled a 'blitz' approach, with an immediate use of direct and heavy violence. The assault itself tends to be over fairly quickly, once the assailant feels he has released his pent-up anger both physically and sexually. Victims will tend to be in the same age range as the rapist and may be selected because they symbolise another person against whom the person has a grudge. For example, if the man has been rejected by a lower class young woman, he may choose a victim who appears to have similar characteristics. This type of rapist will tend to attack again when the anger and resentment build up to levels which he is unprepared to tolerate.

The final type of rapist has been labelled as **anger-excitement**. In this case pleasure and sexual excitement are produced for the assailant by the almost sadistic pleasure of seeing his victim's suffering and fear. Such an attacker might thus inflict pain in order to achieve fear and, subsequently, submission. Contrary to media images, these forms of attack are actually the least common type. Rapists falling into this category will usually plan their attacks in a very clear and methodical way. They may even rehearse the assault and make sure that they have covered all eventualities. They will decide in advance what weapons to use, what mode of transport to employ and they will already have items such as gags or ropes to hand. However, the actual victim may well not have been chosen in advance. She will typically be a stranger who meets the criteria for an attacker's sexual fantasies and desires, but with whom he has not previously come into contact. His sexual and verbal behaviour will be almost entirely selfish and he will tend to use an extreme amount of force, often resulting in the victim's death. This type of attacker tends to restrain his victim physically and this is followed by long periods of control and sexual assault. Torture is not uncommon and the helplessness, degradation and humiliation of his victim appears to be stimulating to this type of offender. He may keep records of his conquests and in some cases may take photographs or make video recordings. The anger-excitement rapist is the least likely to attack at regular intervals, preferring to initiate an assault only when his planning is complete. For this reason it is often difficult to predict when this type of offender will strike again.

One can see from this classification system that it would be naïve to believe that there is only one type of rapist. The stereotype of the sexually frustrated male, intent on degrading and harming his unfortunate victim, may be far too simplistic a view of rape. Clark and Morley (1988) offer an interesting insight into serial rapists. Their work is based on interviews with 41 rapists who had in total committed some 837 sexual assaults. One of the most important points to emerge is that serial rapists do not necessarily fit the stereotype which people may have of this type of offender. Perhaps surprisingly, many serial rapists appear perfectly normal to those around them. Far from being lonely, disadvantaged, socially unskilled characters, serial rapists typically come from an average or above average home background and are intelligent, well presented, in regular employment and living in a family context. Hazelwood and Warren (1989) suggest that serial rapists are more likely to have previous convictions for theft than for minor sexual offences.

What we can learn from the research reviewed here is that a careful examination of the actual circumstances of the offence may well reveal a great deal about the type of offender who committed a certain crime. By careful consideration, valuable clues can be gleaned as to the probable underlying motive for the attack, and, from this, the most likely 'type' of offender. Such consideration and attempts at classification will also help investigators to determine whether a series of offences appears to have been carried out by the same offender or by several. Classification may also assist the police to establish how likely it is that the person will strike again, and if so, when this is most likely to be. It might also be possible to predict whether the assailant's next attack may be more violent and be likely to lead to the victim being killed.

The FBI's analysis does provide some interesting information, and has undoubtedly helped to solve a number of infamous crimes. However, as was noted earlier, some academics have been critical of the FBI's approach (for example Rossmo, 1996; Oleson, 1996; Canter 1994). Much of this criticism has stemmed from the fact that the FBI's system is based on the analysis of a rather small number of cases and on interviews with only a small number of serial rapists and murderers. In addition,

Canter believes that the FBI's approach is fundamentally flawed because it lacks scientific rigour and is more akin to subjective intuition. Despite this, the FBI's techniques have been influential and spread to other countries. Indeed, Jackson and Bekerian note that 'many, if not all, of the psychological profiling units in other countries (such as Canada, the UK and the Netherlands) have been modelled to a large extent on the FBI approach' (Jackson and Bekerian, 1997: 6).

Despite this influence, a somewhat different approach to profiling has been suggested by the British psychologist David Canter. Some of his ideas and theories will now be covered.

Canter's profiling techniques

While Canter's approach shares some similarities with that of the FBI, he has tried to place his approach within accepted psychological frameworks. Canter has labelled his approach *Investigative Psychology* and believes that as a branch of applied psychology, it goes beyond what is traditionally thought of as offender profiling. Canter has tried to understand firstly the type of crime in which any particular individual will be likely to become involved and also the way in which the crime will be carried out. Secondly, Canter has tried to understand the way in which an individual offender's behaviour while committing a crime mirrors their behaviour in everyday life. His research has led him to believe that there are subsets of interrelated activities which occur when a crime is being committed (see below). He also believes that a criminal's actions at the scene of a crime will reveal something about their background. Thus systematic attempts to destroy evidence might suggest that the person has previous convictions. We will return to this notion later in the chapter.

From his research into offending behaviour Canter (1989, 1994) and his colleagues have identified five important characteristics which they believe can help in investigations. These are *residential location, criminal biography, domestic/social characteristics, personal characteristics* and *occupational/educational history*. While all of these have been found to be of some value, residential location and criminal history are thought to be of most benefit (Boon and Davies, 1993).

Canter and Heritage (1990) analysed details of sexual assaults in an effort to identify particular styles and patterns within these offences. They were able to identify those characteristics which were very common in such assaults and those which were much rarer and thus more distinctive. By carrying out such analyses it was hoped that common factors in similar types of sex crimes could be specified and the more individually distinctive features identified. Canter's approach is based on the belief that although there are similarities in many sexual assault cases, there are also identifiable differences in the way in which offences are carried out.

Canter believes that during the commission of a crime, vital clues are left behind and the distinctive personality of the offender shows through in some way. Thus, it is thought that the way in which the crime is committed is in part a reflection of the everyday traits and behaviour of the individual. The interaction between the offender and victim is thus studied closely and categorised along a number of dimensions, e.g. sexuality, violence and aggression, impersonal sexual gratification, interpersonal intimacy and criminality. Canter believes that by this careful study of offence behaviour, patterns can be established and variations between offenders identified. However, unlike the FBI's approach, Canter does not attempt to place offenders into rigid typologies, but rather suggests that their behaviour will mirror other aspects of their day-to-day life (Canter, 1995: 354).

Canter and Heritage (1990) originally developed their views by studying 66 sexual assault cases which had been committed by some 27 different offenders. By studying victims' statements and other information in the case file, they identified 33 offence characteristics which appeared to occur with some frequency. While other characteristics were identified, these were much less common (and thus more distinctive) but were unhelpful in terms of general principles. The common characteristics were identified as:

- style of approach;
- surprise attack;
- sudden/immediate use of violence;
- blindfolding;
- gagging;
- reaction/lack of reaction to resistance;
- compliments victim;
- enquires about victim;
- impersonal towards victim;
- demeaning towards victim;
- disturbing of victim's clothing;
- ripping/cutting of clothing;
- use of weapon;
- demanded items;
- verbal victim participation;
- physical victim participation;
- use of disguise;
- knowledge of victim implied;
- threatened if attack reported;
- stealing property;
- identification of victim;
- violence to produce control;
- violence not controlling;
- verbal violence/aggression;

- vaginal penetration;
- fellatio;
- fellatio in sequence;
- cunnilingus;
- anal penetration;
- anal penetration in sequence;
- apologetic.

By compiling such a list of factors, and then carrying out a sophisticated statistical analysis, Canter was able to establish the relationship between various factors. In particular his analysis showed which factors tended to be associated with each other and which were apparently unconnected. It was also possible to identify those actions which occurred in almost all the cases and those which appeared less frequently. A picture was built up of the factors which appeared to be the most central to the offence of rape. Surprisingly, Canter believed that overtly aggressive behaviour was not the core ingredient in all rape cases. While sexual intercourse was invariably the primary aim of the attacker, there was not the large variety of sexual activity which might have been expected. In some cases there was little evidence of a desire for interpersonal intimacy with the victim. While there was no such thing as a 'typical' rape, a large number of such offences were characterised by a sudden impersonal attack in which the victim's response appeared to make little difference to the outcome. This latter point can be important for, as was noted in the previous chapter, victims might be made to feel that the rape could have been avoided if they had behaved differently.

In order to establish all the relevant factors of an assault, it will therefore be important that victims are questioned using the most appropriate interviewing technique. This might include procedures such as the cognitive interview (Ainsworth, 1998: ch. 7), a technique which has been proven to be more effective than the normal type of interview. Having said that, the use of such techniques with traumatised witnesses can bring about its own problems (Ainsworth and May, 1996). We should also be aware that witnesses are often mistaken in their memories, especially with regard to the exact details of an offence (Ainsworth, 1998: ch. 3). This fact may serve to thwart any profiler wishing to categorise a particular assault accurately.

Canter and Heritage (1990) used their data on rape to test certain previous assumptions about such crimes. For example, some earlier research (Marshall, 1989) suggested that an important motivating factor for rapists was their inability to form intimate relationships with women. If this were true, then we would expect that many rapes would be characterised by an apparent desire by the offender to relate to the woman as a person, rather than just as a sexual object. Canter and Heritage found that some (but by no means all) rapes did show evidence of this, with offenders exhibiting a number of behaviour patterns which together suggested attempts at intimacy. Rapists who showed such signs were hypothesised to have had previous difficulty in forming intimate relationships with women, with perhaps one or more failed attempts in the person's background.

While acknowledging that the primary goal of most rapes is the sexual activity itself, there remains a question as to whether different types of sexual behaviour are related (and form a distinct pattern) or whether the types of sexual behaviour are diffuse and related to other aspects of the offender's lifestyle. Canter and Heritage found that the desire for certain types of sexual experience did appear to be a significant aspect of rape. They argued, therefore, that when a variety of sexual activity does take place, this would suggest either that an offender has a high level of previous sexual experience, or that he shows an interest in certain specific activities, through the possession of specialist pornographic magazines, etc.

Canter and Heritage confirmed the fact that threat and violence is an essential element in rape. They found four aggressive factors which were clearly linked in some rapes, and appeared to form a distinct aspect of the offence. As previous literature has also suggested, there is often a link between these aggressive variables and the sexual variables, with some interaction between the two. Two examples of this are where violence is used for pleasure rather than for control purposes and where aggressive anal intercourse took place.

While acknowledging that some rapes are characterised by an apparent desire for intimacy (see above) Canter and Heritage found that many others are anything but and are characterised by a much colder, sinister and impersonal style. In such cases, the woman is treated merely as an object of desire with absolutely no consideration of her rights or wishes. Canter and Heritage's work suggests that there are six characteristics which typify this type of attack. These include the use of impersonal language (e.g. calling the woman 'bitch' rather than using her name) and an almost total disregard for the victim's reaction. While a number of assaults showed at least some evidence of this type of behaviour, the researchers believed that it was possible to identify some cases where this form of action appeared to be the most prominent aspect of a rapist's behaviour. Canter and Heritage believe that the importance of such findings lies in the fact that attacks of this nature will be more likely to be carried out by offenders whose lives in general reflect an impersonal attitude towards women. Thus, when trying to identify an offender, the police may well be advised to concentrate their efforts on those suspects who fit this pattern of behaviour in their everyday lives.

One final point made by Canter and Heritage concerns the association between rape and other types of criminal activity. Although rape is seen as a distinct offence, with its own motivations, many rapists have previous convictions for other types of crime, including that of a non-sexual nature. This fact means that perpetrators may well be 'sophisticated' in the sense that they will use techniques which hinder police investigations. The use of a mask, the wearing of gloves, or attempts to destroy evidence might be appropriate examples. Such behaviour may well signify that a perpetrator has previous convictions and be known to the police, possibly for other types of crime. It is thus argued that some types of behaviour used in rape cases (e.g. the blindfolding of a victim) may have more to do with the fact that the perpetrator has a criminal record than with some sexual fantasy. Canter and Heritage suggest that those cases in which a rapist warns the victim not to tell, or where he tells her that he knows where she lives, may indicate a previous criminal lifestyle. This can be important, as the police are likely to have more success in identifying a person who already has a criminal record than one who has never come to the notice of the authorities. It is suggested that the more factors of this type that are present, the more likely it is that the perpetrator will have a lengthy criminal record.

Canter and Heritage's research has confirmed a number of previous theories and typologies and has demonstrated that there are a number of different types of rape behaviour. This also means that there are a number of different 'types' of offender. The detailed study of offence behaviour thus allows predictions to be made about the likely motivations and characteristics of a particular offender. As such the contribution is useful to the investigation of rape. However, we must bear in mind that Canter's work, and indeed most research on profiling, is still relatively novel, and the theories may be in need of further refinement. Canter's work is based on probabilities and likelihoods rather than absolutes. If an assailant wears a disguise, ties up his victim and also steals from her, this suggests that he is likely to have convictions for offences other than rape. However this does not necessarily mean that he **will** have such convictions. For example, it is possible that a perpetrator uses a mask because in the past this has proved to be an effective way of avoiding detection. In other words, his actions may be indicative of a previously successful criminal career, rather than evidence of a conviction.

Crime locations

Another interesting part of Canter's work has looked at the area of residence of individual offenders and the location of their crimes. Drawing on research from environmental psychology, Canter introduces the notion of **mental maps** as a way of understanding the geographical pattern of offending. The notion stems from the fact that although many people may live in roughly the same location, each will tend to have slightly different representations or mental maps of the area. These mental maps are internal representations of the external world and are unique to the individual. If one were to ask a car driver and a non-driver to describe the area in which they lived, each would have a different perspective, partly because of the way in which they normally move around the neighbourhood. A person's mental map may also be affected by factors such as whether they have a job which involves travelling to other parts of the area.

Some psychologists believe that is possible to access people's mental maps by asking them to draw a picture of their neighbourhood. While each of these will contain its own individual features, there will also tend to be some consistencies among the maps produced by residents in the same area. For example, it has been found that people tend to draw a map from their own perspective, rather than as it would appear to a cartographer. A good example of how mental maps can distort reality is provided by Milgram (1976). He reports that most Paris residents who were asked to draw a map of their city showed the River Seine as following a straight course, when it does in fact meander through the various parts of the city. The reason why people make such mistakes is that from their perspective, the river does appear to be straight. If they regularly saw the city from a tall building or helicopter, their perspective would be different and the map might be drawn more accurately.

The reason why the study of mental maps may be important is that each criminal will have their own mental map of the area in which they live. When deciding which areas to target, they will tend to draw on this mental map and the person may keep to an area within a given boundary, even if this is not intentional. Canter has found that a majority of the rapes he studied were carried out within two miles of an offender's home. This finding was confirmed by Spivey (1994). Davies and Dale (1995) found that in three-quarters of rape cases the offender lived within five miles of the scene of the crime.

While police forces traditionally plotted crimes onto a map (by for example the placing of different coloured pins) this is a rather crude and unhelpful strategy. The major problem with such unsophisticated methods is that they tend to consider just the geographical location of crime with little consideration of the many factors which might be contributing to this distribution. Thus, while it may be easy to demonstrate the existence of crime 'hot spots' in which there is a higher than average rate of offending, there is little attempt to consider when such crimes tend to occur, nor why. Today, computer programs can provide a much more sophisticated way of plotting crime patterns and analysing crime data.

Geographical mapping and crime pattern analysis are emerging fields which should allow the police to better target their resources. One need think only of the work on repeat victimisation (see Chapter 2) to realise that it is possible to make at least some predictions as to likely future targets. Any analysis of data does however depend on the accurate recording of information in the first place. In the case of many police forces, this has proved rather difficult (see for example Ackroyd *et al.*, 1992; Farrington and Lambert, 1997).

We have noted that mental maps are not a literal or objective portrayal of the outside world. Because they are internally generated, they are influenced by subjective interpretation and personal distortion. For this reason, the simple plotting of crime locations onto a map may reveal little. However, once things such as footpaths, cul-de-sacs, bus routes, location of security cameras, etc. are taken into account, then a pattern is more likely to emerge.

When planning an attack, criminals will tend to draw upon their own internal map in selecting likely targets. Their mental maps may well contain knowledge of possible escape routes, areas which lack CCTV surveillance, or locations which are likely to contain a number of fairly easy targets. The choice of target location will undoubtedly be affected by whether or not the criminal has a vehicle at their disposal, or is able to steal one easily. Perpetrators may choose an area of which they have a detailed knowledge and in which they will not feel conspicuous. Knowing this can help the police to decide where to start looking for an offender. Crimes which are the most difficult to solve tend to be those in which an outsider commits a crime and then returns to their residence in a different part of the country.

Canter believes that there are meaningful and identifiable patterns of space use which are typical of different criminals and that these relate to their place of residence at the time of the offence. In this respect, his research has confirmed that of previous writers in showing that criminals tend to operate from their home base and to commit crimes within an identifiable distance of their home. One interesting and practical facet of this work is that when Canter was able to draw a circle which encompassed all of a criminal's offences, in over 85 per cent of cases the offender lived within that circle. This research presents a picture of most offenders as marauders rather than commuters. Canter concludes that whatever a rapist's motives, his choice of location can be explained by well-established environmental psychology principles.

Canter has undoubtedly made a major contribution to our understanding of offender behaviour. His recent work has involved the use of facet theory as a more sophisticated way of analysing data on crime patterns and criminal behaviour (House, 1997: 181). There have also been other useful British contributions to our understanding (see Ainsworth, 1995a: ch. 10; Jackson and Bekerian, 1997 for reviews). Copson *et al.* (1997) have set out the procedures which profilers might adopt when working with the police. Britton (1997) has adopted an approach which differs somewhat from that of Canter, in that he prefers to view each case as unique, rather than relying on statistical analyses of previous cases. Unfortunately, Canter and Britton appear to have little respect for each other's work and animosity between two of the leading British profilers can hardly help to enhance the reputation of offender profiling. (The interested reader might wish to see Britton, 1997: 101 and *Police Review*, 23 September 1994, for examples of this animosity.)

The limited amount of information available in Britain to date suggests that many senior detectives have somewhat negative views as to the usefulness of information provided by profilers (Copson, 1995; Jackson et al., 1997; Smith, 1998). Copson and Holloway (1997) suggest that profiling helped to solve only sixteen per cent of the crimes in which it was used and led to the identification of an offender in less than three per cent of cases. Britton (1997) also admits that a large number of cases continue to be solved, not by profiling, but by routine police work, or the use of forensic evidence. Such apparently poor results should however be viewed in the light of comments made earlier in respect of police officers' possible reluctance to admit that 'outsiders' did help in an investigation. Profiling does at least allow the police to better focus their investigations. This can be important for as Canter (1994: 21) has noted the alternative is that the police will simply throw more and more resources at a crime in the hope that 'something will turn up'. By using a more scientific approach, profiling, thus, has advantages in terms of the resources needed to solve any particular crime.

When trying to evaluate the usefulness of a profile it may also be important to consider whether the profile is seen in isolation or merely as one part of more general guidance which a psychologist might provide to investigators. Jackson et al. (1997) conclude that '... when profiles are considered as a separate entity, they seldom, if ever, offer enough foundation or impetus to steer or guide an investigation in a new direction' (Jackson et al., 1997: 131).

For this reason, these authors report that in the Dutch profiling unit, profiles are never treated as a separate entity, but rather as a management instrument. As such any profile should be accompanied by practical advice on how best to proceed with a particular investigation. Copson (1995) appears to support this viewpoint. He suggests that some of the negative comments made by senior detectives about profiling may stem from a misunderstanding of what 'profiling' can actually achieve. Psychologists can offer different forms of assistance to an investigation, only one of which might be the drawing up of a profile of the most likely offender characteristics.

We should also be aware of the danger of the self-fulfilling prophecy with respect to profiling (Ainsworth, 1995a: chs 3 and 10). Detectives must bear in mind that a psychological profile may well fit a number of people and may not be totally accurate. The fact that the suspect currently being interviewed happens to fit the profile does not 'prove' that they actually committed the offence. There may be several people who share the suspect's make-up and the police should be cautious before making a presumption of guilt. As was noted earlier, the psychologist will tend to work on probabilities. By contrast, the police may be likely to operate in more absolute terms of guilt or innocence. The danger is that once a person has been labelled as a suspect and brought in for questioning, the police will make a presumption of guilt and see their role as merely to elicit a confession (Ainsworth, 1995b).

One ethical dilemma which profilers will need to address is the possibility that information which they provide might result ultimately in the wrongful conviction of an innocent person. While much of the blame for such a miscarriage of justice might well rest with the police (Gudjonsson, 1992) the profiler must acknowledge that their initial contribution may have been significant.

As we have noted earlier, there is little good scientific research to which one can turn in trying to answer the question of how useful psychological profiling is. Success or failure are not so easily measured when one is dealing with the sort of material used in psychological profiling. If a profiler's information proves to be 50 per cent accurate and 50 per cent inaccurate should this be counted as a success or a failure? As was noted earlier, we also need to be sure whether the information which a profiler provides is of a type which others (e.g. detectives) could not reasonably have deduced for themselves.

Despite these difficulties, it looks likely that psychologists will continue to make valuable contributions to criminal investigations. So long as the public, and indeed the police, realise that the image of profiling provided by fictional characters such as Fitz and Hannibal Lecter are false, expectations might not be raised to an inappropriate level.

Summary

The psychological analysis of criminal behaviour can undoubtedly be a valuable tool in the investigation of crime. The understanding gained from such analysis can be particularly useful in helping the police to focus better their enquiries and, ultimately, to target better their resources. Having said that, the expectation that the police and the public may have with regard to the assistance which psychologists can provide might be unrealistic. Psychological profiling is still in its infancy and as such there are a number of different approaches which are being tried at the present time. There is some disagreement among profilers about how best to offer assistance to investigators. However, there are a number of findings which hold significant promise for the future of the subject. The careful study of the way in which offenders behave while committing their crimes can enable inferences to be drawn as to their most likely characteristics. While this does not generally lead to the level of success which their fictional counterparts achieve, it holds considerable promise for the future of psychologists involved in this area of criminal investigation.

Chapter 7

Jury verdicts and judicial sentencing

We have seen in previous chapters that the road from the commission of a crime to the punishment of an offender is a long and tortuous one. However, a proportion of offenders will find themselves in court and at the mercy of magistrates, stipendiary magistrates, juries and judges. In this chapter we will start to look at two important topics: decisions made by juries and the decisions made by sentencers. We will assess the role which psychology can play in helping to understand what often appear at first glance to be bizarre or irrational decisions made by both juries and sentencers. We will assess whether juries and sentencers are capable of making the sort of objective and rational decisions which our criminal justice system would appear to presume. We will discuss the role of punishment more fully in the next chapter.

Juries and their decisions

Given the fact that the jury system is the cornerstone of many criminal justice processes, it would seem reasonable to expect that a great deal of research would have been carried out into the jury's functioning and efficiency. The criminal justice system does after all place its faith in the abilities of a group of jurors to listen to all the evidence before them and then to reach an objective and appropriate verdict as to a defendant's guilt or innocence. Juries are also seen as important as they allow ordinary members of the public to take an active part in the criminal justice process (Osner *et al.*, 1993). There are, in fact, a large number of arguments both for and against the use of juries in determining guilt (see Kapardis, 1997: 122–9 for a comprehensive summary). We should also note that while juries are an important part of the criminal justice process, many cases are settled without reference to such groups.

Psychological research on groups, juries and jurors

Given that social psychologists have carried out a great deal of research into groups and group decision making it might also be reasonable to expect that psychologists would routinely sit in on jury deliberations and report their findings. In fact this is not the case. Despite the fact that juries' decisions can have far-reaching and even grave consequences for individuals, the criminal justice system has been extremely reluctant to allow academics to study the way in which juries actually make decisions. Most countries ban researchers from entering the jury room and many even forbid jurors from discussing the case. We would want to argue that the criminal justice system's continued and apparently blind faith in a jury's ability to make objective and correct decisions may be misplaced (Cammack, 1995). As Wrightsman (1991) notes:

> Deliberating juries are assumed to be decision-making groups that produce objective and fact-based outcomes. Generally ignored is the possibility that they are subject to the group pressures or irrational impulses that operate in some other groups when they make decisions.
>
> (1991: 290)

It is quite possible, therefore, that a jury may acquit a defendant even if they feel that he/she is actually guilty. They may, for example, feel sympathy for a defendant, or even believe that a prosecution should not have been brought at all (Devons, 1978; Harrower, 1998 for some examples). Juries may also fail to convict a defendant if they feel that the punishment they are likely to receive would be excessive. The recent introduction of policies such as 'Three strikes and you're out' and even the reintroduction of the death penalty in some American states might thus lessen the chances of a guilty verdict being returned (Kerr, 1978). In the USA, jurors who are about to serve on a case for which a death sentence may be passed are now asked specifically about their views on capital punishment. Those who are against the use of capital punishment may actually be excluded on the grounds that they are unlikely to reach a 'fair' verdict. In an interesting piece of research, Ellsworth (1993) found that people who did not oppose the death penalty tended to be biased in favour of the prosecution and to be more likely to find an accused guilty than were those who opposed the death penalty.

The criminal justice system's reluctance to open up jury deliberations to public scrutiny does not mean that psychologists are unable to shed any light on jury decisions. They may for example choose to carry out research using 'shadow juries' or 'mock juries'. In the former case, a shadow jury might sit in the public gallery during a trial and would then retire to discuss the case and to reach a verdict. However, unlike the real jury in the case, the shadow jury's deliberations could be monitored and recorded and the decision-making process analysed. In the case of mock juries, a group of people similar to a real jury might be assembled and asked to listen to or read about a case. They would then be asked to discuss the case and decide upon the guilt or innocence of a defendant. During this process their deliberations would be monitored. (The research by Ellsworth (1993) cited above used this method.)

Shadow juries and mock juries offer one way of simulating what actually goes on in jury rooms. In addition, they allow researchers to test hypotheses with regard to certain aspects of a case. Thus, if researchers wanted to know whether the race of a defendant might affect a jury's decision, they could give each of two mock juries a case transcript which was identical except that the race of the defendant would be varied for the two mock juries.

While mock and shadow juries can offer valuable insights into real juries' decision making, they can never replicate exactly the decision-making process (Hans, 1992). One crucial difference is that decisions made by mock and shadow juries do not have consequences for an individual accused, whereas those made by real juries certainly do. A second difference relates to the composition of real juries compared with mock/shadow juries. Many studies using mock/shadow juries have used undergraduate students as 'jurors' and anyone who has agreed to take part in the study will have been selected for the 'jury'. However, in the case of juries in real criminal cases, there may have been a great deal of discussion and argument over the actual composition of the jury.

Today it is becoming increasingly common for both sides in a case (but particularly the defence) to challenge certain potential jurors, arguing perhaps that a person is biased and will not approach the case with an open mind. Although the right to challenge jurors may originally have been introduced as a way of trying to ensure a fair trial, more recently it has been seen as a way of trying to select a jury which is likely to be the most favourable to one side or another (see Ainsworth, 1995a: 73–80 for a review). We should not underestimate this process. In one case reported by Zeisel and Diamond (1976) a jury of twelve men and women was eventually selected from an original pool of some 196 people. Jury selection is a complex process and, despite what some well-paid consultants might claim, it is not always easy to predict whether individuals will be sympathetic or hostile towards an accused (Dunstan et al., 1995; Hastie, 1993; Kadane, 1993). In fact, Kadane points to the surprising fact that defence and prosecution often agree as to which potential jurors should be eliminated from a jury.

There is however one aspect of jury selection which does deserve further discussion. We know from social psychological research that one of a new group's first roles will be to establish a hierarchy and to identify a leader. Once so identified the leader will, almost by definition, be able to exert some influence over other group members. In the case of juries, the position of leader is formally recognised in the need to appoint a foreman (or, increasingly today, foreperson). Juries are in fact told that their very first task will be to appoint a foreman who will become the spokesperson for the whole group. The foreman, by the nature of his/her role, will be in a better position to influence the group than will other group members. As such, those involved with juror selection would do well to try to identify the person who is perhaps most likely to become the foreman. If such a person appears sympathetic to their side, they may fight to ensure their retention. However if they appear hostile, they may find some grounds to argue for their removal.

Although the amount of influence which leaders can exert will vary from situation to situation, in the case of a jury, the influence may well be substantial. Indeed, in the murky and complex waters of judicial procedure, most first-time jurors might be only too pleased to receive guidance from someone who appears to know what to do. Research suggests, for example, that jurors often have difficulty in understanding instructions given by judges (Kagehiro, 1990) and will turn to a leader for clarification and/or instruction. In such a situation it may be comparatively easy for the foreman to steer the group in the direction which he or she wishes and which might lead ultimately to a perverse decision.

In addition to a jury being 'fair' it has also been argued that juries should be representative of the community. There is a presumption that a jury which is composed of people from differing backgrounds may be more likely to reach an appropriate verdict than will one composed of people from a small subsection of the population. Despite the fact that heterogeneity may increase perceived fairness there is in fact little empirical evidence to suggest that heterogeneity does increase the accuracy of jury decision making (Arce, 1995). The 'representativeness' argument may in any case be flawed as certain groups (e.g. former police officers) are already excluded from jury service and many other groups (e.g. doctors) can claim exemption. In fact, many people's wish to avoid serving on a jury has prompted more than one cynic to suggest, perhaps unfairly, that today, juries are composed almost entirely of people who were simply not bright enough to get themselves excluded from jury service!

How often do juries make mistakes?

Concern about juries and their decision making stems mainly from cases where perverse decisions appear to have been reached. It is, of course, impossible to establish definitively the number of occasions on which juries get their decision wrong. If one were to interview police officers, many might want to argue that juries often acquit defendants despite the 'overwhelming' evidence. By contrast, many defence lawyers and convicted defendants might wish to argue that there are far too few acquittals (Baldwin and McConville, 1979; Zander and Henderson, 1994). The most comprehensive review of jury decisions remains that of Kalven and Zeisel (1966) in the USA. These researchers examined some

3,576 trials and found that in almost 80 per cent of cases the jury's verdict was in agreement with that of the trial judge.

There are a number of ways in which one might interpret these figures. One may argue that as juries appear to get it right most of the time we should not be too concerned. On the other hand one might want to argue that if juries do get their decisions wrong in over twenty per cent of cases, there are a large number of innocent people languishing in jail, and a large number of guilty people still at liberty. In any case, Kalven and Zeisel only compared jury decisions with the trial judge's view. There were presumably some occasions on which the trial judge was wrong and the jury were in fact correct. There may also have been other cases in which the jury's verdict agreed with that of the trial judge, yet both were wrong. Although Kalven and Zeisel's original work marked a milestone in criminal justice research, there were in fact a number of methodological deficiencies in their study. In fact, Stephenson (1992: 181) argues that Kalven and Zeisel's own data does not support the conclusions which they themselves drew.

Many of those who claim to have been wrongly convicted will in any case tend to blame both the judge and the jury for their fate. Those who wish to appeal against their conviction will, of course, not be allowed to do so simply on the grounds that they believe that the jury made a mistake. They may, however, appeal on the grounds that the judge misdirected the jury or was biased in his/her summing up.

Another American survey which concerned itself with errors of a different kind was that of Huff (1987). Huff contacted a large number of people involved in the criminal justice system and asked them for their views on the error rate of convictions. He found that over 70 per cent of those surveyed believed that the error rate was less than one in a hundred, while a further twenty per cent believed it to be between one and five per hundred. Huff concluded from his research that perhaps only about one defendant in every 200 is wrongfully convicted. However, we should note that if this figure is correct, over 7,500 people will be wrongly convicted of a serious offence in the USA each year (Cutler and Penrod, 1995). One may also wish to argue that those who work within the criminal justice system may have a vested interest in making it work and, as such, may be somewhat reluctant to admit that mistakes may be common.

One possible explanation for why juries might make mistakes can be gleaned from Solomon Asch's early research in social psychology. Asch (1956) was able to demonstrate the way in which a majority of people in a group can exert pressure on an individual and persuade him/her to go against their own beliefs. In Asch's classic (1956) study, confederates of the experimenter deliberately gave wrong answers to a series of questions regarding the length of lines. Asch found that the majority of people who took part in the study were unable to resist this 'group pressure' and gave at least one wrong answer, rather than go against the group. One can extrapolate from this study to the jury situation in which the majority may pressurise a dissenting individual until he/she bows to the pressure and goes along with the majority's view. The scenario portrayed by Henry Fonda in the film *Twelve Angry Men* (in which one person succeeds in changing the views of eleven other jurors) may make entertaining viewing, but appears unlikely to occur frequently in real life. Kalven and Zeisel (1966) reported that 98 per cent of juries delivered the same decision which the majority had supported at the outset of their deliberations. However, some writers (e.g. Pennington and Hastie, 1990) suggest that this figure may be misleading.

Examining the effects of majorities on jury decisions, Davis (1980) suggested that if the majority consists of eight or more (from a twelve person mock jury) the eventual decision will tend to go in favour of the majority. However, if the majority is only seven, the split is often much more difficult to resolve and the jury may simply be unable to agree upon a verdict. The pressure on an individual (or on several individuals) to conform to the majority is important because in most countries juries are required to bring in unanimous verdicts. Indeed on returning to the courtroom, the foreman will often be asked the question 'Have you reached a decision upon which you are **all** agreed?' Of course, this question does not require the foreman to disclose **how** the unanimous verdict was reached. The fact that the privacy of the jury room is regarded as sacrosanct means that if bullying or even threats are made by some jury members against others, this is unlikely to come to light.

The courts appear to make a presumption that if all jurors agree with a decision it is more likely to be correct. However, in some countries (including England and Wales) it is possible for a jury to return a majority verdict. Such decisions are not encouraged and are usually only allowed after the foreman of the jury has told the judge that it is unlikely that the jury will be able ever to return a unanimous verdict. Interestingly, research by Hastie *et al.* (1983) suggests that juries which are required only to bring in majority verdicts spend less time discussing the actual case and more time taking votes. In addition, Hastie found that majority juries were more likely to adopt a forceful and persuasive style than was the case with juries from which unanimity was required.

Judges appear reluctant to accept the fact that juries are on occasion unable to reach a verdict of any kind. A foreman who reports this fact to a trial judge is likely (at least initially) to be told to try again. In some cases, a judge may only accept that a decision is not going to be possible after the jury has spent several days in deliberation. One can but speculate as to what judges think will happen if a jury is instructed to go away and spend even more time trying to reach an agreed decision. (The interested reader may wish to consult Hastie (1993) for a review of decision-making models.) Psychologists would suggest that in such circumstances those in the minority will perhaps eventually cave in and agree to go along with the majority. In such cases, however, the individual(s) concerned may not have finally been convinced by the power of the majority's arguments, but may simply have gone along with them in order to avoid further pressure.

This tendency can be partly explained by reference to Asch's work. Subjects in the Asch experiment did not necessarily become convinced that their initial view was incorrect and that they should now change their opinion so that they would be right (i.e. they did not privately accept the view). It seems that many of those who did bow to the group pressure were simply complying in order to avoid some possible rejection, ridicule or further pressure (Kiesler and Kiesler, 1969). This may be relevant to the jury's decision-making process. Those who do not agree with the majority may 'agree to disagree' but finally abandon further resistance. They may not actively agree with the ultimate decision but will simply acquiesce and spare further heated discussion. Of course, if these minority members were wrong all along, we should not be too concerned. However, if they were in fact correct, their acquiescence may lead to an incorrect verdict.

Even if jurors agree broadly on their decision, this does not necessarily mean that the eventual outcome of their deliberations will be a simple averaging of their views. For example, in cases where a jury is asked to make a recommendation (for example, the punishment which an offender should be given, or the amount of compensation which someone should receive) it is possible that the group will produce a result which is in excess of their original or average view. This tendency for groups to become more extreme was first highlighted by Stoner (1968). Stoner labelled the phenomenon the risky shift, although it now appears that while groups do tend to become more extreme, their decisions do not necessarily become more 'risky'. In fact, the tendency is more an example of group polarisation in which whatever initial view is expressed, the view becomes more extreme as a result of prolonged group discussion.

We can see from this brief review of some jury research that the justice system's faith in jury decision making may be misplaced. Like other small groups, juries are subject to a number of forces and pressures some of which have been identified and explained by psychologists. Knowledge of such factors can help us to understand some of the more perverse jury decisions which can lead to miscarriages of justice.

Sentencing of offenders

Although sentencing has been the focus of extensive research and comment by legal scholars, the process also allows opportunity for psychological study. Kapardis (1997: 157) suggests that sentencing offers a 'goldmine of opportunities' for psychologists, a view supported by other writers including Hebenton and Pease (1995).

As was noted in Chapter 7, the public have certain expectations in respect of the courts. They will expect the courts to be capable of separating the innocent from the guilty, but will also expect that those convicted of a crime will receive a punishment which is appropriate. However, different parties within the justice system will often have differing expectations as to what constitutes an appropriate sentence. Perhaps nowhere is the maxim 'you can't please all the people all of the time' more pertinent than in the sentencing of offenders. The media seem regularly to report on the outrage felt by the public when some offender receives a sentence which is considered to be too lenient (or in some cases too harsh). In such cases the outrage stems from a feeling that an offender did not receive his/her 'just deserts' (Von Hirsch, 1995).

It might also be reasonable to expect that, despite the occasional odd decision, sentencers would at least be consistent in their decisions and that those who commit similar crimes would receive similar sentences. In fact, this is too simplistic a notion as sentencers will need to consider a large range of factors before making a final decision (see below). Indeed, if sentencing is more to do with changing offenders' attitudes and behaviour than with ensuring that they receive their just deserts, we might expect to find little consistency across similar types of offence. Those who support this viewpoint may wish to argue that sentencing can only help an offender to change and be rehabilitated if the sentence reflects the offender's own individual needs and circumstances. Why else would courts ask for pre-sentence reports in many cases before making a final decision as to an offender's sentence?

Disparities in sentencing

Public disquiet over sentencing would thus seem to arise from the perceived appropriateness of individual sentences and from inconsistencies between different sentencers. Most judicial systems take the view that the judge (or magistrate) is in the best position to make a judgement about sentencing and, as such, considerable discretion is often given to such people. However, we should note that increasingly an offender's fate may be decided by politicians and policy makers rather than by judges. Ashworth (1997) makes this point forcefully but also points out that there appears to be confusion and equivocation over what the real purpose of sentencing should be. He notes that in England and Wales the Criminal Justice Act 1991 sought to clarify the rationale for sentencing by establishing that 'just deserts' should be the main criterion (except in rare cases where the protection of the public took priority). However Ashworth observes that within a few months of the Act coming into force the Lord Chief Justice established 'general deterrence' as an aim in certain cases. Ashworth also notes that only a few months later the government began to retreat from the 1991 Act to the point where deterrence and incapacitation became prominent in the Criminal Justice and Public Order Act 1984 and the Crime (Sentences) Act 1997.

In fact, judicial discretion is by no means absolute and is subject to an increasing number of constraints. For example, most offences are subject to a maximum sentence, while others such as murder carry a mandatory sentence of life imprisonment. The Crime (Sentences) Act 1997 even introduced minimum sentences for some offences. Judges are also bound at least to some extent by sentencing guidelines and by precedent. Sentencing guidelines may even contain recommendations with regard to which circumstances might serve to reduce a sentence and which might serve to increase it. We should also bear in mind that in many cases, offenders have the right to appeal against their sentence and may be more likely to do so if the sentence is considered too harsh. In England and Wales it is also now possible for the prosecution to appeal if they feel than an offender received a sentence which is too lenient. Plea bargaining and the increasing use of fixed penalty notices serve further to reduce judicial sentencing discretion. Indeed, in 1997 some seven million fixed penalty notices were issued in England and Wales. This compares with almost two million people prosecuted in magistrates' courts and only 84,000 tried in Crown Courts.

Despite these important provisos, there is public concern over what appear to be disparities in sentencing. Kapardis argues that such disparities are only to be expected and are in fact endemic within the criminal justice system. He lists a large number of reasons why this should be the case. These include the large number of different individuals who are involved in sentencing, regional variations between rural and urban courts, the amount and type of information provided to sentencers (e.g. by social workers), and the way in which sentencers perceive different types of case information. Hebenton and Pease (1995), drawing on the work of Ashworth (1992), suggest that a judge's discretion can be influenced by four broad categories of factors, i.e. the demographic features of sentencers, views on crime and punishment, views on the principle of sentencing and views of the facts of the case.

One might expect that the judiciary would respond to concerns over sentencing disparities by allowing researchers such as psychologists to study judicial decision making at close quarters. This has certainly not been the case (Ashworth, 1992). Indeed, one study of sentencing in English Crown Courts was curtailed on the instructions of the then Lord Chief Justice, Lord Lane. Ashworth reports that the reasoning behind Lord Lane's surprising action appeared to be that:

> Research into the attitudes, beliefs and reasoning of judges was not the way to obtain an accurate picture: sentencing was an art and not a science, and the further judges were pressed to articulate their reasons, the less realistic the exercise would become.

(1984: 64)

One is inclined to agree with the view of Hebenton and Pease (1995) who note that 'These assertions, veering from regarding sentencing as an ineffable mystery to a process characterised by strong formalism, fail to convince' (1995: 375). Indeed, the comments attributed to Lord Lane appear to portray judges as almost superhuman individuals who are not subject to the influences, biases and mistakes which afflict other human beings. The argument failed to convince Fitzmaurice and Pease (1986) who argued that as judicial power is substantial, and as the mental processes governing sentencing decisions are so unclear, there should be increased scrutiny of the sentencing process, particularly by psychologists. The fact that most judges oppose the introduction of legislation which introduces more maximum or minimum sentences also suggests that much of the judiciary believes that they should simply be trusted to impose the appropriate sentence in each individual case. While the judiciary's wish to remain independent of political influence is in some cases admirable, their apparent belief in their own infallibility is more disturbing.

Kapardis (1985) conducted an extensive literature review of the important legal factors which might account for sentencing inconsistencies. These included the type of charge, the defendant's criminal record (and the recency of their last conviction), past interactions with the criminal justice system, the type of plea, the defendant's age, gender, community ties, provocation by the victim, the location of the court and probation officers' recommendations as to an appropriate sentence. Writing in 1997, Kapardis suggests that the use of Victim Impact Statements might also now be added to the list.

In addition to these legal factors, Kapardis added a number of important extra-legal factors pertaining to the defendant, the victim and the sentencer. In the case of the defendant this might include their pre-trial status, socio-economic status, race and attractiveness. In relation to the victim, this might include factors such as race. In relation to the sentencer, a large number of factors are seen as important, including their age, religion, education, social background, cognitive complexity, constructs, politics and penological orientation.

Given such a long list of relevant factors it is perhaps unsurprising that sentencing disparities do occur. Even if all the relevant factors could be identified, discrepancies might still arise as a result of the importance attached to each of the factors by individual sentencers. As Hebenton and Pease (1995) note eloquently 'The knee-jerk response of judges and magistrates that each case is treated on its merits is meaningless until there is agreement on which merit is to be judged, and which variables should be deemed irrelevant to merit' (1995: 381). Thus, one sentencer may decide that a defendant's age is the most important variable whereas another might decide that their home circumstances merit the most consideration. Kapardis argues that 'There is no doubt that it is the interaction of both specific legal and extra-legal factors that best explains disparities in sentencing' (1997: 157). In fact, Kapardis goes so far as to suggest that no generalisations are possible particularly given wide regional and temporal variations.

One important point to bear in mind is that the same factors which affect sentencing decisions might also be relevant to other stages of the criminal justice process. For example, if race turns out to be an important sentencing variable, it might also be relevant at earlier stages of the process. It may be that the police are more likely to stop and search black people than they are white people. Black suspects might also be more likely to then be arrested and charged, but less likely to be cautioned. Thus sentencing disparities may mirror or even compound biases at other points in the criminal justice system (Stanko, 1999; Bowling and Phillips, 1999). Bearing this point in mind, we will next consider two variables which appear to be particularly important in explaining sentencing disparities. Although all of the other variables identified above may impact upon sentencing decisions, race and gender are the two most widely researched areas and we will consider these in some detail.

The effects of race

Race is perhaps the most researched area with regard to possible biases in the criminal justice system (see Bowling and Phillips, 1999; Smith, 1997 for recent reviews). A simple look at the prison population would tend to suggest that biases appear to be occurring at some stage(s) of the criminal justice process. If we look for example at the male prison population in England and Wales in 1994, we find that black prisoners made up 11.1 per cent of the 15–39 year olds in prison. However, in the same year black males within this age group made up only 2.3 per cent of the general population. The figures for female offenders in the same age group are even more disparate with 20.4 per cent of female prison inmates being black whereas in the general population black females represent only 2.3 per cent. As with many other statistics, however, it may be unwise to reach simplistic conclusions. For example, significant numbers of the black females were not residents of this country but were in fact foreign nationals convicted of offences relating to the attempted importation of drugs. However, if one considers only British nationals, large discrepancies are still found and black people remain heavily over-represented in the prison population.

Of course, this by no means proves that blacks tend to receive harsher sentences than do whites. As was noted earlier, biases may occur at many other stages of the criminal justice process and it may be these biases which best explain the discrepancy (Smith, 1997: 732–44 for a detailed discussion). We also need to consider the fact that blacks may be over-represented in the prison population because they tend to commit more serious types of crime which are likely to carry heavier penalties.

However, if one controls for offence type, significant differences still emerge. For almost all types of offence, blacks are over-represented and for some categories of offence the differences are extremely large. For example, Smith notes that in the case of drug offences, the rate of imprisonment is almost eleven times as high for black men as for white men.

Interestingly, the figures do not appear simply to point to a prejudice against all non-whites. The rates of incarceration for South Asian men for example is broadly similar to that for white men and, in some cases, the rate is actually lower. Figures taken from magistrates' courts in London (Home Office, 1989b) also suggest that South Asians are more likely to be fined and less likely to be given custodial sentences than both black and white defendants. Smith (1997) points out that this difference is interesting given the fact that prejudice against Asians is common in other arenas such as employment and housing and is often at a level similar to that against blacks from Afro-Caribbean backgrounds.

The same Home Office figures suggest that there are differences in Crown Court sentences. Thus, while 51 per cent of white men were given immediate custody, 57 per cent of black defendants suffered immediate incarceration. In some cases (e.g. sexual offences) the difference could be accounted for by offence seriousness, but in other types of crime such as robbery this was not the case.

Perhaps the best known British study of sentencing and race to date is that of Hood (1992) which looked at a total of 2,884 defendants appearing in Crown Court. Hood found that among his sample, 48.4 per cent of whites were sentenced to custody compared with 56.6 per cent of blacks. Hood noted that there were, however, large differences in the relative sentences of black and white defendants between individual courts and between individual judges. In other words, some judges and some courts (in fact, one particular court) showed significant variation in the way in which black and white defendants were treated. However, most others showed little variation. This was particularly striking for offences which were moderately serious and in which judges had the most discretion in deciding upon a sentence. In fact, Hood found that there was no such variation in the most trivial, nor in the most serious, type of offence.

Interestingly, Hood suggested that where differences did occur they tended to be found only in relation to those who were unemployed. Thus, black unemployed defendants were more likely to receive custodial sentences than were white unemployed defendants, but no differences were found in relation to black and white defendants who were in employment.

In addition, Hood found that black defendants were more than twice as likely to plead not guilty compared with white defendants. This factor may go some way towards explaining the longer average sentences given to black defendants – in general a guilty plea leads to a lesser sentence. This may seem inherently unfair in a country in which some police forces have been accused of being inherently racist and others have admitted to institutional racism. Given such facts, it is possible that a larger proportion of black offenders will in fact be innocent of the charges brought against them in comparison to white offenders.

The decision whether or not to plead guilty does appear to be an important and relevant factor here, as a significant proportion of the variance in custodial sentences between black and white defendants is accounted for by differences in the proportion of not guilty pleas among the two sets of defendants. However, even after controlling for this factor, some unexplained variance in custodial sentences remains and Hood argued that at least some of this could be accounted for by prejudice. We must, however, emphasise the point that in the majority of the courts which Hood studied there was no variation found in the sentences given to black and white defendants, once offence seriousness was taken into account.

We can see from this brief review of some British research that there appear to be some demonstrable effects of race on sentencing decisions. However, we can also see that the relationship is not as straightforward, nor as easy to explain, as one might expect. Perhaps of most relevance to the current discussion is Hood's finding that while some judges and most courts appear to show little bias, others show considerably more. Furthermore, those cases in which judges had the greatest discretion were the ones in which the greatest race variation was found. This fact suggests that we should remain sceptical of those who wish to portray all judges as being almost superhuman and above the prejudices and vices of we lesser mortals! Ethnocentricity and in-group favouritism appear to be universal human traits, yet ones which lead to prejudice or hostility against members of an out-group (Brewer, 1979; Brown, 1986). In a country in which the vast majority of judges are white should we really be surprised if some individuals appear to view blacks differently from whites?

Although we have chosen to concentrate on British research in this section, it should be noted that there is a wealth of American literature on this topic. Many of the findings portray a similar picture to that found in Britain, although as an increasing number of states have reintroduced the death penalty for certain offences, concern over disparities in sentence take on an even greater urgency (Aguirre and Baker, 1990).

Gender differences in sentencing

In almost all countries for which reliable records are available, men are convicted of significantly more criminal offences than are women (Dobash *et al.*, 1995; Heidensohn, 1997; Stanko, 1999). In England and Wales the ratio of men to women in prison in recent years has generally been of the order of 30 to one. Men are also more likely to be involved in serious offences including violent and sexual crimes. However, some authors have suggested that in recent years the gap appears to be closing. It is interesting to note that although most criminal offences are not gender specific, some crimes (e.g. rape in the case of males and infanticide in the case of females) can only be committed by one of the sexes.

Daly (1987) has argued that sexism in sentencing reinforces traditional gender roles. Judges are said to take a paternalistic attitude which aims to protect the social institution of the family. It has also been suggested (e.g. by Henning, 1995) that many judges, the majority of whom are, of course, male, perceive female defendants to be acting out of character (from their normal female role) and assume that they must therefore be psychologically disturbed. This notion was confirmed by Fontaine and Emily (1978) who found that judges appeared to be more interested in the circumstances surrounding female defendants' crimes than was the case with male defendants. It appeared as though judges were searching for reasons why such women might have behaved in this 'uncharacteristic' way. Thus, the focus on male and female defendants when deciding upon a sentence appeared to be different. If a male defendant appeared before the court accused of a violent offence his behaviour might be viewed as almost normal and sentencing deliberation would focus almost exclusively upon the seriousness of the offence. However, with female defendants far more background information would be sought in an effort to account for behaviour which is not (according to the sexist stereotype) within the normal behavioural repertoire of females. Interestingly, Heidensohn (1997) notes that while twenty per cent of males convicted of criminal offences are sent to prison, only five per cent of women are treated in this way.

Further evidence of this tendency is found in the work of Wilczynski and Morris (1993). These researchers found, for example, that a woman found guilty of killing her own child was more likely to be convicted of manslaughter rather than murder, more likely to have a plea of diminished responsibility accepted and less likely to receive a custodial sentence. These same authors note that in their sample, none of the women who were convicted of infanticide received a custodial sentence. There have also been a number of recent cases in which women convicted of killing their partner have been released following the reconsideration of evidence that the women themselves had been abused (in some case for many years) by the victim.

It does then appear that there are gender differences in the sentences imposed on male and female defendants. Writing in 1997, Kapardis observes that with one exception British studies all show that female defendants receive more lenient sentences than do males. He suggests that the tendency is all the more compelling when one realises that the research has looked at both magistrates' and Crown Courts and has covered a wide range of offenders and offences.

Before moving on, we must mention the fact that disparities in sentencing may not always be in the direction which we might expect. For example, while many judges may take the view that women who commit serious offences must be 'mad' and therefore require treatment, others may take the view that such women are in fact very bad and therefore deserve to be punished severely for having behaved in such 'non-feminine' ways. Heidensohn (1997) talks of double deviance and double jeopardy in that such women have transgressed both social norms and gender norms. In these cases we might expect the sentence to be more severe than if a similar crime were committed by a man (Kennedy, 1992). Farrington and Morris (1983) have suggested that the apparent leniency of sentences for females may actually conceal the fact that some female offenders (e.g. those who are not 'domesticated' and who appeared to lack respect) may actually be given more severe sentences than would equivalent men.

There were signs that in the late 1990s the figures for women offenders were showing signs of change. For example, the number of males aged 21 or over who were sentenced for an indictable offence rose by six per cent between 1996 and 1997 (Home Office, 1998). However, the figures for female offenders showed a rise of eleven per cent over the same period. Thus, although six times as many men as women are sentenced for indictable offences, the rate of increase for females was almost twice that for men. Similarly, the figures for 18–20 year olds showed a rise of four per cent for male offenders, but eleven per cent for female offenders. Again, during the course of the 1990s, the percentage of female juveniles who received cautions decreased at a faster rate than that for male juveniles.

The figures for the number of defendants sentenced to immediate custody also provide food for thought. The number of males dealt with in this way rose from eighteen per cent in the early 1990s to 26 per cent by 1997. However, in the case of female offenders, the number rose from six per cent in the early 1990s to thirteen per cent in 1997. Although women are statistically less likely to receive custodial sentences than are men, their chances of being dealt with in this way have more than doubled in the space of only a few years. It has also been suggested that women who are sent to prison are less likely to receive good education and training and are more likely to be expected to carry out domestic chores within the prison. Such anomalies once again point to differences in the perception of male and female roles.

As with race differences, it would appear that sentencers are subject to similar biases and prejudices as are others in society when it comes to considering male and female behaviour. Despite the fact that in the last twenty years there have been some not insubstantial changes in the perception of male and female roles, significant differences are still apparent. While there have been moves to reduce outright sexual discrimination, prejudices have been more difficult to tackle. Although discussing primarily racial prejudice, Cochrane (1991) make an interesting point with respect to humans and their biases. He notes that prejudice is very common and that 'any explanation for it must recognise that it is a statistically "normal" psychological phenomena and not an aberration limited to a minority of unstable or disturbed people' (1991: 127). Under such circumstances we should hardly be surprised if a predominantly male judiciary continues to treat women differently from men.

From this brief review of two important factors, it would thus appear that sentencing may not be the rational and objective process which certain members of the judiciary might wish us to believe. The fact that researchers have experienced great difficulty in being allowed to interview judges about their decisions also raises some concern. Nevertheless, in an attempt to understand sentencing decisions a little more fully various models have been proposed. Some of the models with a psychological focus will be described briefly below.

Understanding sentencing decisions

Michon and Pakes (1995) make a distinction between 'normative' and 'descriptive' models. While descriptive models are concerned with optimal decision making, normative models focus upon how decisions are actually made in real life. In the case of judges' sentencing decisions, descriptive models recognise that there is a limit to the amount of information which can be processed at any one time. As a consequence judges will be selective in what they attend to and will focus predominantly upon those variables which they consider to be the most important when deciding upon a sentence. Ashworth (1997) notes that a judge might have access to five different pieces of information about each individual defendant. These might include the police antecedents statement, the defence plea in mitigation, a pre-sentence report, a medical report, and the offender's appearance.

Although judges might claim to give each factor the appropriate amount of attention, it would be unusual if each judge did not have their own personal view as to which should be considered the most relevant in deciding upon a sentence. Research in the field of cognitive psychology has shown that perception is selective, subjective and individual (Ainsworth, 1998: ch. 1). As such it would be difficult to assert that different judges will be consistent in the weight which each gives to certain factors. It is also possible that a judge would be swayed by one particular piece of information. For example, if the judge were to take an instant dislike to a defendant's appearance and attitude in court, it would take a superhuman effort for the judge not to allow this to have undue influence. We know that people do make presumptions about individuals based upon their personal appearance, especially if that appearance confirms some pre-existing stereotype. Thus, a person who appears to have an honest or attractive face may be treated more leniently than one who appears menacing or threatening. In their study, Kalven and Zeisel found that American judges attributed fourteen per cent of their disagreement with the jury to jurors' impressions of a defendant. Mock jury studies have found that a defendant's appearance can have an effect upon determinations of guilt and on recommended sentences, although the influence may not be as great as some early writers had supposed (see Bull and McAlpine, 1998 for a review). In a number of mock jury studies, a defendant's attractiveness has been shown to lead to a more lenient sentence. However, if the defendant appears to have used their attractiveness to help in the commission of a crime (e.g. in cases of deception) such individuals may be given a more severe sentence.

Michon and Pakes conclude that while the complex task of judicial decision making is often performed quite well, it does not necessarily use methods which would be described by normative models. Further, these authors suggest that judicial decision making can never be described as rational in the pure sense in which the term might be used in economics.

Further insights into sentencing decisions can be gleaned from research drawing on attribution theory (see Chapters 6 and 9). Attribution theory seeks to understand the way in which people explain the causes of others' behaviour. It has been found that people often make a distinction between dispositional (i.e. internal) causes and situational (i.e. external) causes. Such a distinction will be crucial when considering sentences. An offender who is perceived as having offended because 'he is just that sort of person' will generally be given a more severe sentence than will one who appears to have been almost dragged into the offence as a result of strong situational forces. Pre-sentence reports will often try to establish which of these scenarios best describes an individual offender's particular situation.

In addition to the internal/external distinction, attribution theory suggests that people will also try to make a further distinction between stability/instability and between controllability/uncontrollability. In the case of the stability dimension, people will attempt to establish whether another's particular behaviour suggests an enduring pattern or one which is out of character. Thus, an otherwise respectable first time offender may be perceived as having just made a mistake rather than as possessing an underlying deviant personality. In the case of the controllability/uncontrollability dimension, observers might try to establish whether the behaviour in question appeared to be committed wilfully, i.e. deliberately, or was in fact largely out of the individual's conscious control. As we saw in Chapter 6, this is an important consideration when assessing the mental state of individuals appearing in court. Claims by defendants that 'it was the drink that made me do it' is an obvious example of attempts to imply that they were not in control of their faculties at the time of the offence.

Weiner (1980) suggests that attributions of responsibility for criminal acts stem from the way in which an individual sentencer classifies the actions of a defendant in terms of the three dimensions of causality. Thus, a defendant who appears to have committed an offence because of internal factors, who shows a consistent pattern of such behaviour, and who appears to have acted deliberately, will tend to receive a harsher sentence than would one on the opposite ends of these three continuums. This notion is supported by research such as that of Carroll and Payne (1977) and Ewart and Penninton (1987).

Of course, we should not necessarily be concerned about this. The public may well support the judiciary if they impose harsher sentences on those who appear to be acting as a result of internal factors and who also appear to be wilful and persistent offenders. However, concerns might be raised if it were found that the attributions made by judges were in fact incorrect. Research in attribution theory has shown consistently that people can and do make errors when attributing causes to the behaviour of others. The most common error appears to occur in the tendency for people to over-emphasise internal factors and to under-emphasise external factors (see Chapter 9). So common is this tendency that it has been labelled the Fundamental Attribution Error. Thus, if judges do operate in the same way as other human beings they will tend to presume consistently that defendants carry more responsibility for their actions than is actually the case. As such they may impose more severe penalties than might be justified and in some cases recommend treatment which may be inappropriate.

Another apparent example of attributional bias is provided by Oswald (1992). Oswald surveyed a number of German judges and found that their sentencing appeared to vary according to whether they adopted an offender orientation or a victim orientation. Oswald suggested that the more a judge adopted the victim's perspective, the more likely they were to attribute responsibility to the defendant (and presumably then to impose a tougher sentence). Here again then it would appear that judges are not making objective nor even consistent evaluations, but, like other humans, are making subjective, and in some cases inaccurate, assessments.

We can see that psychologists can and do make valuable contributions to the study of judicial sentencing and to an understanding of sentencing disparities. Their scientific approach stands in marked contrast to that of some of those within the legal profession who appear to wish the public to believe that an analysis of judicial decision making is not necessary as judges can always be trusted to make the correct decision. Hebenton and Pease (1995) suggest that in the future psychologists may be able to have a much greater input with regard to sentencing decisions. In particular they suggest that a clearer understanding of criminal careers may make it possible to maximise the effectiveness of crime-reductive sentencing. It also seems that as psychologists develop further their abilities to assess risk and dangerousness in individual offenders, their input may be considerable (Quinsey et al., 1998).

Summary

We have seen in this chapter that, in the two areas chosen for analysis, psychologists have made significant contributions to our understanding of decision making. We have attempted to explode the myth that juries are objective and accurate determiners of guilt and innocence. It has also been argued that some of the more surprising decisions made by juries may become a little more understandable if we consider social psychological research on group behaviour generally. Having said that, a complete understanding of jury decision making may have to wait until such time as the authorities allow jury deliberations to be monitored by psychologists. Unfortunately, it would appear that this is unlikely to happen in the foreseeable future. We should also bear in mind that the majority of convictions are not determined by juries. The vast majority of offences are dealt with at magistrates' courts or involve a guilty plea at Crown Court.

By studying judicial sentencing, psychologists can also help to identify some of the most important factors which appear to affect judges' decisions. By doing so they can offer explanations for at least some of the sentencing disparities which come to light each year. However, through their understanding of psychological processes such as attribution, psychologists can also identify some of the ways in which sentencing decisions may be inappropriate.

Chapter 8

Dealing with offenders

Members of society hope, and in most cases expect, that those who commit a crime will be punished and that the punishment will be 'appropriate'. However, as we saw in Chapters 1 and 2, the number of people who are eventually convicted of a crime is only a small proportion of those who actually break the law. Of those who are convicted, many do not receive what victims might consider to be an appropriate sentence (see Chapter 7).

A debate over the philosophy of the criminal justice process is beyond the scope of this book, but a consideration of the disposal of offenders from a psychological viewpoint is appropriate. This chapter will, therefore, begin with an examination of the role of punishment and go on to consider what methods might be the most effective in trying to prevent offenders from committing further crime. We will challenge the assumption that harsher sentences in and of themselves lead to less offending and consider why prisons are generally ineffective in changing behaviour. We will also challenge the view that 'nothing works' and consider which approaches appear to be the most effective in changing offenders' behaviour. Much of this chapter will focus on the use of custodial sentences, though the reader may also wish to consult Brownlee (1998) for an up-to-date review of community punishments.

This chapter will not attempt to provide a comprehensive review of all psychologically based treatment programmes, but will instead try to identify the characteristics which differentiate successful from unsuccessful programmes. It will also focus on two examples of potentially effective interventions, i.e. anger management programmes and initiatives targeted at men who assault their partners. Readers who wish to learn about other types of programme may wish to see the suggestions for further reading at the end of the book.

Society's expectations of punishment

Each society passes laws which prohibit a wide array of unacceptable or deviant behaviours. However, as we saw in Chapters 1 and 2, 'criminal behaviour' can cover a very wide range of actions. Those who choose to transgress society's rules may, if convicted, expect to be punished. In some cases the actual punishment is prescribed (e.g. life imprisonment for murder), but in most cases courts have some discretion in the sentences which they pass (see Chapter 7). However, punishment may serve a number of different purposes from a psychological viewpoint. For those affronted and distressed by victimisation, punishment of the offender might lead to a feeling of satisfaction. Knowledge that the culprit is also now suffering may well make victims feel that they have obtained at least some of their 'pound of flesh'. In these circumstances, punishment is perhaps best thought of in terms of **retribution** (Von Hirsch and Ashworth, 1992). Both the victim(s) and society seek to redress the balance between offender and offended by seeing the perpetrator punished and thus suffer. In a similar way, society may wish to see an offender punished as a way of signalling to them that society as a whole disapproves of the behaviour.

Part of the satisfaction stemming from an offender's punishment can be explained with reference to the just world hypothesis (Lerner, 1970). As we saw in Chapter 2, victims' distress often arises from a feeling that 'it just isn't fair'. Victims invariably cannot understand why they have been targeted or what they have done to 'deserve' their fate. As there are few ready answers to these questions, the victim can at least take some solace from the fact that the offender has been punished and that there is after all some justice or equity in the world. Those who believe strongly in a 'just world' may derive more satisfaction from an offender's punishment than would individuals who are less concerned with such matters. Allowing victims to give their views in court before sentence is passed can also make them feel that they are not helpless or powerless and that they can (literally) have their voice heard.

In contrast to the notion of retribution is the idea that appropriate punishment will lead to a reduction in crime. This might be achieved by **deterrence** (people might think twice and consider the possible consequences before committing a crime), **reform** (the offender might be persuaded to change his/her ways while serving their sentence), or by **incapacitation** (the offender will be unable to commit further crimes against society while they are incarcerated in prison) (Zimring and Hawkins, 1995). Linked to this is the notion of **public fear** and **public protection**, i.e. that members of the public may feel safer knowing that they will not fall victim to a perpetrator who is locked up.

Society's expectations in respect of punishment may well be based upon crude (or even misunderstood) behaviourist principles stemming from B.F. Skinner's work on operant conditioning. Skinner (1953) put forward an interesting theory to explain some aspects of human behaviour. Working initially with animals such as pigeons and rats, Skinner showed that an animal which is reinforced for behaving in a certain way will be much more likely to behave in that way in the future. (Reinforcement can generally be thought of as a reward, although Skinner preferred not to use this word in his writings.) An animal which receives no reinforcement for a certain behaviour will tend not to repeat such behaviour.

Although Skinner did not generally approve of the use of punishment, the flip side of his argument is that if an animal is not only not reinforced, but is actually punished for certain behaviour, then that behaviour should be even less likely to occur. Thus, a simplistic, if not naïve view might be that a person who commits a crime and gains a material reward, or who receives adulation from friends, will be more likely to commit further crimes. However, the individual who commits a crime and then suffers an unpleasant punishment will be much less likely to repeat the crime.

Of course, one need not look very far to see that the second part of this argument does not appear to hold true – significant numbers of those convicted reoffend within days of being released from the unpleasant and aversive surroundings of a prison. For young adult males, the reconviction rate can be as high as 82 per cent (Home Office, 1994) and the British prison population rose to over 62,000 (a 30 per cent increase) between 1992 and 1997. The figures for female offenders have shown an even more dramatic rate of increase with a 76 per cent rise in the prison population between 1993 and 1997.

There is perhaps an expectation that prison will be effective if only we make it sufficiently unpleasant for offenders. Clear (1994) has labelled this notion the 'penal harm movement'. Cullen and Applegate (1997) describe the basis of this movement:

> The lengthy incarceration of lawbreakers in Spartan living conditions is typically justified by three interrelated considerations ...; offenders deserve to be harmed because they have harmed others; offenders who suffer the pain of imprisonment will be 'scared straight'; offenders who cannot be deterred need to be caged in harsh conditions because they are dangerous and do not warrant our further concern.
>
> (1997: xiii)

Cullen and Applegate note that the penal harm movement is bereft of any notion that criminals can actually change (other than in order to avoid future incarceration). Certainly it fails to consider that interventions might change an individual's attitudes, cognitive patterns or social relationships. If a man is sent to prison after assaulting his wife he may leave prison believing that there is little reason why he should not continue to use her as a punchbag and commit further assaults. The man may not believe that what he is doing is wrong or that he needs to change, but may instead feel justified in committing further assaults against the person who was (in his distorted view) responsible for his incarceration.

Some of the theorising behind the penal harm movement is that a particularly unpleasant experience will motivate the person to avoid exposure to such a situation in the future. The best way in which this might be achieved is by the person avoiding committing crime again. The public's indignation when it hears of the 'easy life' which some prisoners are alleged to lead only adds to the feeling of frustration experienced when offenders fail to change their behaviour. However, the available evidence suggests that the severity of punishment and the harshness of conditions in prison has little effect on recidivism rates, with the one obvious exception of capital punishment (McCord, 1999). When effects are detected, they are sometimes in the opposite direction from what might be expected.

Let us take the example of prison overcrowding. As some societies choose to incarcerate increasing numbers of offenders, crowding within prisons becomes more of a problem. (The prison population in the USA is predicted to top two million by the start of the new millennium.) Like almost all other animals, humans will feel uncomfortable when forced to live in overcrowded conditions. People who are in such a situation will seek to end their exposure to this unpleasant or aversive condition and be motivated to remove themselves (or to avoid a repetition of the experience) if at all possible (Galle *et al.*, 1972).

Much of the early work on the effects of overcrowding was carried out on animals such as mice and rats (Calhoun, 1962). This research suggested that severe overcrowding can lead to a number of forms of pathology, including increasing levels of aggression. In most cases it is not easy to extrapolate directly from research on animals such as mice to human populations. One obvious difference is that, unlike the animals in Calhoun's studies, a human who is feeling the aversive effects of overcrowding can generally walk away from the immediate situation – they might perhaps go for a walk in the countryside. Interestingly, a prison is one environment in which this normal escape is generally not possible. For this reason, some writers (e.g. Ruback and Innes, 1990) have suggested that comparison between animal studies such as those of Calhoun and the study of humans in prison are appropriate.

We might thus reasonably expect to find that those released from overcrowded prisons would be less likely to reoffend than would those released from less crowded prisons. In fact, the opposite appears to be true. For example, Farrington and Nuttall (1980) found that those who left particularly crowded prisons were significantly more likely to reoffend than were those released from less crowded conditions. Farrington and Nuttall suggest that there are a number of reasons why this might be the case. Firstly, those in the more crowded conditions are likely to spend more time locked in their cells with other inmates and thus more likely

to become 'contaminated'. Secondly, it is more difficult to attempt rehabilitative work in overcrowded prisons. Thirdly, inmates in such
conditions may become more stressed and aggressive and these effects
will lead them to commit further crimes upon release. Farrington and
Nuttall concluded that if we wish to lower recidivism rates, reducing
prison overcrowding should become a priority. Many other writers have
echoed this point, although for a variety of reasons psychologists have
not been particularly successful in bringing about policy changes
(Ruback and Innes, 1990).

Why is prison largely ineffective in preventing reoffending?

There are at least two reasons why imprisonment is not effective in the
way that a simplistic presumption about behaviourist principles might
suggest. Firstly, according to Barclay (1993) and Ashworth (1997) over
95 per cent of those who actually commit a crime are not convicted (and
thus not punished). Maguire (1997) suggests that the figure may in fact
be as high as 98 per cent. Secondly, those who are punished are sentenced many months or even years after they committed their crime – as
such the aversive consequences are not so obviously associated with the
crime in question. The current British government has recognised this
problem in relation to young offenders. In a speech to Parliament on 21
July 1998, the Home Secretary pledged to halve the average time it took
for persistent young offenders to be brought to court. At the time of his
speech, the Home Secretary reported that the average length of time
between arrest and sentence was 'an appalling 142 days'.

In fact many offenders will have been 'reinforced' by, for example,
acquiring material possessions as a result of their crime and are perhaps
more likely to see that their criminal behaviour produced a positive outcome. Such offenders may not learn that committing a crime leads to
negative consequences, but rather that getting caught and going to court
does. In these circumstances it would be unsurprising if offenders vow
not to give up their offending but rather to try to give up being caught.

In some ways an offender's failure to 'learn' from the negative reinforcement of imprisonment is like that of the man who has consumed
too much alcohol. Such a person may wake up the next morning with
such a terrible hangover that he vows never to touch another drop. Yet
within days, he may find himself drinking copiously, apparently not
having learned from his previous over-indulgence. Of course, the consumption of alcohol is often followed immediately by a pleasant feeling
(Robinson, 1988). In behaviourist terms, drinking is reinforced by the
good warm feeling which small amounts of alcohol produce. The bad
feeling of the hangover follows many hours after the drinking has ceased
and is thus not so obviously associated with the cause.

The purposes of imprisonment

In Britain at least, prisons have traditionally seen their role as not just the containment of offenders, but also their treatment and (re)training. Despite the fact that prisons rarely fulfil this second purpose (and are increasingly prepared to admit this), King and Morgan (1980) suggest that such an idea allowed prisons to see themselves as having a noble purpose. As Morgan (1997) suggests:

> If imprisonment could be justified on the ground that it could make prisoners less likely to offend, then sentencers were more likely to be deluded into using imprisonment for this purpose.
>
> (1997: 1146)

If treatment and training are seen as primary aims then, paradoxically, prisoners might be given lengthy or indeterminate sentences in the belief that they would not be released until such aims had been fulfilled. However, the prison authorities have begun to accept that treatment and training are no longer important priorities, or, in many instances, achievable aims (May Report, 1979). These days imprisonment is often seen more in terms of the protection it offers to society rather than as an environment which can make an individual renounce their criminal lifestyle (Pease, 1999). Having said that, the current British government has recognised that spending time in prison may in itself do little to change offenders' behaviour. In a speech to Parliament on 21 July 1998 the Home Secretary stated that 'prisons will only fully protect the public if they not only incarcerate prisoners securely during their sentence, but also **reduce offending on release**'. (The emphasis is not the current author's, but is contained within the written release of the Home Secretary's statement.) The increasing use of performance targets in prisons, including the evaluation of regimes to address offending behaviour (especially those targeted at sex offenders) may also have some effect (Vennard and Hedderman, 1998: 103).

In a recent book examining what strategies might work in reducing reoffending, McGuire and Priestley (1995) argue that the rates of reoffending can be reduced, but not by punitive methods. Rather they note that:

> The methods that 'work' for this purpose are those that address the factors that have played a causal or contributory role in an offending act, and that would place the offender at risk of reoffending in the future.
>
> (1995: 4)

Effective treatment: searching for the impossible?

One of the primary aims of the criminal justice system should surely be to persuade those who do offend to cease their criminal activities.

Unfortunately, many of those who work within the criminal justice system disagree as to how this might best be achieved. Nevertheless, a wide range of measures which attempt to reduce reoffending have been tried and will continue to be tried. As we saw earlier, sending people to prison may well satisfy society's demand for retribution and will incapacitate those detained, but may actually do little to change the attitudes or behaviour of those sentenced. Thus, on release from prison, significant numbers will reoffend within a short period of time. In fact, writers such as Lipsey (1992) have concluded that punitive measures have a net destructive effect and, in many cases, actually increase recidivism rates. Such facts have prompted some within the criminal justice system to introduce different forms of intervention.

Strategies differ widely depending upon the type of individual, the type of crime and, in some cases, the philosophy of the psychologist who is introducing a treatment programme. Given that people commit crime for a wide range of different reasons (see Chapter 4) we should hardly be surprised to learn that a wide range of different approaches have been used. We should also bear in mind that as most criminal acts are the result of a combination of a large number of contributory factors, there are few simple and effective treatment strategies which can be applied across a broad range of offenders. This is a particular issue when we consider some of the mental elements in criminal behaviour (see Chapter 5).

Attempts to rehabilitate rather than simply punish offenders was seen as the guiding philosophy of corrections in many countries (but especially in the USA) between the early 1900s and the 1960s. There was a belief that as each person committed crime for a specific, and individual, reason sanctions should be contingent upon the nature of the offender, rather than the nature of the offence. As a result, it was argued that sanctions should be individualised and should target the factors underlying a person's offending behaviour. Attention was also paid to the effectiveness and quality of the sanction which was 'to move beyond inflicting pain on offenders to the daunting task of changing them from lawbreakers to the law-abiding' (Cullen and Applegate, 1997: xv).

Many of those who were involved in trying to rehabilitate offenders were somewhat rocked by the publication in 1974 of a now famous paper by Robert Martinson. Martinson examined some 231 studies which had been published between 1945 and 1967. These covered a wide range of treatment programmes including counselling, probation and parole. Martinson's somewhat disturbing conclusion was that:

> ... these data, involving over two hundred studies and hundreds of thousands of individuals as they do, are the best available and give us very little reason to hope that we have in fact found a sure way of reducing recidivism through rehabilitation.

(1974: 50)

Many who read (or in most cases read of) the findings interpreted Martinson's paper as proving that 'nothing works'. The results were seen as powerful ammunition by those who would prefer that resources were targeted at the simple incarceration of offenders rather than at their rehabilitation. It is interesting to go back to Martinson's seminal paper 25 years after it was published to see what he did actually say. The quote cited above and the oft-quoted line that rehabilitative efforts 'have had no appreciable effects on recidivism' (1974: 26) do sound an extremely pessimistic note, but Martinson did qualify his remarks. Thus he did not say categorically that **nothing** works or will work. Indeed, he conceded that there were a few isolated exceptions which **did** work. In fact, Andrews (1994) argues that almost half of the studies which Martinson reviewed actually showed positive results. However, one of Martinson's frustrations was the fact that, because of poor research designs and poor evaluation, it was not easy to tell whether or not different forms of inter-vention were working and why. As he states: 'It is just possible that some of our treatment programs *are* working to some extent, but that our research is so bad that we are incapable of telling' (1974: 51).

Although Martinson's main concern was with the apparent ineffective-ness of rehabilitation attempts, he did make a number of other interesting points. For example, he suggested (1974: 52) that while many high-risk prisoners might well be kept in prisons which were nothing more than custodial institutions, many low-risk offenders could be released. He does however point out that this would bring about its own problems and inequities and, more worryingly, compromise the deter-rent effect which the threat of prison is presumed to signify.

Martinson's main comments, however, were seized upon by those who had already started to lose faith in the philosophy of rehabilitation but were greeted with despair by many of those involved in rehabilitation programmes (Blumstein, 1997). As Cullen and Applegate observe elo-quently, many who opposed rehabilitation took the findings:

> ... not as a provocative scientific proposition to be viewed sceptically but as empirical confirmation for what they already 'knew': rehabilitation, con-ducted by 'corrupt' agents of the state, had little chance of improving the object of its power.

> (1997: xv)

By the time Gottfredson wrote about 'treatment destruction techniques' in 1979, he acknowledged that the lack of effectiveness in rehabilitation attempts 'is agreed upon by criminologists of every persuasion and theo-retical orientation' (1979: 39). Gottfredson suggested that critics of rehabilitation quickly became adept at dismissing any findings which showed that rehabilitation could work. Such studies were attacked for their alleged lack of scientific validity, whereas those studies which sup-ported their viewpoint were accepted unconditionally. Gottfredson argued that the conditions which the anti-rehabilitation movement laid down before they would accept research findings made it all but impossible to 'prove' that rehabilitation did work.

Writing ten years later, Andrews (1989) suggested that treatment destruction techniques were still being used by those opposed to the notion of rehabilitation. He notes that many of the strategies adopted made it impossible ever to satisfy the critics. For example, studies which used official records were criticised because they did not use self-report measures. However, studies which used self-report measures were also attacked because they did not use official records. Studies which showed a reduced rate of offending after a one year follow-up were criticised for not having used a two year follow-up period. However, those studies which did use a two year follow-up period were attacked for not using a three year period!

Attacks on rehabilitation continued in the 1990s. For example, Logan and Gaes (1993) argued against attempts at rehabilitation and suggested that the main priority of prison officials should be 'to administer justice, not treatment' (1993: 245). Logan and Gaes attacked many of the meta-analysis studies which appeared to show that some forms of treatment could be effective. They argued further that 'individualised treatment muddles the message of punishment, making it less principled and not necessarily more humane' (1993: 245). Whitehead and Lab (1989) also argued that, as few treatment programmes can be proved to have worked, such attempts at rehabilitation might just as well be abandoned. Pitts (1992) concurred with this view.

What most writers from the 'nothing works' school fail to mention is the fact that Robert Martinson did in fact withdraw and revise many of his own conclusions in 1979. In his later paper, Martinson acknowledged some errors in his earlier review and drew on newer research which provided evidence that some things did in fact work. However, as McGuire and Priestley (1995) observe, by that stage the 'nothing works' view 'had become deeply embedded in the thinking of a majority of professionals at most levels of the criminal justice system' (1995: 7).

There would thus appear to be a polarisation of views with regard to rehabilitation. As we have seen above, there have been a succession of loud voices which have attacked rehabilitation. Yet there have also been a number of perhaps less vociferous individuals who have carried on regardless and have developed a number of apparently effective strategies (see McGuire, 1995 for a recent review). The danger inherent in the 'nothing works' voice is that in the rush to rubbish all rehabilitation strategies, some which may prove to be effective are brushed aside. If as much time and energy had been devoted to establishing which strategies were useful for which groups of prisoners and why, it is likely that our knowledge would be considerably more advanced than it is today. As it is we are in a position to identify some methods which do work and for the remainder of this chapter we will consider a few of the more effective strategies which have been employed.

We should, however, bear in mind that whether or not one believes that offenders can be encouraged to change depends very much on one's presumptions about why people start committing crime in the first place. If, for example, one feels that most people are propelled towards criminality because of their genetic make-up, attempts to change offending behaviour by changing attitudes will be unlikely to meet with much success. On the other hand, if one takes the view that the majority of offenders commit criminal acts because of their inappropriate attitudes, it may be easier to effect a change.

There may however be a view that if people **choose** to commit crime rather than to obey the law, then they should be punished, rather than treated. Conversely, those who commit crime mainly because of some defect or deficiency should be helped. This dilemma is often highlighted in the discussion of offenders who appear to have a drug addiction and commit crime mainly to finance their addiction (Walters, 1998). On the one hand some would argue that as such people have chosen to start taking drugs in the first place, they should simply choose to stop taking them and thus stop committing crime. On the other hand, it might be argued that as such people are mainly committing crime because of their addiction, treatment programmes which treat the addiction will also prevent offending (Falkin *et al.*, 1994; Wexler *et al.*, 1990).

In Chapter 5 we attempted to make a distinction between those who are 'bad' and those who are 'mad'. As was noted in that chapter, this distinction can be very important in terms of the disposal of offenders. Essentially, the reasoning might be that if people are 'bad' they deserve to be punished, but if they are 'mad' they should not be held fully responsible for their actions and might benefit more from treatment as opposed to punishment. However, a third category of offenders might be labelled not so much bad or mad, but rather 'sad'. Such individuals may be considered legally responsible for their actions, yet may be inadequate in one or more ways. In some cases such 'sad' people may lack normal life (or social) skills and have difficulties in dealing with a number of common situations in their lives. In some cases, their offending might well be linked to their lack of skills or other deficits.

To take one example, a person may lack the necessary social skills to be able to communicate effectively with others. This may well lead to perpetual feelings of frustration which may in turn lead to the person becoming aggressive. In treatment terms, such individuals may prove to be the easiest to deal with as in many cases their deficits can be addressed and they can be taught new (or more appropriate) skills (Trower, Bryant and Argyle, 1977). Once the skills have been learned then the person is (hopefully) less likely to reoffend. We will discus some of these forms of treatment later in the chapter.

Which forms of treatment are likely to be the most effective?

As was noted earlier, there is a danger that in the rush to prove that 'nothing works', many schemes which do have an effect on recidivism rates will have been dismissed unfairly. In addition, the move to pour scorn on all attempts at rehabilitation will inevitably mean that lessons are not necessarily learned from the more successful schemes. For example, Fagan (1990) has argued that the actual length of time that a young violent offender spends in custody is not necessarily a crucial factor in determining reoffending rates. What appears more important is that such high-risk youths are prepared for their release back into the community through the provision of well run reintegration programmes which are rooted in sound theory and advanced practices. In addition, Fagan argues that on release there should be intensive supervision with an emphasis on a gradual re-entry. Reviewing a number of such programmes, he notes that: 'The well-implemented programs resulted in significant reductions in the number and severity of arrests ... as well as in significantly greater time until rearrest' (1990: 258).

This view is supported by more recent writers including Lipsey and Wilson (1997) who argue that although research on programmes which target violent offenders is rather sparse, many effective strategies have been identified (see also Quinsey *et al.*, 1998).

Andrews *et al.* (1990) have identified a number of characteristics which appear to differentiate successful rehabilitation programmes from the less successful ones. They observe importantly that 'The effectiveness of correctional treatment is dependent upon what is delivered to whom in particular settings' (1990: 372).

Andrews *et al.* argue that successful programmes are those which have the following characteristics:

(1) They are highly structured and focused and address a distinct problem in a distinct way.
(2) They employ staff who are firm but fair and who reinforce anti-criminal values. In addition, the staff are committed and enthusiastic and are supported by good management.
(3) The programmes target in particular those attitudes and values which support offending behaviour.
(4) The programmes employ problem-solving procedures based on cognitive and social learning perspectives.
(5) Programmes are matched to offender characteristics.
(6) Programmes are monitored and evaluated in relation to both recidivism rates and personal growth.
(7) Programmes target medium and high risk offenders.
(8) Programmes attempt to generalise beyond the institutional setting.

Programmes with these characteristics appear to have what Hollin

(1995) refers to as 'high treatment integrity' and are likely to be more successful than treatment programmes which lack these attributes (also Andrews *et al.*, 1990; Van Hoorhis *et al.*, 1995). However, Hollin (1995) notes that integrity can be threatened when programmes drift away from their original aims, when staff fail to model appropriate behaviour, or when programmes change their objectives or targets mid-way through their course.

Andrews' views on successful regimes have been largely supported by other writers including Vennard and Hedderman (1998). In their recent review these authors suggest that good programmes are those which:

(a) attempt a risk classification and target more intensive programmes at high risk offenders;
(b) target criminogenic needs, i.e. those factors which contribute directly to criminal behaviour. These would include antisocial attitudes, drug dependency, low level of education and skills, poor cognitive and interpersonal skills;
(c) have high programme integrity;
(d) are responsive in that they match teaching methods to offenders' learning styles;
(e) use a skills-based intervention which helps to improve problem solving and social interaction, but which also addresses and challenges the attitudes, values and beliefs which support offending behaviour;
(f) are community based (although it is acknowledged that programmes which incorporate the previous five principles can be successful irrespective of the treatment setting).

In their overview of recent programmes which do appear to reduce reoffending, McGuire and Priestley (1995) suggest that there are important lessons to be learned by those who manage intervention programmes. These are identified as:

(a) the need for those managing service delivery to become more familiar with the relevant research evidence;
(b) the need to develop reliable risk-needs assessment methods for client selection and allocation to different types of programme;
(c) the need for managers to accept that if practitioners are to be effective, appropriate resources for the development, delivery and evaluation of programmes must be provided; McGuire and Priestley recognise that in some cases managers will need to convince others of the need for changes in resource allocation;
(d) the need for managers to have better knowledge of staff members' skills;
(e) the need to recognise that new types of programme provision will necessitate considerable staff retraining;

(f)   the need to recognise the importance of evaluation of programmes, not least so that funding for effective programmes can be maintained.

We will now consider one example of a psychological intervention which may reduce future offending and which incorporates a number of the principles outlined above. In this case we will examine anger reduction schemes.

Anger reduction schemes

It is recognised that significant numbers of offenders, especially young people, come to the attention of the authorities because they have lost control of themselves and behaved in a violent way. As we saw in Chapter 4, there are a very large number of predisposing factors which are associated with violence and aggression. However, one of the most prominent precursors would appear to be an inability to deal with feelings of anger. While everyone will experience anger from time to time, most people are able to keep at least some control over this emotion and do not feel the need to resort to physical violence in response to such angry feelings. However, a number of people appear to have more difficulty in dealing with their angry feelings and it is these individuals who might be targeted for anger management programmes.

Some of our current understanding of anger stems from the work of Novaco (1975). Novaco stressed the role which cognition plays in the emotional arousal which generally precedes aggressive and violent acts. Novaco argued that anger is often quick to surface because the individual is already upset about other things in their life. The individual tends to displace angry feelings onto an available target, even if this is entirely inappropriate. In this case, expressing anger may be one way in which the individual feels that he/she can take control of a situation. This is particularly likely in circumstances in which the person feels insecure or threatened. In behaviourist terms, becoming angry is reinforced by the individual's feeling of control in the situation.

Novaco suggests that any intervention should not try to stop the individual from experiencing anger – rather it should allow him/her to monitor, control and manage angry reactions. Thus, the individual will need to be taught new strategies for regaining self-control, and be encouraged to develop techniques which allow the resolution of conflict situations without resort to violence. Most anger management programmes involve individuals working in groups and comprise three distinct stages.

1. Cognitive preparation

In this phase, individuals are encouraged to think about and to analyse their own patterns of anger. In particular, group members would be encouraged to try to identify the specific situations which have triggered an angry response in the past. By doing this it is hoped that individuals can learn to recognise the types of situation which are potentially dangerous (in terms of invoking an angry response). Individuals would also be encouraged to try to recall their pattern of thought during the interaction. By doing this, the therapist/counsellor may be able to challenge some of the irrational thoughts and assumptions which the individual makes (for example, about what another's actions signify). By tracing the individual's pattern of behaviour, it is hoped that it will be possible to break what may have become an almost automatic response. For example, the individual might recognise that teasing by others invariably leads to physiological arousal, which quickly leads to a violent outburst.

Individuals would also be encouraged to think about the consequences of their anger. Specifically they would be taught that although their anger may have served some purpose at the time, it probably had long-term negative consequences. For example, the individual may be left with feelings of guilt, may be banned from a favourite pub, lose a girlfriend or be punished by the courts.

2. Skill acquisition

As the name implies, this stage allows individuals to learn a range of new skills which can allow them to deal with potentially anger-provoking situations in a more effective way. The skills to be learned are both cognitive and behavioural. Cognitive skills would be predominantly concerned with challenging the automatic thought processes which are perhaps irrational yet well rehearsed. Thus, the individual might be instructed simply to say 'stop' to themselves when the normal thought patterns emerge. Alternatively, they might practise saying to themselves something along the lines of 'I can deal with this situation in an effective way' rather than relying on previous maladaptive responses.

There are a number of different behavioural skills which might be taught including relaxation, assertiveness, social and communication skills and problem-solving strategies. Relaxation training may be particularly helpful as it serves two purposes: it teaches the individual to relax, thus making him/her less tense generally and, secondly, it teaches the individual that it is possible to take control of emotions, rather than be ruled by them. Assertiveness training can also be very useful for some individuals, as the techniques learned can allow the person to achieve an objective without resorting to violence. Many people confuse assertiveness with aggressiveness, but the two are very different. In the case of assertiveness training, the individual learns to make his/her point in a calm and effective way. The individual is also encouraged to acknowledge others' feelings and wishes, but to stick to their legitimate request.

3. Application practice

In the final phase, individuals would be allowed the opportunity to practise their skills in controlled conditions. Each person might, through
role-play, be exposed to a range of situations which have caused problems in the past. The person would typically begin with situations which
were only slightly problematic and would then gradually work up to
other more difficult scenarios. Throughout these exercises the individual would be encouraged to monitor their progress, but would also
receive encouragement (or reinforcement) from others. The individual
would then need to transfer the skills from the controlled situation
within the group to everyday occurrences.

There is no doubt that anger management programmes can be very
useful as a way of helping individuals to change their established patterns
of behaviour. However, programmes can only work if sufficient resources
are devoted to the initiative, the appropriate individuals are assigned to
the programme and careful monitoring takes place. While anger management can be useful as a general method of reducing aggression in an
offender population, in some cases a more individual and targeted programme is necessary. For this reason we will next consider a more
specific intervention, in this case, programmes designed to treat men
who have been convicted of violence against their female partner.

Tackling male violence against a partner

As Dobash *et al.* (1999) note, male violence in the home is a widespread
phenomenon affecting a large number of women. However, it is only relatively recently that the extent of the problem has been recognised
(Campbell and Lewandowski, 1997). Growing acknowledgement of the
situation has led to moves to try to help women who have been assaulted
in their homes. Battered women's refuges, help lines, improved police
receptiveness and responsiveness and public education campaigns have
all helped to address at least some aspects of the problem. However, as
Dobash *et al.* note, while most initiatives have understandably been
aimed at helping, supporting, and protecting the victims of such crimes,
relatively little attention has been paid to the perpetrators of domestic
assaults. These authors note that:

> Criminal justice innovations aimed at perpetrators of violence are still the
> exception in Great Britain although pro-arrest and prosecution policies are
> much more established in North America.
>
> (1999: 207)

Certainly in the USA the increasing prosecution of domestic violence
perpetrators has been matched by the introduction of a variety of treatment programmes (Dobash and Dobash, 1992; Pence and Paymer,

1993). However, this has not tended to happen in Britain. One can per-haps understand why there has been a reluctance to offer treatment programmes for such offenders. It has taken campaigners many years to convince the authorities of the seriousness of the problem and to per-suade such authorities to take action against perpetrators. Having achieved this not inconsiderable goal, it would be understandable if the primary aim was to see perpetrators punished. The idea that resources should be devoted to the treatment of such offenders may be anathema to many campaigners.

The first two British criminal justice programmes for violent men were set up in 1989 in Scotland – these were in fact the first initiatives to be established in Europe. By 1994 only 23 programmes had been set up throughout Britain (Scourfield, 1995). Most programmes which have been established have avoided a psychodynamic approach in favour of one which is largely pro-feminist or cognitive-behavioural. In fact Dobash and Dobash (1999) suggest that these latter two terms are often com-bined when describing most current programmes. They note that:

> When combined, the terms usually reflect a common view about the nature of the problem as generated within a context of gender relations, socialisation and learning and an orientation to treatment that focuses on changing behav-iour and ways of thinking.
>
> (1999)

Thus according to Dobash and Dobash, men who use violence against a partner are seen to be acting within a culturally defined role in which the man has greater power and authority and uses violence as a way of con-trolling and punishing his partner. In this situation, violence is regarded as a learned behaviour and is often used as a way of resolving conflicts. The violence is seen as an intentional act designed to intimidate and control. Typically, men who behave in this way are egocentric, lack empa-thy, minimise the harm done, deny responsibility and try to deflect the blame onto others (usually the victim). Intervention thus tries to instil different attitudes towards women and the learning of new forms of behaviour in conflict situations. It also aims to analyse and help the offender to understand his own behaviour and to persuade the offender to accept responsibility for his actions.

This pro-feminist, cognitive-behavioural approach stands in marked contrast to psychodynamic (or insight) approaches. The latter generally analyse the problem in terms of trauma which may have occurred early in an offender's life. Violence in later life is seen as displacement of anger and hostility which originated in early life. There is, therefore, a focus on childhood loss, frustration or rejection which is presumed to be at the root of the later violent behaviour. Unlike the cognitive-behav-ioural approaches there is little attention given to the circumstances of the violence itself.

In recent years cognitive-behavioural approaches have taken over from psychodynamic work, partly because the former appear to be more successful (McGuire, 1995; Saunders, 1996; Vennard *et al.*, 1997). In their recent review, Vennard and Hedderman suggest that offenders who attend cognitive-behavioural programmes achieve a 10–15 per cent lower reconviction rate than those who do not attend such programmes. Further, the authors report that programmes which stick closely to effectiveness principles achieve a recidivism rate twenty per cent lower than control groups. In addition, those programmes which include social skills training show the most positive results. It is, however, discouraging to learn that although many probation services in England and Wales recognise the benefits of a cognitive-behavioural approach, many programmes have not achieved good results. Hedderman and Sugg (1987) suggest that the main reasons are threefold: a lack of programme integrity and inadequate staff training, a failure to adopt specialised programmes and a failure to examine whether specialist programmes are effective.

Dobash *et al.* provide an interesting evaluation of two court mandated programmes first set up in Scotland (CHANGE and The Lothian Domestic Violence Probation Project (LDVPP)). Their purpose was to establish whether the two programmes studied were more successful than more orthodox sanctions in reducing violence and changing attitudes over a one year period. They note that in this field it can be particularly difficult to provide good objective evaluations. Although there have been more than 30 evaluation studies of interventions in the USA and Canada (most of which claim a success rate of between 50 and 80 per cent), many such evaluations suffer from methodological inadequacies. The main deficiencies concern small sample sizes, selection bias, lack of control groups, insufficient follow-up period and a reliance on offender's self-reports or official arrest records. In addition, many evaluation studies have failed to control for the possible termination of contact between the two parties concerned. Thus, in some cases, a man's conviction for domestic assault may result in separation or divorce. In these cases there may be no subsequent contact between the perpetrator and victim and thus no arena for violence to re-emerge. Interestingly, Dobash *et al.* report that post treatment evaluations rarely include follow-up interviews with women who have been victims – such a measure may well provide a better indicator of an offender's subsequent behaviour and thus the programme's success.

Dobash *et al.*'s evaluation study was designed to eliminate most of the inadequacies of previous studies, although for a number of reasons it was not possible to use a randomised design. It was, therefore, necessary to show that people assigned to the two programmes under scrutiny were broadly similar to those given other sentences/treatment. Dobash *et al.* suggest that this was indeed the case. Their evaluation used a number of different measures and it is interesting that different types of evaluation gave very different impressions. For example, an examination of court records showed that only seven per cent of men on the programmes and ten per cent of men dealt with by alternative means came before the courts for a repeat offence in the following twelve months. Such figures taken alone might suggest that most of those convicted of domestic assault do not commit further offences and that treatment programmes are only marginally better than other forms of disposal.

However, an examination of other data reveals a rather different picture. For example, three months after the initial interview, 30 per cent of women whose partners were in the programme group reported having suffered further violence. This compares with 62 per cent of women whose partners were given other sentences. This difference was statistically significant. Data gathered after twelve months showed a similar pattern – 34 per cent of men who had been on the treatment programme committed further violence over the year, compared with 75 per cent who had received other disposals. Such figures do not, however, give the whole picture as they take no account of the frequency of further violence. In fact Dobash *et al.* found that after one year, only seven per cent of women whose partners had been on the programmes reported 'frequent' violence. This compares with 37 per cent of the women in the other group, a difference which was again statistically significant.

Dobash *et al.* conclude that:

> ... in contrast to other criminal justice sanctions, programmes for violent men can have significant effects on the prevalence and frequency of violence over a twelve month period following the imposition of a sanction.
>
> (1999: 229)

However, the authors note that such a conclusion can only be reached as a result of the data obtained from victims over the twelve month follow-up period – evaluations based on court records alone would have given a very different and incorrect impression. There are in fact a number of reasons why simplistic measures such as reconviction rates do not offer a reliable measure of treatment effectiveness. Lloyd *et al.* (1994) suggest that the main reasons are:

(1) Reconviction rates take no account of changes in the severity of offences nor of changes in the frequency of offending.
(2) As Dobash *et al.* discovered, reconviction rates underestimate the real level of reoffending, as many types of crime have low rates of reporting and detection.
(3) Different areas and different police forces have differing recording and clear-up rates and so the chances of being arrested and convicted can differ from one area to another (see Chapter 1).
(4) There is inconsistency in the follow-up period used in many reconviction studies. Some studies which follow up for a year may claim a

low reconviction rate, whereas those which use a longer period may show a higher rate. An additional problem is that, as we saw earlier, there is invariably a significant time lag between an offender's crime and their appearance in court. Offenders may actually commit further offences during the follow-up period but these would not be counted as the offender's court appearance would be up to a year after the actual offence.

(5) The follow-up period for community sentences begins from the date of sentence, whereas that for custodial sentences begins with the date of release. It is, therefore, not always possible to make valid comparisons between the two types of sentence.

Dobash *et al.* suggest that their results are in line with a number of evaluation studies carried out in the USA in recent years. Successful programmes appear to be mainly educational and have a core of central characteristics, including high programme integrity, good management and the delivery of structured interventions focusing on the offender and his offending behaviour. Successful programmes also appear to have a cognitive-behavioural focus. As such they attempt to change the values, attitudes, beliefs and actions of offenders. Dobash *et al.* suggest that successful programmes are those which improve a person's internal control, develop appropriate social skills, increase critical reasoning about the offence, establish good problem-solving strategies and increase empathy. However, the authors also note that in order to be successful, programmes should not be voluntary, but rather should be part of an overall process or package of sanctions. The process of being arrested, charged and prosecuted provides a lever or incentive for the individual to participate in the programme and, hopefully, to avoid more severe punishment in the future.

Summary

We have seen in this chapter that there is continued debate as to the purpose and effectiveness of punishment for those who commit criminal offences. Many of the simplistic notions of punishment appear to be myths and it appears not to be the case that harsher punishments lead to less reoffending upon release. There has been a concerted effort by some to try to prove that 'nothing works' and that attempts at rehabilitation may just as well be abandoned in favour of simple containment and incapacitation. However, a more careful review of recent research shows that a number of well-planned psychological interventions can be successful in reducing reoffending.

The current rate of increase in the prison population causes concern as many of those currently being imprisoned will receive little in the way of effective intervention and treatment. As such, many of those released back into the community will have changed little and will reoffend within a short space of time. Unfortunately, such failures may be seized upon by some as an excuse to impose longer prison terms in the future. Many psychologists would want to argue that resources would be better targeted at changing offenders' attitudes, behaviour and skills. In the long term such interventions may be more successful and perhaps even more cost effective.

Chapter 9

Mistakes and the criminal justice system

As we have seen throughout this book, the criminal justice system aims to identify and then punish those who break society's laws. However, we have also seen that only a small proportion of those who commit crime are actually punished and end up in prison. In most cases, perpetrators are simply not caught, or are dealt with in ways other than by a custodial sentence (Brownlee, 1998). There are, however, a small number of cases in which a crime appears to have been solved, but in reality the wrong person has been convicted. Mistakes can be made at many different stages within the criminal justice process. This chapter will not attempt a comprehensive coverage of all these possible sources of error, but will instead concentrate on two areas in which psychologists have made considerable contributions. These are mistakes made by eyewitnesses and the elicitation of what may be false confessions by the police.

As with many aspects covered in other chapters of this book, there are a number of myths which surround the criminal justice process and its (in)fallibility. For example there appears to be a belief that eyewitnesses are generally correct in their memories and can produce objective and largely accurate testimony when they appear in the witness box. However, as we will see below, this is often not the case. In their desire to solve crimes, the police may also act in an over-zealous manner and persuade innocent people to confess to crimes which they have not committed. In both these cases an individual may be wrongly convicted. We should bear in mind that when such miscarriages of justice do occur, they represent a double failure of the legal system – not only is an innocent person convicted, but the real perpetrator is still free and may go on to commit further crimes.

Eyewitness testimony

The vast majority of crimes which are committed are not witnessed by the police nor are they captured on videotape. As such the authorities have to rely on eyewitnesses to report what happened and, in some cases, to identify the perpetrator. The criminal justice system places its trust in eyewitnesses and presumes that they will be able to recall accurately and objectively when called upon to do so. However, many psychologists would take issue with such a view and would want to argue that witnesses' memory is usually incomplete, fallible, subjective and malleable. As such it has been suggested that the criminal justice system may have unrealistic expectations of eyewitnesses (Ainsworth, 1998).

When called upon to give evidence, witnesses will be expected to take an oath and to promise to tell the truth. The exact content of this oath varies from country to country but in Britain witnesses are normally asked to take the Bible in their right hand and to read the lines: 'I swear by almighty God that the evidence I shall give shall be the truth, the whole truth, and nothing but the truth'. Such an oath is considered necessary in order to ensure that witnesses do not deliberately lie when giving evidence. Those who do lie may be deemed to have committed perjury and may be punished for this crime. Although there are undoubtedly a number of cases in which an innocent person has been convicted as a result of lies told in the witness box, we are here more concerned with witnesses who make 'honest' mistakes in their testimony. Such witnesses may well believe that they are telling the truth, but in reality they are not.

The courts appear to presume that memory works like a video camera. Information enters the eyes or ears and is then stored in the brain. When a witness is asked to recall the details they simply have to locate the stored memory, press the 'play' button and an accurate and objective record of events is presented. Unfortunately, this is not the way in which perception and memory work. There are three stages in the memory process, i.e. perception, storage and retrieval. At each of these stages errors can occur and such errors may affect the story which is eventually told in court. We will consider each of these stages in turn.

1. Perception

This is the stage at which information is taken in from the outside world. Although people may believe that their memories are accurate, they may in fact have been distorted by the many factors which can affect perception. If ten people were asked to watch a videotape of a crime taking place and then to write down what they saw, each story would be slightly different. Some witnesses may have paid closer attention to the video than others and thus be able to give a more detailed account. Some will have concentrated on one specific aspect of the crime while others may have paid more attention to other features. Some may have prejudiced views about one of the characters in the video and thus interpreted their actions in a negative way.

The point is that perception is not an objective process but rather is a subjective and individual one. People do not simply take in every aspect of a scene in the way that a video camera might. People's perception is selective. Because humans are unable to take in all the information which bombards their senses, they are selective in what they choose to attend to. Thus, when witnesses swear to tell 'the whole truth' they may honestly believe that they are doing so, but are in fact only recounting those parts to which they originally paid attention. No amount of probing of a witness's memory will produce results if the information never entered their memory in the first place. However, as we will see later, repeatedly pressurising a witness to come up with more information may lead the witness to fill in gaps in their memory and to suggest what may have happened.

Witnesses are prone to make errors of omission, in that they omit certain details which may be important. However, perhaps more worrying, are cases in which a witness believes that they have an accurate memory for an event, but in reality that memory is based on prejudices or on errors which were made at the perceptual stage. Attitudes and prejudices can all too easily affect the way in which we perceive the world and lead us to draw inappropriate conclusions. Let us consider one example from the social psychological literature on prejudice in a study carried out by Duncan (1976).

Duncan set out to establish whether actions committed by a person of one race might be perceived differently from identical actions performed by a member of a different race. Subjects in his study watched a videotape of an altercation between two people. An argument became gradually more heated until eventually one person pushed the other. After viewing the videotaped incident, Duncan's subjects were asked to describe what they had seen. All the subjects were white, American college students.

Duncan did in fact use two different versions of the videotape and showed the different versions to differing groups of subjects. In one version, the person who pushed the other was white, but in another version the person was black. The videotapes were otherwise identical and were all viewed by groups of white students.

The subjects were then asked whether the behaviour of the person who pushed the other could best be categorised as 'playing around' or as 'violent behaviour'. When the perpetrator was white, only thirteen per cent of subjects chose to label the actions as violent behaviour. However, when the perpetrator was black, some 70 per cent labelled the behaviour in this way. This difference is highly significant considering that the students all saw the exact same actions, with only the race of the perpetrator changed. The results of this study have obvious implications for eyewitness testimony. If Duncan's subjects were to appear as witnesses in court, their version of what they saw (or, more correctly, perceived) would clearly be affected by whether the defendant was black or white.

Witnesses may claim that because they 'saw it with their own eyes' their version of events must be true. Most witnesses will, however, remain blissfully unaware of the way in which their own prejudices and stereotypes will have affected their perception of events. Because perception is a creative, subjective and personalised process, any one witness's version of events may be slightly different from that of another. However, the fact that many people's categorisation of behaviour can be affected by the race of a perpetrator suggests that some systematic biases can occur. The reader may wish to consult Ainsworth (1998: ch. 1) for further examples and a fuller discussion of these points.

There are many other factors which will affect witnesses' ability to perceive (and perhaps recall) accurately. One obvious example is stress. An incident which is extremely traumatic may result in a victim-witness being so stressed that they fail even to take in some important aspects of the event. Such a witness may well claim that he/she will 'never forget this day as long as I live', yet may have an incomplete or inaccurate memory of what actually took place. Common sense might suggest that the more serious an incident is, the more likely it would be to be perceived and remembered accurately. It would appear that this is too simplistic a view, and in fact stress (or more correctly arousal) affects perception and memory in a curvilinear fashion. By that we mean that too little arousal tends to produce inaccuracies in the same way that too much arousal does. However, there is an optimum level of arousal which ensures that an individual is stimulated enough to pay close attention, but not so stressed that they are unable to concentrate on what is taking place. In highly stressful incidents there is a tendency for witnesses to narrow their focus of attention and to concentrate on one feature. Thus, a victim who has a loaded gun pointed at their head may pay a great deal of attention to the gun itself, but take in little about the clothing worn by the assailant (Steblay, 1992).

2. Storage

If we accept that inaccuracies can be produced when a witness first perceives an event, then we might at least expect that once the information is in the memory store it will retain its original form and content. Unfortunately, this appears not to be the case. While research confirms the common sense notion that memories do often fade with time, it may not be quite so obvious that original memories can actually be transformed while in the memory store.

Unlike the videotape which lies undisturbed until it is replayed, memories can undergo significant transformation. Let us take an example. Suppose an individual witnesses a car accident in which a vehicle skids off the road on a bad bend and strikes a pedestrian. Shortly after viewing the accident the witness talks to a friend who informs him that the driver is a 'maniac' who always drives too fast and should not be allowed on the roads. Two days later the witness is interviewed by the police and gives a statement about the accident. Although the police would be interested only in what the witness actually saw, it is quite likely that the subsequent information about the driver would have affected his 'memory' of the incident. Thus, if the interviewing police officer asks whether the driver appeared to be driving too fast, it is possible that the new information about the driver will affect the witness's answer to the question.

The problem for the courts is that once a memory has been altered it is all but impossible for the witness to retrieve the original, uncontaminated version. While the court may instruct a witness only to recall those details which arose from the original, witnessed event and to ignore any subsequent information, this would actually be almost impossible. Witnesses are invariably unable to separate out an original memory from an amended version based upon more recent information. In a large number of experiments, Beth Loftus and her colleagues have demonstrated how easy it can be for witnesses to incorporate misleading information into their memory of an incident (see Ainsworth, 1998, ch. 4 for a review). This can be a particular problem when there has been widespread media coverage of a case and a witness has read or seen a great deal of information about the incident. Loftus's work suggests that witnesses can come to believe that they have seen objects which did not actually exist and are even prepared to describe such objects! Witnesses can even be persuaded that a suspect who clearly had no facial hair did in fact have a moustache. In an interesting variation of the usual misinformation study, Weingardt, Toland and Loftus (1994) have shown that witnesses who have been deliberately misled are often unaware of the fact and are even willing to bet money on the fact that their memory is original and accurate.

3. Retrieval

The final stage of the memory process is that of the retrieval of information previously stored. Here again there are a number of factors which can affect the likely accuracy of information recovered from memory. Perhaps most obvious is the influence of stress at the time of recall. In the same way that stress can interfere at the perceptual or encoding stage (see above) it can also affect a witness at the time of any attempted recall. For most witnesses, attending an identification parade or giving evidence in open court will be a particularly stressful experience. One piece of research (Ainsworth and King, 1988) showed for example that witnesses who were very nervous were less likely to pick out a suspect from an ID parade than were witnesses who were less nervous.

A witness who experiences a particularly high level of stress will invariably have great difficulty in recalling much about an incident which may have occurred years earlier. Yet the courts fail to address this important question and expect witnesses to provide accurate and objective testimony and to deliver this in a competent manner. Psychological research has a great deal to say about the accuracy or inaccuracy of witness recall, yet only on rare occasions are psychologists called upon to advise the courts on such matters (Ainsworth, 1998: ch. 11).

One area in which advice would be appropriate would be that of witness confidence. A common-sense view would be that a witness who is very confident about his/her testimony would be more likely to be accurate than would one who was less confident. Yet perhaps surprisingly, psychological research suggests that there is little correlation between eyewitness confidence and the accuracy of accounts (Ainsworth, 1998: 44). In other words, the most confident eyewitness will not necessarily be any more accurate than one who appears faltering and unsure. As Loftus (1979: 101) notes 'one should not take high confidence as any guarantee of anything'.

There are of course many other factors which will affect both the completeness of a witness's account and its likely accuracy. Only recently have police forces come to realise that the way in which witnesses are interviewed can be important in determining the quality of information obtained. While techniques such as hypnosis have attracted much interest, the use of such procedures is fraught with danger. The major problem with the use of hypnosis is that, while hypnotised, the witness can be easily led and encouraged to make up (or confabulate) information for which no actual memory exists (Orne, 1984). Following hypnosis, it will be all but impossible for the witness to disentangle the original memory from what went on in the hypnotic interview. Although hypnosis may have some success in retrieving memories of a particularly traumatic incident, its incorrect use may contribute to miscarriages of justice (Ainsworth, 1998: ch. 8). Police officers would be far better advised to use techniques such as the cognitive interview which can increase the amount of information obtained but without an increase in fabrications (Ainsworth, 1998: ch. 7).

Facial identification

Most of what has been said so far has been concerned with the way in which witnesses might recall details of an event which they have seen. A great deal of psychological research has shown how inaccuracies can creep in and how these might contribute to a possible miscarriage of justice. However, mistakes are perhaps even more likely when a witness is called upon to identify the face of a perpetrator. Evidence suggests that there are a number of reasons why such errors might occur and we will consider some of these below.

Over 25 years ago, the Devlin Committee was asked to look into the possibility that mistaken identifications could lead to the wrongful conviction of innocent people. The committee had been established in response to public and judicial concern over a number of high profile cases in which miscarriages of justice had taken place. Among many concerns, the committee expressed misgivings over the number of cases in which eyewitness identification was the sole, or main, evidence against an accused. They noted that in England and Wales in 1973 there were some 347 cases in which eyewitness testimony was the only evidence against a defendant. In almost three-quarters of these cases the defendant was in fact convicted, despite the fact that in half of the trials the evidence consisted of just one eyewitness identification. Brandon and Davies (1973) listed 70 cases in which an innocent person had been convicted mainly as a result of eyewitness testimony. Huff (1987) found that eyewitness error was a significant factor in approximately 60 per cent of the 500 cases of wrongful conviction which he studied in the USA.

After considering a great deal of evidence (including a comparatively limited amount of psychological research) the Devlin Committee recommended that cases in which the only evidence against an accused was that of eyewitness testimony should not proceed. Further, the committee recommended that if such cases were brought to trial then they should fail. It is perhaps surprising then that some 25 years since that recommendation, the provisions have not been implemented and it is still possible for an accused to be convicted mainly on eyewitness evidence. A couple of examples of how things can go wrong will highlight the potential dangers.

In October 1992 a London taxi-driver was accosted and threatened by a man with a gun. The taxi-driver had a bomb placed in his cab and was told that he must deliver the bomb to the London street in which the British Prime Minister lived. The driver did in fact abandon the cab in Whitehall and was able to shout a warning shortly before the bomb exploded. Following the attack, the police arrested an Irishman by the name of Patrick Murphy. Murphy was so confident that his innocence would soon be proved that he refused the offer of legal representation and agreed to take part in an identification parade. To his great surprise and dismay, Murphy was picked out from the ID parade by three people, including the taxi-driver. The authorities were convinced of Murphy's involvement and he was detained in custody while the Crown Prosecution Service commenced proceedings against him. Murphy was, however, able to produce some eleven witnesses, all of whom were prepared to testify that at the time of the offence he had been at a meeting of Alcoholics Anonymous. Faced with this evidence the CPS agreed to drop the charges against Murphy and he was released. One can only speculate as to what might have happened had Murphy not been able to provide an alibi for his movements on the day in question.

A case from the USA (cited in Cutler and Penrod, 1995) also highlights the mistakes which eyewitnesses can make. In this case one Shaun Deckinga was accused of robbing a number of banks in Minnesota. A rather blurred picture of the actual robber had been shown on television and a caller had identified the face as that of Deckinga. The main evidence against the accused was the fact that the three bank tellers who had been in the bank at the time of one of the robberies had identified him and stated that they were either 'positive' or 'fairly sure' that he was the culprit. This identification convinced the jury of Deckinga's guilt and he was convicted of two of the robberies, despite protesting his innocence. However, while Deckinga was in custody an almost identical robbery was carried out and a clearer picture of the robber was obtained. A prison guard recognised the face of this robber as that of Jerry Clapper, a man recently released from prison. Clapper was arrested and confessed to the robberies, including those for which Deckinga had been convicted. As a result Deckinga was released from custody and his conviction quashed.

One wonders how, in both of these cases, apparently well-intentioned witnesses could make such fundamental mistakes and identify the wrong person. Psychological research has been able to provide some answers to this question and today psychologists (at least in the USA) are increasingly being called upon to provide expert testimony on the problems associated with eyewitness identifications. (It is interesting to note, however, that in the Deckinga case, the court actually refused permission for the defence to call an expert psychologist witness.)

If, as we saw above, memory for events is plagued with possible sources of confusion, then facial memory and identification are perhaps even more error-prone. Although the rape victim may state with conviction that 'she will never forget her attacker's face as long as she lives', it appears quite possible that such confidence may be ill-founded. Many of the variables which affect event memory will also affect facial memory – factors such as stress may well interfere with a witness's ability both to recall facial features accurately and to identify a perpetrator's face in, say, an identification parade. However, facial recognition also brings about its own particular problems which any criminal justice system should acknowledge. For example, we now know that identifying faces from a different race is more difficult than identifying faces from one's own race (Bothwell *et al.*, 1989; Chance and Goldstein, 1996). We also know that in some cases an unconscious transference can occur in which a witness recognises a face as being familiar, but wrongly labels it as that of a perpetrator (Ainsworth, 1995c). It would also appear that, as we will see below, many of the procedures which the police use to try to identify a perpetrator afford potential sources of error.

It has been suggested by many researchers (e.g. Bruce, 1988) that facial recall and recognition are different from many other types of memory task. While most people will experience little difficulty in recognising the face of an old friend, describing and identifying the face of an attacker seen only once (and probably in difficult or unusual circumstances) may prove to be much more problematic. People do not routinely study and try to memorise each feature of a face. Rather, they tend to perceive faces as an entity and to form an overall impression, perhaps by noticing that a person has a friendly face or that he is good looking. Unfortunately, such descriptions may be seen as being of little use to police officers who are used to noting and classifying offenders' hair, eyes, nose, chin, etc.

Because descriptions of an offender's physical characteristics can prove to be so difficult to elicit, techniques such as photofits or artists' impressions may be used. Unfortunately, such techniques often bring about their own difficulties and are not always particularly helpful (Ainsworth, 1998: 80–2). Most witnesses will tend to produce rather sketchy descriptions which will be of little help to the police in identifying a suspect. In any case, it would be inappropriate to presume that a suspect who happens to match the description given by a witness is necessarily the perpetrator. Even more worrying will be those cases in which a witness, possibly under pressure from a police officer, provides a description which contains inaccuracies and which leads to the arrest of an innocent person. Some of these mistakes can be explained by reference to the techniques used by the police when trying to identify a suspect. Some of the more common techniques will be described below.

Mugshot inspections

Given that most witnesses will have difficulty in describing the physical features of an assailant's face it may be better to test whether they can recognise the face. Indeed, many witnesses may claim that although they are unable to provide a good description, they would certainly recognise the face if they did encounter it again. In such circumstances, the police may ask the witness to examine the mugshot files to see whether they can identify the person. The mugshot files will contain photographs of local criminals who have convictions, often for crimes similar to that currently under investigation.

Although mugshot file searches can be beneficial in helping to identify a perpetrator, they do pose some problems. For example, the files will contain only photographs of those individuals who have been convicted of a criminal offence. Thus, crimes committed by an assailant who has no previous convictions would cause obvious difficulties. One might reasonably assume that in such circumstances a witness would simply report that their attacker was not in the files, but, this may not always happen. The police might, for example, ask the witness to go through the files a second time, or perhaps ask them to look at more sets of photographs. In such cases, it would appear increasingly likely that a witness will pick someone out, if only to bring the procedure to a close.

Research evidence suggests that the greater the number of photographs a witness is asked to examine, the more likely it is that an incorrect identification will be made (Ellis *et al.*, 1989). The problem is compounded by the fact that mistakes made at this stage may well be repeated by mistakes made further along the criminal justice process. For example, a witness who has selected a suspect from a mugshot inspection might later be asked to attend an identification parade. In such cases, it would perhaps hardly be surprising if the witness picked out the same person whom he/she had selected from the earlier procedure. Yet this second identification merely proves that the witness is being consistent, not that they have definitely identified the right person.

This tendency to be consistent (though not necessarily accurate) was demonstrated by Brigham and Cairns (1988). These researchers showed that when mistakes are made at the first stage of an identification procedure, the mistake tends to be carried forward to any future identification attempts (see also Cutler and Penrod, 1995: 107). Thus, in the Brigham and Cairns study, witnesses who incorrectly picked out a face from a mugshot inspection, tended to pick out the same wrong face from a later photospread identification procedure. If the police take such identifications as 'proof', their enquiries will then tend to focus almost exclusively upon the individual named and presumptions will be made about his/her guilt (Ainsworth, 1995b).

Show-ups

In cases where the police have some idea as to who might be responsible for a crime, they will usually ask the witness to try to identify the person concerned. Such formal identification procedures range from photospreads and live identification parades to what are known as show-ups. In this latter case, the witness will simply be shown one person and asked whether this is or is not the person responsible for the crime under investigation. This is by far the most simple type of identification procedure, yet it is also the one most likely to lead to false identifications (Kassin *et al.*, 1989). The problem has been described thus:

> Witnesses, especially those who are victims, may be highly motivated to try to identify an assailant, and if given a choice of only one suspect may be more likely to claim that they do recognise the person as the perpetrator.
>
> (1989: 85)

This tendency will be heightened if the police apply pressure to a witness to make an identification. For example, police officers might tell the witness that they are sure that they have the right person and that they need the witness simply to confirm this (Wagenaar and Veefkind, 1992; Wrightsman, 1991: 138). It is perhaps surprising to learn that even if witnesses are given a choice of only one suspect, they are not necessarily very accurate. For example, Yarmey (1992) found that when subject-witnesses were shown a photograph of someone with whom they had interacted only two minutes earlier only 57 per cent identified the picture correctly.

Given the vagaries of show-ups, it is perhaps surprising to learn that although such procedures are not actively encouraged, they are not actually banned in most countries (Kapardis, 1997: 239). Furthermore, there is one form of show-up which is accepted almost unconditionally. This is the scenario in which a witness who is giving evidence in court is asked if the perpetrator is in the court and if so to point him/her out. Such so-called dock identifications are thought to reassure the court that the person in the dock is indeed the right person. However, such dock identifications can hardly be considered a fair way of identifying a perpetrator. Given that the accused will tend to be in the dock and perhaps flanked by uniformed prison officers it would be almost unimaginable for the witness to point to anyone else in the courtroom (Ainsworth, 1998: 86–7).

Photospread identifications

Photospreads would tend to be used in situations where the police have a suspect in mind, but need a witness to confirm the identification. A typical procedure would involve a witness viewing an array of perhaps twelve photographs and being asked if they recognised anyone in the array. If the witness indicated that they did recognise anyone then they should be asked to say which photograph they recognise and from where. Photospreads have a number of advantages over the procedures discussed so far. For example, they are preferable to mugshot inspections in that they allow the witness to peruse a much smaller number of photographs before making a decision. They are also fairer than show-ups because the witness is asked to make a decision about an array of possible alternatives rather than just about one face.

However, photospreads are not without their own problems. For example, a witness who has seen a 'live' perpetrator may have difficulty in relating that image to a static photograph. Further, the photograph itself may not be a particularly good likeness, or may have been taken when the accused's appearance was somewhat different. Many studies carried out in the psychology laboratory suggest that people can be quite good at identifying a face seen previously (Cutler *et al.*, 1994). However, many of these studies lack ecological validity and their results are perhaps not easily related to real life studies. For example, most lab-based studies involve showing subject-witnesses a photograph and then later asking them to identify the same photograph from an array. In such cases, however, the target person's appearance is identical in both view-ings, making recognition somewhat easy. Furthermore, most studies of this kind will use an array which **does** contain the photograph shown pre-viously. In real criminal investigations it is possible that on some occasions the police will have the wrong suspect in mind and will thus show the witness a photospread which does not contain the real perpe-trator.

It would be naïve to presume that on all such occasions the witness will simply tell the investigators that the perpetrator is not present and that they should start looking elsewhere. The pressures on a witness, espe-cially one who has been a victim, may encourage him/her to guess or to point to the photograph which is most like the face of the real perpetra-tor. Such 'guesses' will not, however, be distributed randomly across the twelve photographs presented. In all likelihood the police will have plumped for a particular suspect because they match the verbal descrip-tion given by the witness originally. If one face in the photo array matches all the elements provided by the witness, it is quite likely that the witness, even if unsure, will choose that photograph. But, of course, this does not necessarily prove that the face which is picked out is that of the real perpetrator – it may simply be that it matches the description more closely than do the others.

Although the regulations governing the conduct of identifications would not allow investigators to use foils whose appearance was com-pletely different from that of the suspect, there will inevitably be some foils which can be rejected immediately because some aspect of their appearance is at odds with that of the real perpetrator. Furthermore, the fact that the witness can view all the photographs at once makes the pro-cedure similar to a multiple choice examination question. The witness may go over the array a number of times and gradually eliminate the less likely foils until they are left with perhaps just one or two from which to choose. In such situations, an identification would not necessarily prove that the face picked out was that of the real perpetrator, but instead may simply signify that it was the one whose appearance was most like them. Laboratory studies which have used a 'target absent' array show that peo-ple do on occasion pick out an innocent person, rather than admit that they are unable to spot the face seen earlier. This can be a particular problem with younger children (Davies *et al.*, 1988) who may feel pres-sured into picking someone out even when they are unsure.

The authorities are aware of some of the potential problems of photo-spread identifications and in many cases will try to prevent mistakes from occurring. For example, it is now routine practice for witnesses to be told in advance that the person whom they saw 'may or may not be in the photo array' and that witnesses should only identify someone if they are certain. However, such warnings may be ineffectual when a victim-witness is highly motivated and wants desperately to see his/her attacker brought to justice. Regulations also dictate that when a photospread is used it should be made available to the court so that jurors and defence counsel can see for themselves whether the procedure was fair.

Before closing our discussion of photospreads, we should point out that such procedures can have some advantages over the traditional live identification parade discussed below. For example, photospreads may be considered more suitable for young witnesses or for those who are particularly nervous. For such individuals, attending a live ID parade might be particularly nerve-wracking and they may find the mere physical presence of a perpetrator intimidating. In such situations, the real perpetrator may be more likely to be identified if witnesses view a photoarray than if they attend a live ID parade.

Identification parades (line-ups)

Perhaps the best know type of formal identification process is the identification (or ID) parade. In such procedures a suspect stands among a number of innocent foils and a witness is asked to inspect the parade and then to decide whether the perpetrator is present. The technique is in some ways similar to that of the photospread and as such is prone to the same types of errors discussed above. Thus, a witness may feel under pressure to pick someone out even if they are unsure; the appearance of the foils may allow the witness to eliminate some immediately, etc. As with photospreads, there are regulations which govern the fair conduct of ID parades, including the need to inform a witness that the perpetrator may or may not be present and that they should make an identification only if they are sure. It is also normal for the accused's legal representative to be present at the parade and for the whole procedure to be video-recorded. However, guidelines and advice can never guarantee that mistakes will not be made. As has been noted recently:

> Such guidelines may have eliminated some of the more questionable tactics used in the past, but as some recent cases of wrongful conviction have shown, there is still room for bias and error to creep in.
>
> (Ainsworth, 1998: 92)

There are a number of distinctive aspects of live ID parades which may contribute to possible errors. One obvious consideration is the number of foils who should be put into a parade in order to make the procedure fair. Rules concerning this vary from country to country, though in Britain the minimum acceptable number is generally seven. Research carried out in the USA suggests that the minimum acceptable number to ensure fairness is five foils plus the suspect (Wells et al., 1994). However, the actual number of foils on the parade is perhaps less important than their similarity to the suspect. As with photospreads, foils should only be included if their appearance is broadly similar to the description given by the witness. Any foils which can be immediately rejected (because their appearance does not match the description) may just as well not be there at all, as their rejection will be almost automatic. Brigham and Pfeiffer (1994) suggest that the fairness of a line-up should be judged not with reference to its actual size, but rather to its functional size. Thus an eight-person parade containing three foils which can be immediately rejected might be considered unfair while one which contains five appropriate foils may be considered fair.

The choice of foils is thus crucial in determining the ease or difficulty of an identification procedure (Lindsay, 1994). The police may wish to increase the likelihood of a witness picking out the suspect by choosing foils who are significantly different from the suspect. By contrast, defence counsel might prefer to have foils whose resemblance is very similar to the suspect, thus making it less likely that the witness will be able to identify the suspect. In practice, the police now have lists of foils whom they can call upon to attend an ID parade. Such people's physical appearance is kept on record so that in theory it should be possible to call only those whose physical appearance resembles that of a suspect. This is a considerable improvement on past procedures in which it was not unheard of for police officers who were about to go off duty to be called onto a parade to act as foils. In many cases, the physical appearance, stance and behaviour of the 'foils' made it very easy for any witness to spot the one person on the parade who stood out from the rest!

Even if the foils' physical appearance is broadly similar to that of the suspect, it may still be possible for a witness to identify who the real suspect is on the parade by studying participants' behaviour carefully. For example, it is feasible that the real suspect may be extremely nervous while the foils will be much more relaxed. Sweating, trembling or even more subtle non-verbal behaviour may send a signal to the witness as to who the 'real' suspect is. One might want to argue that this is not necessarily a problem as a perpetrator deserves to have to 'sweat it out'. In any case, it could be claimed that their extreme nervousness may simply prove their guilt and so they 'deserve' to be picked out.

There is however a flaw in such logic. While a guilty suspect may well be nervous, it might also be the case that a genuinely innocent person will also show signs of tension. A man who has been arrested and accused wrongly may well be extremely anxious about the outcome of the ID parade. Although he may know that he did not commit the crime in question he might well be afraid that the mistakes made so far will be compounded by his being picked out by a witness. While many humans may be quite adept at spotting when an individual appears to be experiencing stress, they may be less accurate in their presumptions about the factors underlying the tension. Although laboratory-based research studies examining identification procedures have been helpful in many areas, they are unable to replicate the tension which a real suspect on a real ID parade might experience. For this reason, it is not easy to call upon reliable research evidence to establish the extent to which wrongly accused suspects are likely to be picked out as guilty.

A further worry concerning ID parades is that, as with photospreads, the witness can look at the whole parade at once and make a decision on that basis. In theory, a witness's task is to study each face in turn and to decide whether or not that face belongs to the person who they saw commit the crime. However, in practice, the witness may actually narrow down the possibilities by rejecting those which are the most dissimilar to their memory of the accused and eventually select the one whose appearance is most similar to the image in their memory (Thomson, 1995).

This latter problem could be eliminated if witnesses were prevented from seeing the whole parade at once. An alternative would be to have the witness simply view each face in turn and to say whether the face was or was not that of the accused. The witness would not necessarily be told in advance how many faces there would be on the parade, thus possibly making their decision more reliable. When such procedures have been used, they appear to be successful in reducing significantly the number of false positives which normal identification parades produce. (In this case a 'false positive' would be where a witness incorrectly identifies a face on the parade as that of the suspect.) Despite the demonstrated advantages of this method over traditional ID parades (Cutler and Penrod, 1995; Thomson, 1995), psychologists have to date been unsuccessful in persuading the authorities to adopt such procedures.

We can see from this section that there are a large number of ways in which even well-intentioned witnesses can make mistakes which could result in the conviction of an innocent person. In the next section we will examine a different source of possible error stemming from the way in which the police interview suspects.

Interviewing suspects and eliciting confessions

The interviewing or interrogation of suspects is often seen by police officers, especially detectives, as a good way of demonstrating their professional prowess. A great deal of respect will be given to the police officer who is able to persuade a reluctant suspect finally to confess to the crime in question – the more serious the crime, the greater will be the kudos. It is interesting that many television dramas focusing on the police devote a great deal of time to interactions in the interview room. Increasing pressure on the police to improve their detection rate might also mean that police officers are highly motivated to try to solve crimes and in some cases may be willing to cut corners in order to do so. In this section we will not deal with cases where police officers might 'fit-up' a suspect by lying deliberately, or perhaps even planting evidence, but will instead look at situations in which police officers' over-enthusiasm or dubious tactics might lead ultimately to a wrongful conviction.

Many police officers will see the interviewing of a suspect mainly as a way of obtaining a confession from a person who is guilty, but unwilling initially to admit their guilt. Police officers may take the view that the suspect would not have been arrested unless he/she was guilty. Thus, the interview is seen primarily as a way of obtaining further evidence which will prove the person's guilt absolutely (Ainsworth, 1995b). Such views may be common in the everyday world of policing (Inbau, Reid and Buckley, 1986) but may be confirmed by messages given during training courses or even in academic texts. One American book (MacHovec, 1989) suggests that 'Experienced interrogators agree that most offenders want to confess and have a psychological and emotional need to do so' (1989: 119).

This same author advocates that stress, pressure and threat might be applied during interrogations and that 'These behaviors increase fear, anxiety, guilt or anger, depending on the interviewee's attitude, personality and mental state. If the person is a suspect this technique can test for "guilty knowledge"' (1989: 110).

Such techniques might well be effective when used against a guilty person, but are extremely questionable from an ethical standpoint. Perhaps more worrying though is the possibility that if such techniques are used against an innocent suspect they may result in extreme distress and perhaps a false confession.

One British study (Moston, Stephenson and Williamson, 1992) found that in almost three-quarters of cases examined, the police interviewer stated that he/she was already sure of the suspect's guilt before the interview even began. In almost 80 per cent of cases, the police officer saw the aim of the interview as being simply to obtain a confession. McConville and Hodgson (1993) discovered similar presumptions by police officers about a suspect's guilt in their research. It is, therefore, not surprising if the interview rarely serves two of its supposed aims, i.e. to obtain valuable facts and to eliminate the innocent (Swanson, Chamelin and Territo, 1988).

In cases where a police officer is unable to obtain a confession, this failure may not be interpreted as proof of a suspect's innocence but rather may be put down to the suspect's shrewdness, perhaps stemming from their previous experience of interrogations. In such circumstances it will be extremely difficult for the genuinely innocent suspect to persuade the interviewer that they really did not commit the crime under investigation. Whatever methods the suspect uses will be reinterpreted as further evidence of their guilt. Thus, a suspect's anxiety might be presumed to stem from guilt rather than from nervousness about the interview situation (Ainsworth, 1995a: 43–7; Vrij, 1998a). Similarly, a suspect who becomes increasingly frustrated and angered by the police's refusal to accept his/her story may be presumed to be exhibiting classic signs of fear of discovery.

Police officers' general air of cynicism often makes them believe that almost all suspects will lie in order to avoid a conviction. Furthermore, police officers often believe that they can spot when someone is lying (Oxford, 1991) though research suggests that this faith may be misplaced (Vrij 1998a; Vrij and Winkel, 1993; Ekman and O'Sullivan, 1989). Mistakes appear to occur because police officers attend to the wrong cues when attempting to spot whether a suspect is lying. In Vrij and Winkel's (1993) study it was found that police officers often focus on a person's clothing and general appearance when trying to decide whether or not he/she is lying. Such cues are in fact unreliable indicators of deception.

Legislation such as the Police and Criminal Evidence Act 1984 (PACE) has contributed to the reduction of some of the more dubious police practices by, for example, insisting that all suspect interviews are tape recorded. However, the introduction of such safeguards may not have affected police officers' underlying attitudes towards the interview situation and officers may still be inclined to presume guilt even before the full facts are known. It is perhaps surprising to learn that a number of researchers (e.g. Baldwin, 1993; Moston, 1995; Pearse and Gudjonsson, 1996; Shepherd, 1993) suggest that the police are often ill-prepared when it comes to conducting interviews and may behave in unprofessional and ineffectual ways. Such tactics may make it less likely that a guilty suspect will confess.

False confessions

Perhaps until relatively recently, most juries would have had little hesitation in convicting a defendant if a signed confession was produced in court (Underwager and Wakefield, 1992). However, as a number of recent well-publicised cases have shown, false confessions can be made by innocent people (Gudjonsson, 1992; Ainsworth, 1995a: ch. 3). Despite such documented cases, it may still be difficult for most members of a jury to accept that a genuinely innocent person would ever sign a confession and admit to committing a crime in which he/she was not involved. Such a view may, however, be misplaced and fail to acknowledge the powerful situational forces which are present in the interview room.

Research in social psychology offers some valuable insights into the fact that people do often underestimate the situational (or external) forces when trying to explain others' behaviour and instead have a tendency to assume that others behave the way they do for internal (i.e. dispositional) reasons. This tendency has been labelled the Fundamental Attribution Error (Jones and Nisbett, 1972). According to attribution theory, the person who makes a confession will be presumed by others to have done so simply because he/she was guilty. In reaching this conclusion, people may well imagine what they think they would do if in the suspect's position. They may well conclude that if they really were innocent, no amount of pressure would persuade them to sign a confession. Even police officers who are familiar with the pressures of the interview situation will find it hard to accept that an innocent person would ever confess (Williamson, 1990).

There are in fact a number of reasons why people might make false confessions. Kennedy (1986) suggests that the most common reason is an over-zealousness on the part of the police officer carrying out the interview. Starting with the belief that the person in the interview room must be guilty (see above), police officers will often adopt an accusatorial or confrontational style of questioning (Moston, 1990). This can serve to exert pressure on the suspect until they see that a confession is the only way in which they can escape from the immediate situation (Irving and Hilgendorf, 1980). Although the number of manipulative and persuasive tactics used by detectives fell dramatically following the introduction of PACE (Irving and McKenzie, 1989), some of this early fall was reversed in later years. Williamson (1990) suggested that more recently, British police officers are likely to use professional rather than coercive tactics in the interview room.

Nevertheless, some people may still make false confessions, even when not subjected to a coercive or threatening interview style. It is, for example, not uncommon for certain individuals to claim responsibility for committing some notorious crime or other, despite the fact that they clearly did not commit the offence. Individuals who display this odd behaviour may be doing so in an attempt to become famous, to try to impress others, or even to improve their low self-esteem. However, others may confess because of some specific or generalised guilt complex. This type of person may wish to relieve themself of a burden of guilt over some other matter and try to achieve this by confessing to the crime under investigation. As Gudjonsson (1992) notes, this type of behaviour may be more likely in people who are mentally ill, especially those suffering from major psychoses such as schizophrenia.

There are a number of other reasons why an individual might confess falsely. The person may, for example, be prone to confusing fantasy with reality – if such a person fantasises about killing, say, a former employer, they may confess if the ex-employer is subsequently killed, albeit by someone else. A second possibility is that an individual may confess in order to save the real perpetrator from being identified. In such a case, one family member might lie and admit to committing a crime in order to protect another family member. It may be difficult for the police to detect such cases, especially if a conspiracy has been agreed previously by other family members.

While such false confessions are worrying and may lead to a miscarriage of justice, we should perhaps be even more concerned by those cases in which a suspect confesses falsely because of the pressure exerted on him/her in the interview room. Gudjonsson (1992) refers to this type of confession as **coerced-compliant**. In such cases, the suspect will seek to end the interrogation ordeal by doing what the interviewer wants and admit (falsely) their guilt. This apparently incomprehensible behaviour becomes slightly more meaningful when one considers the immediate pressure which a suspect may feel at the time of the interview. The fact that the confession may have serious long-term consequences for the individual may be dismissed in the pressing need to bring a halt to an unbearable situation.

When an innocent person does confess in this way, he/she will usually try to retract the admission once they have escaped from the aversive situation in the interview room. However, attempts at retraction may prove to be difficult and might be viewed by others as simply the actions of a guilty person who is now trying to save their own skin.

Another type of false confession identified by Gudjonsson is labelled **coerced-internalised**. In such cases, the suspect may believe initially that they are innocent but will eventually admit and accept that they did in fact commit the crime. This change may come about as a result of the tactics used by the police officer(s) carrying out the interrogation (Ofshe, 1989). In such cases, the suspect may have little or no memory for the incident or may even be persuaded to distrust their own memory. Eventually, the person may come to believe that the version of events suggested by the police is in fact true, and that they did indeed commit the crime.

Such an acceptance is perhaps most likely when police officers convince a suspect that there is incontrovertible evidence linking him/her to the crime. The officer must also be able to provide the suspect with an acceptable explanation for why their memory is missing or inaccurate. Ofshe (1989) has examined a number of such cases and notes that although most did not involve people who would be defined as mentally ill, there were certain personality variables which were linked with the tendency to confess falsely. For example, individuals who trusted in authority, lacked self-confidence, and were highly suggestible were most likely to confess and then to come to believe that they had committed the crime. Police officers who elicit such confessions might not even be aware that they are false – as was noted earlier, it may be difficult for a police officer to accept that the same techniques which might persuade a guilty person to confess might also lead to a confession by an innocent person.

Although coerced-internalised confessions might well lead to a change in an individual's belief about their involvement in the crime, this change might not be permanent. For example, the person may have accepted the interviewing officer's version of events while they were in the interview room but once removed from such a pressured environment will have an opportunity to reassess the evidence. Conversations with friends or family may allow the person to check out reality and lead them to later reassert their innocence.

From what has been said so far it seems likely that individuals who are highly suggestible may be more likely to confess falsely and then to accept their guilt. For this reason it would be helpful to be able to measure an individual's suggestibility, ideally before any interview commences. Gudjonsson (1989) has developed a psychometric test designed to identify those individuals who may be particularly vulnerable to the more forceful type of interview technique. He identifies two variables which he labels **suggestibility** and **compliance** and seeks to make a distinction between the two. In the case of an individual scoring high on suggestibility, they may well come to believe and internalise the suggestions made by the interviewer. However, the individual who scores highly in terms of compliance may appear to accept the version of events suggested by an interviewer, but will never really accept or believe in them.

Gudjonsson claims that his scales enable a distinction to be made between highly suggestible/compliant individuals and others and that the distinction may explain the behaviour of those individuals who make false confessions. Gudjonsson cites the case of the Birmingham Six, who were falsely convicted of planting bombs in Birmingham (England) and killing 21 people. Gudjonsson claims that the four accused who did (falsely) confess showed higher scores on his suggestibility and compliance scales than did the two individuals who did not confess.

Gudjonsson sees suggestibility essentially as a personality trait and as such it will tend to make some people more vulnerable than others. However, Gudjonsson and other writers have also suggested that mood can have a powerful influence on an individual's ability to resist persuasion. Vrij (1998b) suggests that this raises a potential problem. For example, if an individual's mood when completing the test is substantially different from their mood when being interviewed by the police, the suggestibility score may not be an accurate reflection of the individual's true vulnerability.

In this section we have highlighted some of the ways in which an individual might confess to a crime which they did not commit and which might lead ultimately to a miscarriage of justice. However, it may be appropriate to end on a more positive note. By carrying out research into police interrogation techniques, psychologists are in a better position to be able to understand the effects of some of these practices. Similarly, by identifying those individuals who may be vulnerable to certain types of questioning, psychologists may be able to raise doubts about the likely truthfulness of some disputed confessions. Psychologists might also be able to offer advice to those who wish to change current practice and thus perhaps to make it less likely that miscarriages of justice will occur in the future. Included in this would be the suggestion that particularly vulnerable suspects should be interviewed only in the presence of an 'appropriate adult'. Such a provision may go some way towards ensuring that advantage is not taken of those who may be the most susceptible to attempts at persuasion.

Summary

This chapter has focused upon two important areas within the criminal justice process which can lead to errors and possibly to miscarriages of justice. We have seen that the courts' expectations as to the abilities of eyewitnesses to offer complete and objective testimony may be misplaced. We have also seen that many of the procedures used by the police in an effort to identify suspects may lead to serious errors of misidentification. We should also bear in mind that in addition to making errors, witnesses may also suffer intimidation, be that at the hands of the accused or their defence counsel.

In the second part of this chapter we have seen how police tactics used in the interviewing of suspects can lead to an inappropriate presumption of guilt. In some cases, the techniques used by the police to persuade a guilty person to confess may actually lead to an innocent person making a false confession. However, the introduction of tighter controls on police practices has gone some way towards reducing some of the more inappropriate forms of interview technique.

Conclusion

Throughout this book we have seen many examples of the way in which psychology is relevant to the criminal justice process. In some cases, psychology can help us to understand better the actions of offenders, victims and officials within the system. But psychology can also be useful as a way of producing change. Such changes might include the introduction of better crime prevention strategies, more effective help for crime victims, more efficient (and less prejudiced) police procedures and better intervention strategies to prevent reoffending. We must, however, bear in mind that, compared with most other sciences, psychology is still at an embryonic stage in its development. One consequence of this is that many of those who work within the criminal justice process have not always been eager to embrace input from psychologists. This is particularly the case in Britain where the number of psychologists working within and around the criminal justice system lags far behind that in the USA (Blau, 1998; Hess and Weiner, 1999). However, things are changing slowly and it seems likely that in the future far more psychologists will become involved in the criminal justice process. The introduction of an increasing number of postgraduate courses in forensic psychology in Britain suggests that this will indeed be the case.

It has been suggested that many members of the public have what appears to be an insatiable appetite for crime-related material. The amount of coverage given to the subject in national and local newspapers and on television and in film, bears testament to this (Howitt, 1998). However, it has been argued throughout this book that members of the public may have misconceptions about crime and misunderstandings as to the role which psychology can play. It is hoped that this book will have gone some way towards challenging some erroneous assumptions and exploding some myths about psychology's role. However, psychologists will need to continue to strive to educate both those within the system and members of the public as to the role which psychology can play. We have seen that many of those within the legal system, especially the judiciary, often fail to recognise the potential value of psychology and continue to believe in both their own, and the system's, ability to work efficiently. A cursory look at some of the material covered in Chapter 7 of this volume suggests that such faith may be misplaced.

One of the most important skills which psychologists can bring to the criminal justice arena is the systematic study and analysis of human behaviour using appropriate scientific methodologies. The criminal justice process contains many examples of procedures and processes which have remained in place for years simply because 'that's the way it's always been done' or because of the power held by some within the system. Psychologists approaching the criminal justice arena will tend not to accept the *status quo* in the same way which others with vested interests might. Having said that, psychologists will need to be sure of their facts before advocating change. As Allen and Miller (1995) have noted eloquently:

> The law is a hostage to the knowledge possessed by others; it needs data, good data. It can well do without the biases and prejudices of related disciplines – it has enough of its own to deal with.
>
> (1995: 337)

One example of how psychology can help is provided by the example of the police's attempts at preventing crime. For years the police claimed to be interested in crime prevention yet often marginalised this activity by appointing a small number of crime prevention officers in each force. Many such officers contented themselves with offering standard advice relating to the fitting of better locks and the like, while most other officers got on with 'real' police work (usually meaning the locking up of villains). While individual police officers may have noticed that the same people were being victimised time and time again, they appeared unable or unwilling to translate this knowledge into a strategy which would reduce crime (Hough and Tilley, 1998). It took the pioneering efforts of psychologists such as Ken Pease to analyse the problem of repeat victimisation and to translate this into effective practice (see Chapter 2).

Many years after Ken Pease's pioneering work in Kirkholt, the British government has acknowledged the importance of local crime audits and compelled the police to work with other agencies in tackling the issues which most concern local residents. Ken Pease has also drawn attention to many other ways in which crime might be prevented, focusing, for example, on government strategies and actions by manufacturers (Pease, 1998b). Such lateral thinking is to be applauded and stands in marked contrast to the unimaginative views of many professionals and politicians.

Only in the last couple of years have magazines such as *What Car?* included an evaluation and rating of new cars' security systems. It does seem somewhat odd that at a time when most car owners express great concern over the possible theft of their vehicles, consumers appear to show little interest in security matters when deciding upon their next means of transport. In fact, the vehicle which came top of the British *Top Gear/JD Power* customer satisfaction survey in 1998 and 1999 actually came bottom of a recent *What Car?* league table of car security. It does appear that the car which is the easiest to break into and to steal is also the one which leads to the highest level of customer satisfaction. Perhaps some of those who responded to the survey were working from memory and nostalgia had affected their recollections of a now-stolen vehicle. One might be even more cynical and suggest that at least some of those who responded to the survey had every right to be pleased with their acquisition as it cost them nothing! If nothing else, this story shows how difficult it can be to introduce good crime prevention strategies.

Other forms of interaction between psychologists and the police have also been examined in the preceding pages. In some cases, psychologists can offer help in the detection of crime by the development of techniques such as offender profiling. However, as we saw in Chapter 6, such techniques may not be particularly useful in the vast majority of criminal investigations. The large number of students who embark upon an undergraduate psychology degree in the hope of becoming the next *Cracker* may be sadly disappointed! They may however find that skills such as crime pattern analysis, and an ability to carry out good research, will be in demand.

There are many other areas in which psychology is relevant to policing and some of these have been considered in this volume (see Ainsworth, 1995a for a fuller discussion). The way in which suspects are interviewed continues to raise some concerns, although a better understanding of the situational pressures in the interview room can alert us to the possibility that some innocent people will confess to crimes which they have not committed. A better understanding of the processes of perception and memory can also help police officers to elicit more accurate information from witnesses (Ainsworth, 1998 for a fuller discussion).

Increasing knowledge of memory processes may also help to lower the chances that miscarriages of justice might occur as a result of mistakes made by eyewitnesses. Psychologists have already had some influence on such things as identification procedures and, in the future, they may be able to advise on further improvements to the present systems. It also appears increasingly likely that psychologists will be appearing as expert witnesses in cases where eyewitnesses may have made serious (if unintentional) errors. The legal system still appears unwilling to allow psychologists to study jury deliberations, but some of the knowledge gained from other studies of group behaviour helps to shed some light on jury decisions (Chapter 7).

For any criminal justice system to command respect from its citizens it must demonstrate that it is efficient and effective. Crime costs society billions of pounds each year, yet the resources devoted to crime prevention are, by comparison, minuscule. While psychologists may be able to do relatively little to secure more funds for crime prevention initiatives, by the use of scientific analysis and evaluation they can at least suggest the best and most effective ways in which resources might be deployed.

Similarly, psychologists are in a good position to be able to evaluate offender treatment programmes. For far too long interventions were introduced because it was thought that they 'might' or 'should' work. Martinson's oft-quoted message that 'nothing works' stemmed not so much from a review of carefully controlled evaluations, but rather from a review of programmes which could not actually show whether or not they were being effective (see Chapter 8). Psychologists are now in a much better position to understand which strategies work and why. While incapacitation and public protection may remain the primary goals of the criminal justice system, there are some signs that rehabilitation attempts will become more prominent in the future (see Chapter 8). Recent books, such as those by McGuire (1995), Cullen and Applegate (1997) and Hollin (1999) point the way to more effective intervention and evaluation. As we saw in Chapter 8, the development of good cognitive-behavioural approaches shows considerable promise for the future.

Psychologists can also add to our understanding of the factors which appear to contribute towards the commencement and continuation of criminal behaviour. While there is currently some disagreement as to which factors should be considered to be the most important, a much better understanding of the myriad of contributory elements is emerging. As knowledge increases further, psychologists should be in an even better position to be able to recommend policy initiatives designed to reduce offending behaviour.

Psychologists (along with psychiatrists) are also in a good position to be able to evaluate an offender's mental state and to comment upon this in court. Although such inputs are still more common in the USA than in Britain (Hess and Weiner, 1999), it seems likely that as clinical and forensic psychologists gain greater status, so their views will assume more importance. It is to be hoped that such increased involvement might lead to a larger proportion of those who require treatment (as opposed to punishment) actually receiving help. The alarming prospect of individuals with personality disorders being incarcerated because of what they **might** do (as opposed to what they have done) would, however, raise great concerns for most psychologists.

It seems likely that crime will continue both to fascinate and distress many members of society. The reason why some individuals commit crime, and the way in which the police solve some crimes, will remain subjects of great interest to many people. However, victimisation will mean that many citizens will suffer trauma and distress and, in some cases, have their whole lives changed. We can but hope that the ever-increasing knowledge gained by psychologists will go some way towards preventing or alleviating the suffering of large numbers of victims. While many sociologists suggest that crime in society is endemic and inevitable, it may still be possible to have some influence on the level of crime and the suffering of victims. It would be nice to imagine that at some future point in time all the crime dramas on television will, of necessity, be set in the past rather than the present. However, from today's perspective, that vision seems very distant if not unattainable. In the meantime, both psychologists and members of the public will continue to look at crime. Let us hope, though, that the fascination is not of the hopeless kind and that we can do something other than 'sit and watch it for hours'.

Suggestions for further reading

Below, under the chapter headings of this book, we present some suggestions for further reading.

Chapter 1: The extent and fear of crime

Barclay, G.C. (ed.) (1993) *Information on the Criminal Justice System in England and Wales*, London: Home Office Research and Statistics Department.

Howitt, D. (1998) *Crime, the Media and the Law*, Chichester: Wiley.

Mirrlees-Black, C. and Allen, J. (1998) *Concern about Crime: Findings from the British Crime Survey*, Research, Development and Statistics Research Findings No. 83, London: Home Office.

Mirrlees-Black, C., Budd, T., Partridge, S. and Mayhew, P. (1998) *The 1998 British Crime Survey England and Wales: Home Office Statistical Bulletin 21/98*, London: Home Office.

Walker, M. (ed.) (1995) *Interpreting Crime Statistics*, Oxford: Oxford University Press.

Chapter 2: The psychology of victimisation

Farrell, G. and Pease, K. (eds) (1999) *Repeat Victimization*, New York: Criminal Justice Press.

Joseph, S., Williams, R. and Yule, W. (1997) *Understanding Post Traumatic Stress Disorder: A Psychological Perspective on PTSD and Treatment*, Chichester: Wiley.

Pease, K. (1998) *Repeat Victimization: Taking Stock*, Police Research Group Crime Detection and Prevention Series, Paper 90, London: Home Office.

Zedner, L. (1997) 'Victims' in Maguire, M., Morgan, R. and Reiner, R. (eds) *The Oxford Handbook of Criminology* (2nd ed.), Oxford: Oxford University Press.

Chapter 3: Preventing crime and offending

Crawford, A. (1998) *Crime Prevention and Community Safety*, Harlow: Longman.

Hough, M. and Tilley, N. (1998) *Getting the Grease to the Squeak: Research Lessons for Crime Prevention*, Crime Detection and Prevention Series Paper 85, London: Home Office.

Pease, K. (1997) 'Crime Prevention', in Maguire, M., Morgan, R. and Reiner, R. (eds) *The Oxford Handbook of Criminology* (2nd ed.), Oxford: Oxford University Press.

Tonry, M. and Farrington, D.P. (1995) *Building A Safer Society: Strategic Approaches to Crime Prevention*, Chicago III: University of Chicago Press.

Chapter 4: Psychology and criminal behaviour

Blackburn, R. (1993) *The Psychology of Criminal Conduct: Theory, Research and Practice*, Chichester: Wiley.

Feldman, P. (1993) *The Psychology of Crime*, Cambridge: Cambridge University Press.

Shoemaker, D.J. (1996) *Theories of Delinquency* (3rd ed.), Oxford: Oxford University Press.

Chapter 5: Crime, intention and mental illness

Blackburn, R. (1993) *The Psychology of Criminal Conduct: Theory, Research and Practice*, Chichester: Wiley.

Howells, K. and Hollin, C.R. (1993) *Clinical Approaches to the Mentallly Disordered Offender*, Chichester: Wiley.

Peay, J. (1997) 'Mentally Disordered Offenders', in Maguire, M., Morgan, R. and Reiner, R. (eds.) *The Oxford Handbook of Criminology* (2nd ed.), Oxford: Oxford University Press.

Quinsey, V.L., Harris, G.T., Rice, M.E. and Cormier, C.A. (1998) *Violent Offenders: Appraising and Managing Risk*, Washington DC: American Psychological Association.

Chapter 6: Crime analysis and offender profiling

Canter, D. (1993) *Criminal Shadows: Inside the Mind of the Serial Killer*, London: HarperCollins.

Canter, D. and Alison, L.J. (eds) (1999) *Profiling in Policy and Practice*, Abingdon: Ashgate.

Holmes, R. and Holmes, S. (1996) *Profiling Violent Crimes: An Investigative Tool*, London: Sage.

Jackson, J.L. and Bekerian, D.A. (eds) (1997) *Offender Profiling: Theory, Research and Practice*, Chichester: Wiley.

Note: At the time of writing, Ashgate were about to publish a new series of books on offender profiling. These are edited by David Canter and his colleagues and will probably all be available by late 1999.

Chapter 7: Jury verdicts and judicial sentencing

Ashworth, A. (1992) *Sentencing and Criminal Justice*, London: Weidenfeld & Nicolson.

Hastie, R. (ed.) (1993) *Inside the Juror: The Psychology of Juror Decision-making*, New York: Cambridge University Press.

Pennington, D. and Lloyd Bostock, S. (1987) *The Psychology of Sentencing*, Oxford: The Centre for Socio-Legal Studies, University of Oxford.

Chapter 8: Dealing with offenders

Cullen, F.T. and Applegate, B.K. (eds) (1997) *Offender Rehabilitation: Effective Correctional Intervention*, Aldershot: Dartmouth.

Goldblatt, P. and Lewis, C. (1998) *Reducing Offending: An Assessment of Research Evidence on Ways of Dealing with Offending Behaviour*, Home Office Research Study 187, London Home Office Research and Statistics Directorate.

Hollin, C.R. (ed.) (1999) *Handbook of Offender Assessment and Treatment*, Chichester: Wiley.

McGuire, J. (1995) *What Works? Reducing Reoffending: Guidelines from Research and Practice*, Chichester: Wiley.

Chapter 9: Mistakes and the criminal justice system

Ainsworth, P.B. (1998) *Psychology, Law and Eyewitness Testimony*, Chichester: Wiley.

Gudjonsson, G.J. (1992) *The Psychology of Interrogations, Confessions and Testimony*, Chichester: Wiley.

Memon, A., Vrij, A. and Bull, R. (1998) *Psychology and Law: Truthfulness, Accuracy and Credibility*, Maidenhead: McGraw-Hill.

Bibliography

Ackroyd, S., Harper, R., Hughes, J.A., Shapiro, D. and Soothill, K. (1992) *New Technology and Practical Police Work*, Milton Keynes: Open University Press.

Adhami, E. and Browne, D.P. (1996) *Major Crime Enquiries: Improving Expert Support for Detectives*, Police Research Group Special Interest Series, Paper 9.

Aguirre, A. and Baker, D.V. (1990) 'Empirical research on racial discrimination in the imposition of the death penalty', *Criminal Justice Abstracts*, 135–51.

Ainsworth, P.B. (1982) 'British police officers' perceptions of Psychology', paper presented to *International Conference on Psychology and Law*, Swansea: July.

Ainsworth, P.B. (1995a) *Psychology and Policing in a Changing World*, Chichester: Wiley.

Ainsworth, P.B. (1995b) 'Police folklore and attributions of guilt: Can psychology challenge long held assumptions?', paper presented to the *5th European Conference on Law and Psychology*, Budapest: 2 September.

Ainsworth, P.B. (1995c) 'Turning heroes into villains: the role of unconscious transference in media crime reporting', paper presented to the *5th European Conference on Law and Psychology*, Budapest: 2 September.

Ainsworth. P.B. (1998) *Psychology, Law and Eyewitness Testimony*, Chichester: Wiley.

Ainsworth, P.B. (2000) 'Psychology and Police Investigation', in J. McGuire, T. Mason and A. O'Kane (eds) *Behaviour, Crime and Legal Processes*, Chichester: Wiley (in press).

Ainsworth, P.B. and Armitage, S.J. (1989) 'Viewing of Videos and Violent Behaviour', paper presented to the *British Psychological Society Conference*, St Andrews, Scotland.

Ainsworth, P.B. and King, E. (1988) 'Witnesses' perception of identification parades', in M.M. Gruneberg, P.E. Morris, and R.N. Sykes (eds) *Practical Aspects of Memory: Current Research and Issues, Vol. 1*, Chichester: Wiley.

Ainsworth, P.B. and May, G. (1996) 'Obtaining information from traumatized witnesses through the Cognitive Interview Technique', paper presented to the *Trauma and Memory International Research Conference*, Durham, New Hampshire, 27 July.

Allen, R.J. and Miller, J.S. (1995) 'The expert as educator: Enhancing the rationality of verdicts in child sexual abuse prosecutions', *Psychology, Public Policy and Law*, 1, 323–38.

Andrews, D.A. (1989) 'Recidivism is predictable and can be influenced: Using risk assessment to reduce recidivism', *Forums on Correction Research*, 1 (2), 11–18.

Andrews, D.A. (1994) *An Overview of Treatment Effectiveness: Research and Clinical Principles*, unpublished paper, Carleton University. Cited in Cullen, F.T. and Applegate, B.K. (1997) (see below).

Andrews, D.A., Zinger, I., Hoge, R.D., Bonta, J., Gendrau, P. and Cullen, F.T. (1990) 'Does Correctional Treatment Work? A clinically relevant and psychologically informed meta-analysis', *Criminology*, 28 (3), 369–404.

Arce, R. (1995) 'Evidence evaluation in jury decision making', in R. Bull and D. Carson (eds) *Handbook of Psychology in Legal Contexts*, Chichester: Wiley.

Arce, R., Farina, F. and Sobral, J. (1995) 'From Juror to Jury Decision Making: A Non-Model Approach', in G. Davies, S. Lloyd-Bostock, M. McMurran and C. Wilson (eds) *Psychology, Law and Criminal Justice: International Developments in Research and Practice*, Berlin: De Gruyter.

Aronson, E. (1988) *The Social Animal* (5th ed.), New York: Freeman.

Asch, S.E. (1956) 'Studies of independence and conformity: a minority of one against a unanimous majority', *Psychological Monographs*, 70, 416.

Ashton, J., Brown, I., Senior, B. and Pease, K. (1998) 'Repeat Victimization: Offender Accounts', *International Journal of Risk, Security and Crime Prevention* (in press).

Ashworth, A. (1992) *Sentencing and Criminal Justice*, London: Weidenfeld & Nicolson.

Ashworth, A. (1997) 'Sentencing', in M. Maguire, R. Morgan and R. Reiner (eds) *The Oxford Handbook of Criminology* (2nd ed.), Oxford: Oxford University Press.

Ashworth, A., Genders, E., Mansfield, G., Peay, J. and Player, E. (1984) *Sentencing in the Crown Court: Report of an Exploratory Study*, Oxford: Centre for Criminological Research, Occasional Paper No. 10.

Ault, R.L. and Reese, J.T. (1980) 'A Psychological Assessment of Crime Profiling', *FBI Law Enforcement Bulletin* 49, 22–5.

Baldwin, J. (1993) 'Police interview techniques: establishing truth or proof', *British Journal of Criminology*, 33, 325–52.

Baldwin, J. and McConville, M. (1979) *Jury Trials*, Oxford: Clarendon Press.

Bandura, A. (1977) *Social Learning Theory*, Englewood Cliffs: Prentice Hall.

Barclay, G.C. (ed.) (1993) *A Digest of Information on the Criminal Justice System in England and Wales*, London: Home Office Research and Statistics Department.

Barclay, G.C. (1995) *Information on the Criminal Justice System in England and Wales*, London: Home Office.

Barr, R. and Pease, K. (1990) 'Crime placement, displacement and deflection', in N. Morris and M. Tonry (eds) *Crime and Justice: A Review of Research* Vol. 12, Chicago Ill: University of Chicago Press.

Barr, R. and Pease, K. (1992) 'A place for every crime and every crime in its place', in D.J. Evans, N.R. Fyfe and D.T. Herbert (eds) *Crime, Policing and Place: Essays in Environmental Criminology*, London: Routledge.

Beck, J.C. (1994) 'Epidemiology of mental disorder and violence: beliefs and research findings', *Harvard Review of Psychiatry*, 2, 1–6.

Belson, W.A. (1975) *Juvenile Theft: The Causal Factors*, New York: Harper Collins & Row.

Belson, W.A. (1979) *Television Violence and the Adolescent Boy*, London: Saxon House.

Bennett, T. (1995) 'Identifying, Explaining and Targeting Burglary Hot Spots', *European Journal of Criminal Policy and Research*, 13, 113–23.

Bennett, T. and Wright, R. (1984) *Burglars on Burglary: Prevention and the Offender*, Aldershot: Gower.

Bisbey, S. and Bisbey, L.B. (1998) *Brief Therapy for Post Traumatic Stress Disorder: Traumatic Incident Reduction and Related Techniques*, Chichester: Wiley.

Blackburn, R. (1975) 'An empirical classification of psychopathic personality', *British Journal of Psychiatry*, 127, 456–60.

Blackburn, R. (1993a) *The Psychology of Criminal Conduct*, Chichester: Wiley.

Blackburn, R. (1993b) 'Clinical programmes with psychopaths', in K. Howells and C.R. Hollin (eds) *Clinical Approaches to the Mentally Disordered Offender*, Chichester: Wiley.

Blackburn, R. (1995a) 'Psychopaths: are they bad or mad?' in N.K. Clark and G.M. Stephenson (eds) *Criminal Behaviour: perceptions, attribution and rationality, Issues in Criminological and Legal Psychology*, 22, Leicester: British Psychological Society.

Blackburn, R. (1995b) 'Violence', in R. Bull and D. Carson (eds) *Handbook of Psychology in Legal Contexts*, Chichester: Wiley.

Blair, R.J.R. (1998) paper presented to the *British Psychological Society London Conference*, December.

Blair, R.J.R., Jones, L., Clark, E., and Smith, M. (1997) 'The psychopathic individual: A lack of responsiveness to distress cues?' *Psychophysiology*, 34, 192–8.

Blau, T.H. (1994) *Psychological Services for Law Enforcement*, New York: Wiley.

Blau, T.H. (1998) *The Psychologist as Expert Witness* (2nd ed.), New York: Wiley.

Bluglass, R. and Bowden, P. (eds) (1990) *Principles and Practice of Forensic Psychiatry*, Edinburgh: Churchill Livingstone.

Blumstein, A. (1997) 'Interaction of Criminological Research and Public Policy', *Journal of Quantitative Criminology*, 12, 349–361.

Bohman, M. (1995) 'Predisposition to criminality; Swedish adoption studies in retrospect', in *Genetics of Criminal and Antisocial Behaviour*, Ciba Foundation Symposium 194, Chichester: Wiley.

Boon, J. and Davies, G. (1993) 'Criminal Profiling', *Policing*, 9 (8), 1–13.

Bothwell, R.K., Brigham, J.C. and Malpass, R.S. (1989) 'Cross-racial identification', *Personality and Social Psychology Bulletin*, 15, 19–25.

Bouchard, T.J., Lykken, D.T., McGue, M., Segal, N.L. and Tellegen, A. (1990) 'Sources of human psychological differences; The Minneapolis study of twins reared apart', *Science*, 250, 223–8.

Bowlby, J. (1953) *Child Care and the Growth of Love*, London: Penguin.

Bowling, B. and Phillips, C. (1999) *Race, Crime and Criminal Justice*, Harlow: Longman.

Brandon, R. and Davies, C. (1973) *Wrongful Imprisonment: Mistaken Convictions and their Consequences*, London: George, Allen & Unwin.

Brantingham, P.J. and Faust, F.L. (1976) 'A conceptual model of crime prevention', *Crime and Delinquency*, 22, 130–46.

Brewer, M.B. (1979) 'Ingroup bias in the minimal intergroup situation: A cognitive motivational analysis', *Psychological Bulletin*, 86, 307–24.

Brigham, J.C. and Cairns, D.L. (1988) 'The effect of mugshot inspections on eyewitness identification accuracy', *Journal of Applied Social Psychology*, 18, 1394–410.

Brigham, J.C. and Pfeiffer, J.E. (1994) 'Evaluating the fairness of line ups', in

D.F. Ross, J.D. Read and M.P. Toglia (eds) *Adult Eyewitness Testimony: Current Trends and Developments*, Cambridge: Cambridge University Press.

Britton, P. (1997) *The Jigsaw Man*, London: Bantam.

Brown, R. (1986) *Social Psychology* (2nd ed.), New York: Free Press.

Brownlee, I. (1998) *Community Punishment: A Critical Introduction*, Harlow: Longman.

Bruce, V. (1988) *Recognising Faces*, Hove: L.E.A.

Brussel, J.A. (1968) *Casebook of a Crime Psychiatrist*, New York: Simon and Schuster.

Bull, R. and McAlpine, S. (1998) 'Facial Appearance and Criminality', in A. Memon, A. Vrij and R. Bull, *Psychology and Law: Truthfulness, Accuracy and Credibility*, Maidenhead: McGraw-Hill.

Burgess, A.W. and Holmstrom, L.L. (1974) *Rape: Victims of Crisis*, Bowie, MD: R.J. Brady Company.

Butler, Lord (1995) *Report of the Committee on Mentally Abnormal Offenders*, Cmnd 6244. London: Home Office.

Calhoun, J.B. (1962) 'Population density and social pathology', *Scientific American*, 206, 139–48.

Cammack, M. (1995) 'In search of the post positivist jury', *Indiana Law Journal*, 70(2), 405–89.

Campbell, C. (1976) 'Portrait of a mass killer', *Psychology Today*, 9, 110–19.

Campbell, J.C. and Lewandowski, L.A. (1997) 'Mental and physical health effects of intimate partner violence on women and children', *Anger, Aggression and Violence*, 20, 353–74.

Canter, D. (1989) 'Offender Profiling', *The Psychologist*, 2, 2–16.

Canter, D. (1994) *Criminal Shadows: Inside the Mind of the Serial Killer*, London: Harper Collins.

Canter, D. (1995) 'Psychology of Offender Profiling', in D. Canter and L.J. Allison (eds) *Criminal Detection and the Psychology of Crime*, London: Ashgate and Dartmore.

Canter, D. and Heritage, R. (1990) 'A multi-variate model of sexual offence behaviour', *Journal of Forensic Psychiatry*, 1 (2), 185–21.

Carroll, J.S. and Payne, J.W. (1977) 'Judgements about crime and the criminal: A model and a method for investigating parole decisions', in B.D. Sales (ed.), *Perspectives in Law and Psychology Vol 1: The Criminal Justice System*, New York: Plenum.

Chance, J.E. and Goldstein, A.G. (1996) 'The other-race effect and eyewitness identification', in S.L. Sporer, R.S. Malpass and G. Kohnken (eds) *Psychological Issues in Eyewitness Identification*, New York: Lawrence Erlbaum.

Christiansen, K.O. (1977) 'A preliminary study of criminality among twins', in S. Mednick and K.O. Christiansen (eds) *Biological Bases of Criminal Behaviour*, New York: Gardner Press.

Clark, S. and Morley, M. (1988) *Murder in Mind*, London: Boxtree.

Clarke, R.V. (1983) 'Situational crime prevention: its theoretical basis and practical scope', in M. Tonry and N. Morris (eds) *Crime and Justice: An Annual Review of Research*, Vol 4, Chicago: University of Chicago Press.

Clarke, R.V. (1991a) 'Deterring obscene phone callers: The New Jersey experience', in R.V. Clarke (ed.), *Situational Crime Prevention: Successful Case Studies*, Albany, NY: Harrow & Heston.

Clarke, R.V. (ed.) (1992) *Situational Crime Prevention: Successful Case Studies*, Albany NY: Harrow & Heston.

Clarke, R.V. (1995) 'Situational crime prevention', in M. Tonry and D.P. Farrington (eds) *Building a Safer Society: Crime and Justice, a Review of Research*, Vol. 19, Chicago: University of Chicago Press.

Clarke, R.V. and Felson, M. (eds) (1993) *Routine Activity and Rational Choice: Advances in Criminological Theory*, London: Transaction.

Clarke, R.V. and Mayhew, P.M. (eds) (1980) *Designing out Crime*, London: HMSO.

Clear, T.R. (1994) *Harm in American Penology: Offenders, Victims and their Communities*, Albany: SUNY Press.

Cleckley, H. (1976) *The Mask of Sanity*, St Louis: Mosby.

Cochrane, R. (1991) 'Racial Prejudice', in R. Cochrane and D. Carroll (eds) *Psychology and Social Issues*, London: Falmer.

Cohen L. and Felson, M. (1979) 'Social change and crime rate trends: A routine activity approach', *American Sociological Review*, 44, 588–608.

Coleman, A. (1985) *Utopia on Trial*, London: Hilary Shipman.

Copson, G. (1995) *Coals to Newcastle? Part 1; A Study of Offender Profiling* (paper 7), London: Police Research Group Special Interest Series, Home Office.

Copson, G., Badcock, R., Boon, J. and Britton, P. (1997) 'Articulating a systematic approach to clinical crime profiling', *Criminal Behaviour and Mental Health*.

Copson, G. and Holloway, K. (1997) 'Offender profiling', paper presented to the Annual Conference of the British Psychological Society's Division of Criminological and Legal Psychology, Cambridge, England.

Cornish, D.B. and Clarke R.V. (eds) (1986) *The Reasoning Criminal: Rational Choice Perspective on Offending*, New York: Springer-Verlag.

Cornish, D.B. and Clarke R.V. (1990) 'Crime specialisation, crime displacement and rational choice', in H. Wegener, F. Losel and J. Haisch (eds) *Criminal Behaviour and the Criminal Justice System: Psychological Perspectives*, New York: Springer Verlag.

Crawford, A (1998) *Crime Prevention and Community Safety: Politics, Policies and Practices*, Harlow: Longman.

Cullen, F.T. and Applegate, B.K. (1997) *Offender Rehabilitation: Effective Correctional Intervention*, Aldershot: Dartmouth.

Cumberbatch, G. (1989) 'Violence and the mass media: the research evidence', in G. Cumberbatch and D. Howitt, *A Measure of Uncertainty: The Effects of the Mass Media*, London: Broadcasting Standards Council/John Libbey.

Cutler, B.L., Berman, G.L., Penrod, S. and Fisher, R.P. (1994) 'Conceptual, practical and empirical issues associated with eyewitness identification test media', in D.F. Ross, J. D. Read and M.P. Toglia (eds) *Adult Eyewitness Testimony: Current Trends and Developments*, Cambridge: Cambridge University Press.

Cutler, B.L. and Penrod., S.D. (1995) *Mistaken Identification: The Eyewitness, Psychology and the Law*, Cambridge: Cambridge University Press.

Daly, K. (1987) 'Structure and Practise of familial-based justice in a criminal court', *Law and Society Review*, 27, 267–90.

Davies, A. and Dale, A. (1995) *Locating the Stranger Rapist*, Police Research Group Special Interest Paper 3.

Davies, G.M., Stevenson-Robb, Y. and Flin, R. (1988) 'Tales out of school: Children's memory for an unexpected incident', in M.M. Gruneberg, P.E. Morris, and R.N. Sykes (eds) *Practical Aspects of Memory: Current Research and Issues*, Vol. 1, Chichester: Wiley.

Davis, J.H. (1980) 'Group decision and procedural justice', in M. Fishbein (ed.) *Progress in Social Psychology*, Hillsdale NJ: Erlbaum.

Davis, R.C. and Friedman, L.N. (1985) 'The emotional aftermath of crime and violence', in C.R. Figley (ed.) *Trauma and its Wake: The Study and Treatment of Post Traumatic Stress Disorder*, New York: Bruner/Mazel.

Devons, E. (1978) 'Serving as a juryman in Britain', in J. Baldwin and A.K. Bottomley, *Criminal Justice: Selected Readings*.

Ditton, J., Farrall, S., Bannister, J., Gilchrist, E. and Pease, K. (1999) 'Why has anger been ignored?' paper awaiting submission.

Dobash, R.E. and Dobash, R.P. (1979) *Violence against Wives: a Case against Patriarchy*, New York: Free Press.

Dobash, R.E. and Dobash, R.P. (1992) *Women, Violence and Social Change*, London: Routledge.

Dobash, R.P. and Dobash, R.E. (1999) 'Criminal Justice Programmes for Men Who Assault Their Partners', in C.R. Hollin (ed.), *Handbook of Offender Assessment and Treatment*, Chichester: Wiley.

Dobash, R.P., Dobash, R.E., Cavanagh, K. and Lewis, R. (1999) 'A research evaluation of British programmes for violent men', *Journal of Social Policy*, April (in press).

Dobash, R.E., Dobash, R.P. and Noaks, L. (eds) (1995) *Gender and Crime*, Cardiff: University of Wales Press.

Dryden, W. and Gordon, J. (1990) *Think Your Way to Happiness*, London: Sheldon Press.

Duncan, B.L. (1976) 'Different social perceptions and attribution of intergroup violence: testing the lower limits of stereotyping of blacks', *Journal of Personality and Social Psychology*, 34, 590–8.

Dunstan, S., Paulin, J. and Atkinson, K.A. (1995) *Trial by Peers? The Composition of New Zealand Juries*, Wellington, New Zealand: Department of Justice.

Ekblom, P. (1995) 'Less crime by design', *The Annals*, 539, 114–29.

Ekman, P. and O'Sullivan, M. (1989) 'Hazards in detecting deceit', in D.C. Raskin (ed.) *Psychological Methods in Criminal Investigation and Evidence*, New York: Springer.

Ellingworth, D., Tseloni, A. and Pease, K. (1997) 'Prior victimization and crime risk', *International Journal of Risk, Security and Crime*, 2, 201–14.

Ellis, H.D., Shepherd, J.W., Shepherd, Flin, R. and Davies, G. (1989) 'Identification from a computer-driven retrieval system compared with a traditional mugshot album search: A new tool for police investigations', *Ergonomics*, 32, 167–77.

Ellsworth, P.C. (1993) 'Some steps between attitudes and verdicts', in R. Hastie (ed.) *Inside the Juror: The Psychology of Juror Decision Making*, New York: Cambridge University Press.

Ewart, B. and Pennington, D.C. (1987) 'An attributional approach to explaining sentencing disparity', in D. Pennington and S. Lloyd-Bostock (eds) *The Psychology of Sentencing*, Oxford: The Centre for Socio-Legal Studies, University of Oxford.

Eysenck, H.J. (1970) *The Structure of Human Personality*, London: Methuen.

Eysenck, H.J. (1977) *Crime and Personality* (3rd ed.) London: RKP.

Eysenck, H.J. and Gudjonsson, G.H. (1989) *The Causes and Cures of Criminality*, New York: Plenum Press.

Eysenck, S.B.G. and Eysenck, H.J. (1971) 'Crime and personality: item analysis of questionnaire responses', *British Journal of Criminology*, 11, 49–62.

Eysenck, S.B.G. and McGurk, B.J. (1980) 'Impulsiveness and venturesomeness in a detention centre population', *Psychological Reports*, 47, 1299–306.

Fagan, J.A. (1990) 'Treatment and reintegration of violent juvenile offenders: Experimental results', *Justice Quarterly*, 7, 233–63.

Falkin, G.P., Prendergast, M. and Anglin, M.D. (1994) 'Drug treatment in the criminal justice system', *Federal Probation*, 58, September, 31–6.

Farrell, G. (1995) 'Predicting and Preventing Revictimization', in M. Tonry and D.P. Farrington (eds) *Building a Safer Society: Crime and Justice*, 19, Chicago: University of Chicago Press.

Farrell, G. and Pease, K. (1993) *Once Bitten, Twice Bitten: Repeat Victimization and its Implications for Crime Prevention*, Crime Prevention Unit Paper 46, London: Home Office.

Farrington, D.P. (1991) 'Anti-social personality from childhood to adulthood', *The Psychologist*, 4, 389–94.

Farrington, D.P. (1997) 'Human development and criminal careers', in M. Maguire, R. Morgan and R. Reiner (eds) *The Oxford Handbook of Criminology* (2nd ed.), Oxford: Oxford University Press.

Farrington, D.P. and Lambert, S. (1997) 'Predicting offender profiles from victim and witness descriptions', in J.L. Jackson and D. A. Bekerian (eds) *Offender Profiling: Theory, Research and Practice*, Chichester: Wiley.

Farrington, D.P. and Morris, A. (1983) 'Sex, sentencing and reconviction', *British Journal of Criminology*, 23, 229–48.

Farrington, D.P. and Nuttall, C.P. (1980) 'Prison size, overcrowding, prison violence and recidivism', *Journal of Criminal Justice*, 8, 221–31.

Feldman, P. (1993) *The Psychology of Crime*, Cambridge: Cambridge University Press.

Felson, M. (1993) *Crime and Everyday Life*, London: Pine Forge.

Felson, M. (1995) 'Those who discourage crime', *Crime Prevention Studies*, 4, 53–66.

Fitzmaurice, C. and Pease, K. (1986) *The Psychology of Judicial Sentencing*, Manchester: Manchester University Press.

Fitzmaurice, C., Rogers, D. and Stanley, P. (1995) 'Predicting Court Sentences: A Perilous Exercise', in G. Davies, S. Lloyd-Bostock, M. McMurran and C. Wilson (eds) *Psychology, Law and Criminal Justice: International Developments in Research and Practice*, Berlin: De Gruyter.

Fontaine, G. and Emily, C. (1978) 'Causal attribution and judicial discretion: a look at the verbal behaviour of municipal court judges', *Law and Human Behavior*, 2, 323–7.

Forrester, D., Frenz, S., O'Connor, M. and Pease, K. (1990) *The Kirkholt Burglary Prevention Project Phase II*, Crime Prevention Unit Paper 23, London: Home Office.

Franzini, L.R. and Grossberg, J.M. (1995) *Eccentric and Bizarre Behaviors*, New York: Wiley.

Gale, A. (ed.) (1988) *The Polygraph Test: Lies, Truth and Science*, London: Sage.

Galle, O.R., Grove, W.R. and McPherson, J.M. (1972) 'Population density and pathology: What are the relations for man?', *Science*, 7 April, 23–30.

Garberth, V.J. (1983) *Practical Homicide Investigation*, New York: Elsevier.

Garland, D. (1985) 'The criminal and his science', *British Journal of Criminology*, 25, 109–37.

Garland, D. (1996) 'The limits of the sovereign state: Strategies of crime control in contemporary society', *British Journal of Criminology*, 36, 445–71.

Garland, D. (1997) 'Of crimes and criminals: The development of Criminology in Britain', in M. Maguire, R. Morgan and R. Reiner (eds) *The Oxford Handbook of Criminology* (2nd ed.), Oxford: Oxford University Press.

Geen, R.G. (1998) *Human Aggression* (2nd ed.), Milton Keynes: Open University Press.

Genn, H. (1988) 'Multiple victimization', in M. Maguire and J. Pointing (eds) *Victims of Crime: A New Deal?*, Milton Keynes: Open University Press.

Gerbner, G., Gross, L., Eley, M.E., Jackson-Beeke, M., Jeffries-Fox, S. and Signorielli, N. (1977) 'Television violence profile No. 8', *Journal of Communication*, 27, 171–80.

Gerbner, G., Gross, L., Morgan, M. and Signorielli, N. (1980) 'The mainstream of America: violence profile No. 11', *Journal of Communication*, 30(3), 10–29.

Gerbode, F. (1993) *The Traumatic Incident Reduction Course* (3rd ed.), California: IRM Press.

Gill, M. and Pease, K. (1998) 'Repeat Robbers: How are they Different?', in M. Gill (ed.) *Crime at Work: Studies in Security and Crime Prevention*, Leicester: Perpetuity Press.

Glueck, S. and Glueck, E.T. (1956) *Physique and Delinquency*, New York: Dodd Meade.

Goldblatt, P. and Lewis, C. (1998) *Reducing Offending: An Assessment of Research Evidence on Ways of Dealing with Offending Behaviour*, Research Study No. 187, London: Home Office Research and Statistics Directorate.

Gostin, L. (1986) *Mental Health Services – Law and Practice*, London: Shaw and Sons.

Gottfredson, M.R. (1979) 'Treatment Destruction Techniques', *Journal of Research in Crime and Delinquency*, 16, 39–54.

Griew, E. (1986) 'Reducing murder to manslaughter: Whose job?', *Journal of Medical Ethics*, 12, 18–23.

Griffiths, M. (1993) 'Are computer games bad for children?', *The Psychologist*, September 401–7.

Groth, A.N., Burgess, A.W. and Holmstrom, L.L. (1977) 'Rape, Power, Anger and Sexuality', *American Journal of Psychiatry*, 134, 1239–48.

Gudjonsson, G.H. (1989) 'Compliance in an interrogation situation: A new scale', *Personality and Individual Differences*, 10, 535–40.

Gudjonsson, G.H. (1992) *The Psychology of Interrogations, Confessions and Testimony*, Chichester: Wiley.

Gudjonsson, G.H., Clare, I., Rutter, S. and Pearse, J. (1993) *Persons at Risk During Interview in Police Custody: The Identification of Vulnerabilities*, RCCJ Research Study No. 12.

Gudjonsson, G.H. and Copson, C. (1997) 'The role of the expert in criminal investigation', in J.L. Jackson and D.A. Bekerian (eds) *Offender Profiling: Theory, Research and Practice*, Chichester: Wiley.

Gunter, B. (1987) *Television and the Fear of Crime*, London: John Libbey.

Halgin, R.P. and Whitbourne, S.K. (1993) *Abnormal Psychology: The Human Experience of Psychological Disorders*, Fort Worth TX: Harcourt Brace Jovanovich Inc.

Hall, S., Crilcher, C., Jefferson, T., Clarke, J. and Roberts, B. (1978) *Policing the Crisis: Mugging, the State and Law and Order*, London: Macmillan.

Hans, V.P. (1992) 'Jury decision making', in D.K. Kagehiro and W.S. Laufer (eds) *Handbook of Psychology and Law*, New York: Springer.

Hare, R.D. (1991) *The Hare Psychopathy Checklist* (revised), Toronto: Multi Health Systems.

Hare, R.D. (1996) 'Psychopathy: A clinical construct whose time has come', *Criminal Justice and Behavior*, 23, 25–54.

Hare, R.D. (1998) 'The Hare PCL-R: Some issues concerning its use and misuse', *Legal and Criminological Psychology*, 3, 99–119.

Hare, R.D., Strachan, C.E. and Forth, A.E. (1993) 'Psychopathy and Crime: A Review', in K. Howells and C. R. Hollin (eds) *Clinical Approaches to the Mentally Disordered Offender*, Chichester: Wiley.

Harrower, J. (1998) *Applying Psychology to Crime*, London: Hodder and Stoughton.

Hart, S.D. (1998) 'The role of psychopathy in assessing risk from violence: Conceptual and methodological issues', *Legal and Criminological Psychology*, 3, 121–137.

Hastie, R. (ed.) (1993) *Inside the Juror: The Psychology of Juror Decision Making*, New York: Cambridge University Press.

Hastie, R., Penrod, S. and Pennington, N. (1983) *Inside the Jury*, Cambridge MA: Harvard University Press.

Hazelwood, R.R. (1983) 'The behavior-oriented interview of rape victims; The key to profiling', *FBI Law Enforcement Bulletin*, 52.

Hazelwood, R.R. (1987) 'Analyzing the Rape and Profiling the Offender', in R.R. Hazelwood and A.W. Burgess (eds) *Practical Aspects of Rape Investigation: A Multidisciplinary Approach*.

Hazelwood, R.R. and Burgess, A.W. (1987) *Practical Aspects of Rape Investigation: A Multidisciplinary Approach*, New York: Elsevier.

Hazelwood, R.R. and Douglas, J.E. (1980) 'The Last Murderer', *FBI Law Enforcement Bulletin*, April, 1–5.

Hazelwood, R.R. and Warren, J. (1989) 'The Serial Rapist', *FBI Law Enforcement Bulletin*, February, 1989.

Heal, K. and Laycock, G. (eds) (1986) *Situational Crime Prevention: From Theory into Practice*, London: HMSO.

Hebenton, W. and Pease, K. (1995) 'Weighing the pound of flesh: The psychology of punishment', in R. Bull and D. Carson (eds) *Handbook of Psychology in Legal Contexts*, Chichester: Wiley.

Hedderman, C. and Sugg, D. (1997) *The Influence of Cognitive Approaches: A Survey of Probation Programmes*, HORS No. 171, London: Home Office.

Heidensohn, F. (1997) 'Gender and Crime', in M. Maguire, R. Morgan and R. Reiner (eds) *The Oxford Handbook of Criminology* (2nd ed.), Oxford: Oxford University Press.

Heider, F. (1958) *The Psychology of Interpersonal Relations*, New York: Wiley.

Hemphill, J.F., Hare, R.D. and Wong, S. (1998) 'Psychopathy and recidivism: A review', *Legal and Criminological Psychology*, 3, 139–170.

Henning, T. (1995) 'Psychological explanations in sentencing women in Tasmania', *Australian and New Zealand Journal of Criminology*, 28, 298–322.

Hess, A.K. and Weiner, I.B. (eds) (1999) *The Handbook of Forensic Psychology* (2nd ed.), New York: Wiley.

Hesseling, R.B.P. (1994) 'Displacement: A review of the empirical literature', in R.V. Clarke (ed.), *Crime Prevention Studies 2*, Monsey NY: Willow Tree Press.

Hindelang, M.J., Gottfredson, M.R. and Garofalo, J. (1978) *Victims of Personal Crime: An Empirical Foundation for a Theory of Personal Victimization*, Cambridge Mass: Balinger.

Hodge, J.E., McMurran, M. and Hollin, C.R. (1997) *Addicted to Crime?*, Chichester: Wiley.

Hoggett, B. (1996) *Mental Health Law* (4th ed.), London: Sweet and Maxwell.

Hollin, C.R. (1989) *Psychology and Crime: An Introduction to Criminological Psychology*, London: Routledge.

Hollin, C.R. (1995) 'The meaning and implications of programme integrity', in J. Maguire (ed.), *What works? Effective Methods to Reduce Reoffending*, Chichester: Wiley.

Hollin, C.R. (ed.), (1999) *Handbook of Offender Assessment and Treatment*, Chichester: Wiley.

Holmes, T.H. and Rahe, R.H. (1967) 'The social readjustment rating scale', *Journal of Psychosomatic Research*, 11, 213–18.

Home Office (1989a) *Report of the Working Group on the Fear of Crime*, Standing Conference on Crime Prevention, London: Home Office.

Home Office (1989b) *The Ethnic Group of Those Proceeded Against or Sentenced by the Courts in the Metropolitan Police District in 1984 and 1985*, Home Office Statistical Bulletin, 6.89, London: Home Office.

Home Office (1994) *Criminal Statistics*, London: Home Office.

Home Office (1998) *Criminal Statistics, England and Wales 1997* (Cmnd 4162) London: Home Office.

Home Office/DHSS (1987) *Report of the Interdepartmental Working Group of Home Office and DHSS Officials on Mentally Disturbed Offenders in the Prison System*, London: Home Office/Department of Health and Social Security.

Hood, R. (1992) *Race and Sentencing*, Oxford: Clarendon Press.

Horn, J. (1988) 'Criminal personality profiling', in J. Reese and J. Horn (eds) *Police Psychology: Operational Assistance*, Washington DC: US Government Printing Office.

Horne, C.J. (1996) 'The case for: CCTV should be introduced', *International Journal of Risk, Security and Crime Prevention*, 1, 317–26.

Hough, M. (1996) 'The police patrol function: what research can tell us', in W. Saulsbury, J. Mott and T. Newburn (eds) *Themes in Contemporary Policing*, London: PSI/Police Foundation.

Hough, M. and Mayhew, P. (1983) *The British Crime Survey: First Report*, London: HMSO.

Hough, M., Clarke, R.V. and Mayhew, P. (1980) 'Introduction', in R.V. Clarke and P. Mayhew (eds) *Designing Out Crime*, London: HMSO.

Hough, M. and Tilley, N. (1998) *Getting the Grease to the Squeak: Research Lessons for Crime Prevention*, Crime Detection and Prevention Series Paper 85, London: Home Office.

House, J.C. (1997) 'Towards a practical application of offender profiling: the RNC's criminal suspect prioritization system', in J.L Jackson and D.A. Bekerian (eds) *Offender Profiling: Theory, Research and Practice*, Chichester: Wiley.

Howard, J.A. (1984) 'Societal influences on attribution: Blaming some victims more than others', *Journal of Personality and Social Psychology*, 47, 270–81.

Howitt, D. (1998) *Crime, the Media and the Law*, Chichester: Wiley.

Huff, C.R. (1987) 'Wrongful convictions: societal tolerance of injustice', *Research in Social Problems*, 4, 99–115.

Inbau, F.E., Reid, J.E. and Buckley, J.P. (1986) *Criminal Interrogations and Confessions*, Baltimore MD: Williams & Wilkins.

Irving, B.L. and Hilgendorf, L. (1980) *Police Interrogation: The Psychological Approach*, Research Study No. 1, Royal Commission on Criminal Procedure, London: HMSO.

Irving, B.L. and McKenzie, I.K. (1989) *Police Interrogation: The Effects of the Police and Criminal Evidence Act, 1984*, London: The Police Foundation.

Ito, K. (1993) 'Research on the fear of crime; perceptions and realities of crime in Japan', *Crime and Delinquency*, 29, 385–92.

Jackson, J.L. and Bekerian, D.A. (eds) (1997) *Offender Profiling: Theory, Research and Practice*, Chichester: Wiley.

Jackson, J.L., van den Eshof, P. and De Kleuver, E.E. (1997) 'A research approach to offender profiling', in J.L. Jackson and D.A. Bekerian (eds) *Offender Profiling: Theory, Research and Practice*, Chichester: Wiley.

Jacobs, F.G. (1971) *Criminal Responsibility*, London: Weidenfeld & Nicolson.

Jacobs, J. (1961) *The Death and Life of Great American Cities*, New York: Vintage.

Jaffe, P.D. (1998) 'Necrophilia: Love at last sight', in J. Baros, I. Munnich and M. Szegedi (eds) *Psychology and Criminal Justice: International Review of Theory and Practice*, Berlin: Walter de Gruyter.

Jarvik, L.F., Klodin, V. and Matsyama, S.S. (1973) 'Human aggression and the extra Y Chromosome', *American Psychologist*, 28, 674–82.

Jeffrey, C.R. (1971) *Crime Prevention Through Environmental Design*, California: Sage.

Jones, B. (1992) *Voice From an Evil God*, London: Blake.

Jones, E.E. and Nisbett, R.E. (1972) 'The actor and the observer: Divergent perceptions of the causes of behaviour', in E.E. Jones, D.E. Kanouse, H.H. Kelly, S. Valins and B. Weiner (eds) *Attribution: Perceiving the Causes of Behaviour*, Morristown NJ: General Learning Press.

Joseph, S., Williams, R. and Yule, W. (1997) *Understanding Post-Traumatic Stress: A Psychosocial Perspective on PTSD and Treatment*, Chichester: Wiley.

Kadane, J.B. (1993) 'Sausages and the law: Juror decisions in the much larger justice system', in R. Hastie (ed.), *Inside the Juror*, Cambridge: Cambridge University Press.

Kagehiro, D.K. (1990) 'Defining the standard of proof in jury instructions', *Psychological Science*, 1 (3), 194–200.

Kahn, A. (1984) *Victims of Violence: Final Report of APA Task Force on the Victims of Crime and Violence*, Washington: American Psychological Association.

Kalven, H. and Zeisel, H. (1966) *The American Jury*, Boston: Little Brown.

Kapardis, A. (1985) *Sentencing by English Magistrates as a Human Process*, Nicosia, Cyprus: Asselia Press.

Kapardis, A. (1997) *Psychology and Law: A Critical Introduction*, Cambridge: Cambridge University Press.

Kassin, S.M., Ellsworth, P.C. and Smith, V.L. (1989) 'The "general acceptance" of psychological research on eyewitness testimony: A survey of experts', *American Psychologist*, 44, 1089–98.

Kendall, P.C. and Hammern, C. (1995) *Abnormal Psychology*, Boston: Houghton-Mifflin.

Kennedy, H. (1992) *Eve was Framed*, London: Chatto & Windus.

Kennedy, L. (1986) 'Foreword', in N. Fellows (ed.) *Killing Time*, Oxford: Lion.

Kerby, J. and Rae, J. (1998) 'Moral identity in action: Young offenders' reports of encounters with the police', *British Journal of Social Psychology*, 37, 439–56.

Kerr, N.L. (1978) 'Beautiful and blameless: The effects of victim attractiveness and responsibility on mock jurors' verdicts', *Journal of Personality and Social Psychology*, 4, 479–82.

Kidd, R.F. (1985) 'Impulsive bystanders: Why do they intervene?', in D.P. Farrington and J. Gunn (eds) *Reactions to Crime: The Public, the Police, Courts and Prisons*, Chichester: Wiley.

Kiesler, C.A. and Kiesler, S.B. (1969) *Conformity*, Reading MA: Addison Wesley.

Kilpatrick, D.G., Saunders, B.E., Veronen, L.J., Best, C.L. and Von, J.M. (1987) 'Criminal victimization: Lifetime prevalence reporting to police and psychological impact', *Crime and Delinquency*, 33, 479–89.

King, R.D. and Morgan, R. (1980) *The Future of the Prison System*, Aldershot: Gower.

Koch, B. (1996) *National Crime Prevention Policy in England and Wales, 1979–1995*, unpublished D.Phil thesis, Cambridge: Institute of Criminology, cited in Pease, K. (1997) (see below).

Kohnken, G. (1996) 'Social Psychology and the Law', in G.R. Semin and K. Fiedler (eds) *Applied Social Psychology*, London: Sage.

Kranz, H. (1936) *Lelenschicksale Kriminiller*, Berlin: Springer Verlag.

Lange, J.S. (1931) *Crime as Destiny*, London: Allen & Unwin.

Latané, B. and Darley, J.M. (1968) 'Group inhibition of bystander intervention in emergencies', *Journal of Personality and Social Psychology*, 10, 215–21.

Lerner, M.J. (1970) 'The desire for justice and reactions to victims', in J. Macauley and L. Berkowitz (eds) *Altruism and Helping Behaviour*, Orlando FL: Academic Press.

Lerner, M.J. and Meindl, J.R. (1981) 'Justice and Altruism', in J.P. Rushton and R.M. Sorrentino (eds) *Altruism and Helping Behavior*, Hillsdale NJ: Erlbaum.

Levey, S. and Howells, K. (1994) *Journal of Community and Applied Psychology*, 4, 313–28, cited in Howitt, D. (1998) above.

Lewin, K. (1943) 'Defining the field at a given time', *Psychological Review*, 50, 292–310.

Lindsay, R.C.L. (1994) 'Biased line-ups: where do they come from?', in Ross, D.F., Read, J.D. and Toglia, M.P. (eds) *Adult Eyewitness Testimony: Current Trends and Developments*, Cambridge: Cambridge University Press.

Lion, J.R. (1978) 'Outpatient treatment is psychopaths', in W.H. Reid (ed.) *The Psychopath: A Comprehensive Study of Antisocial Disorders and Behaviors*, New York: Brunner/Mazel.

Lipsey, J.W. (1992) 'Juvenile delinquency treatment: A meta-analytical enquiry into the variability of effects', in T. Cook (ed.), *Meta-analysis for Explanation: A Casebook*, New York: Russel Sage Foundation.

Lipsey, M.W. and Wilson, D.B. (1997) 'Effective intervention for serious juvenile offenders: A synthesis of research', paper prepared for the OJJDP study group on serious and violent juvenile offenders, cited in F.T. Cullen and B.K. Applegate, *Offender Rehabilitation* (see above).

Litwack, T.R. and Schlessinger, L.B. (1999) 'Dangerousness risk assessment: research, legal and clinical considerations', in A.K. Hess and I.B. Weiner (eds) *The Handbook of Forensic Psychology* (2nd ed.), New York: Wiley.

Lloyd, C., Mair, G. and Hough, M. (1994) *Explaining Reconviction Rates: A Critical Analysis*, Home Office Research Study No. 136, London: HMSO.

Loftus, E.F. (1979) *Eyewitness Testimony*, Cambridge, Mass: Harvard University Press.

Logan, C.H. and Gaes, G.C. (1993) 'Meta-analysis and the rehabilitation of punishment', *Justice Quarterly*, 10(2), 245–63.

Lombroso, C. (1876) *L'Uomo Delinquente*, Turin: Fratelli Bocca.

Lupfer, M.B., Doan, K. and Houston, D.A. (1998) 'Explaining unfair and fair outcomes: The therapeutic value of attributional analysis', *British Journal of Social Psychology*, 37 (4), 495–512.

MacHovec, F.J. (1989) *Interview and Interrogation: A Scientific Approach*, Springfield Il: Charles C Thomas.

Maguire, M. (1997) 'Crime statistics, patterns and trends: Changing perspectives and their implications', in M. Maguire, R. Morgan and R. Reiner (eds) *The Oxford Handbook of Criminology* (2nd ed.), Oxford: Oxford University Press.

Marshall, W.L. (1989) 'Intimacy, Loneliness and Sexual Offenders', *Behavioural Research in Therapy*, 27 (5), 491–503.

Martinson, R. (1974) 'What works? – Questions and answers about prison reform', *The Public Interest*, 35, 22–54.

Martinson, R. (1979) 'New findings, new views: A note of caution regarding sentencing reform', *Hofstra Law Review*, 7, 243–58.

Maslow, A. (1954) *Motivation and Personality*, New York: Harper.

Mawby, R.I. (1977) 'Defensible Space: A Theoretical and Empirical Appraisal', *Urban Studies*, 14, 169–80.

May Committee (1979) *Report of the Committee of Inquiry into the United Kingdom Prison Services*, Cmnd 7673, London: HMSO.

Mayhew, P. (1979) 'Defensible space: the current status of a crime prevention theory', *Howard Journal*, 18, 150–9.

Mayhew, P., Clarke, R.V., Sturman, A. and Hough J.M. (1976) *Crime as Opportunity*, Home Office Research Study No 34, London: HMSO.

Mayhew, P., Mirrlees-Black, C. and Muang, N.A. (1994) *Trends in Crime: Findings from the 1994 British Crime Survey*, London: HMSO.

McConville, M. and Hodgson, A. (1993) 'Custodial legal advice and the right to silence', *Royal Commission on Criminal Justice Research, Research Study No. 16*, London: HMSO.

McCord, J. (1999) 'Interventions, punishment, diversion, and alternative routes to crime prevention', in A.K. Hess and I.B. Weiner (eds) *The Handbook of Forensic Psychology* (2nd ed.), New York: Wiley.

McGuire, J. (ed.) (1995) *What Works: Reducing Reoffending*, Chichester: Wiley.

McGuire, J. and Priestley, P. (1995) 'Reviewing what works: Past, present and future', in J. McGuire (ed.), *What Works: Reducing Reoffending*, Chichester: Wiley.

Mednick, S.A., Moffitt, T.E. and Stack, S.A. (eds) (1987) *The Causes of Crime: New Biological Approaches*, Cambridge: Cambridge University Press.

Merry, S.E. (1981) 'Defensible space undefended', *Urban Affairs Quarterly*, 16(4), 397–422.

Michon, J.A. and Pakes, F.J. (1995) 'Judicial decision-making: A theoretical perspective', in R. Bull and D. Carson (eds) *Handbook of Psychology in Legal Contexts*, Chichester: Wiley.

Milgram, S. (1976) 'Psychological Maps of Paris', in H.H. Proshansky *et al.* (eds)

Environmental Psychology: People and Their Physical Settings, New York: Holt Rinehart & Winston.

Mirrlees-Black, C. (1998) *Rural Areas and Crime: Findings from the British Crime Survey*, Home Office Research and Statistics Directorate Research Findings No. 77, London: Home Office.

Mirrlees-Black, C., Budd, T., Partridge, S. and Mayhew, P. (1998) *The 1998 British Crime Survey, England and Wales*, Home Office Statistical Bulletin 21/98, London: Home Office.

Mirrlees-Black, C., Mayhew, P. and Percy, A. (1996) *The 1996 British Crime Survey, England and Wales*, Home Office Statistical Bulletin 19/96, London: Home Office.

Mirrlees-Black, C. and Ross, A. (1995) *Crime Prevention against Retail and Manufacturing Premises: Findings from the 1994 Commercial Victimization Survey*, Research Study 146, London: Home Office RSD.

Monahan, J. (1992) 'Mental disorder and violent behaviour', *American Psychologist*, 17, 511.

Monahan, J. (1997) 'Clinical and Actuarial Measures of Violence', in D. Faigman, D. Kaye, M. Saks and J. Flanders (eds) *West's Companion to Scientific Evidence*, St Paul MI: West Publishing Company.

Monahan, J. and Steadman, H.J. (eds) (1994) *Mental Disorder: Developments in Risk Assessment*, Chicago: University of Chicago Press.

Moos, R.H. (1976) *The Human Context: Environmental Determinants of Behavior*, New York: Wiley.

Morgan, R. (1997) 'Imprisonment: Current concerns', in M. Maguire, R. Morgan and R. Reiner (eds) *The Oxford Handbook of Criminology* (2nd ed.), Oxford: Oxford University Press.

Moston, S. (1990) 'The ever so gentle art of police interrogation', paper presented to the *British Psychological Society Annual Conference*, Swansea University, 5 April.

Moston, S. (1995) 'From denial to admission in police questioning of suspects', in G. Davies, S. Lloyd-Bostock, M. McMurran and C. Wilson (eds) *Psychology, Law and Criminal Justice: International Developments in Research and Practice*, Berlin: Walter de Gruyter.

Moston, S., Stephenson, G.M. and Williamson, T.M. (1992) 'The effects of case characteristics on suspect behaviour during police questioning', *British Journal of Criminology*, 32, 23–40.

Murray, D.J. (1989) *Review of research on Re-offending of Mentally Disordered Offenders*, Research and Planning Unit Paper 55, London: Home Office.

Newburn, T. (1997) 'Youth, Crime and Justice', in M. Maguire, R. Morgan and R. Reiner (eds) *The Oxford Handbook of Criminology* (2nd ed.), Oxford: Oxford University Press.

Newman, O. (1972) *Defensible Space: People and Design in the Violent City*, London: Architectural Press.

Newman, O. (1976) *Design Guidelines for Achieving Defensible Space*, National Institute of Law Enforcement and Criminal Justice, Washington DC: Government Printing Office.

Nicholson, R.A. and Krugler, K.E. (1991) 'Competent and incompetent criminal defendants: A quantitative review of comparative research', *Psychological Bulletin*, 109, 355–70.

Nicolson, P. (1994) *The Experience of Being Burgled: A Psychological Study of Domestic Burglary on Victims*, Sheffield: Sheffield University.

Nietzel, M.T. (1979) *Crime and its Modification: A Social Learning Perspective*, New York: Pergamon.

North, C.S., Smith, E.M. and Spitznagel, E.L. (1994) 'Post-traumatic stress disorder in survivors of a mass shooting', *American Journal of Psychiatry*, 151, 82–8.

Novaco, R.W. (1975) *Anger Control: The Development and Evaluation of an Experimental Treatment*, Lexington: D.C. Heath.

Ofshe, R. (1989) 'Coerced confessions: the logic of seemingly irrational action', *Cultic Studies Journal*, 6, 1–15.

Oleson, J.C. (1996) 'Psychological profiling; Does it actually work?', *Forensic Update*, 46, 11–14.

Orne, M. (1984) 'Hypnotically Induced Testimony', in Wells, G.L. and Loftus, E.F. (eds) *Eyewitness Testimony: Psychological Perspectives*, New York: Cambridge University Press.

Osborn, S.G. and West, D.J. (1979) 'Conviction records of fathers and sons compared', *British Journal of Criminology*, 19, 120–33.

Osner, N., Quinn, A. and Crown, G. (eds) (1993) *Criminal Justice Systems in Other Jurisdictions*, London: HMSO.

Oswald, M.E. (1992) 'Justification and goals of punishment and the attribution of responsibility in judges', in F. Losel, D. Bender and T. Bleisener, *Psychology and Law: International Perspectives*, New York: Walter de Gruyter.

Owens, R. G. (1995) 'Legal and Psychological Concepts of Mental Status', in R. Bull and D. Carson (eds) *Handbook of Psychology in Legal Contexts*, Chichester: Wiley.

Oxford, T. (1991) 'Spotting a Liar', *Police Review*, 328–9.

Palmer, C. and Hart, M. (1996) *A PACE in the right direction?*, Institute for the Study of the Legal Profession, Faculty of Law, University of Sheffield.

Patrick, C.J., Bradley, M.M. and Lang, P.J. (1993) 'Emotion in the criminal psychopath: Startle reflex modulation', *Journal of Abnormal Psychology*, 102, 82–92.

Patrick, C.J., Cuthbert, B.N. and Lang, P.J. (1994) 'Emotion in the criminal psychopath: Fear image processing', *Journal of Abnormal Psychology*, 103, 523–34.

Pearse, J. and Gudjonsson, G.H. (1996) 'Police interviewing techniques at two south London police stations', *Psychology, Crime and Law*, 3, 63–74.

Pease, K. (1996) *Repeat Victimization and Policing*, unpublished manuscript: University of Huddersfield.

Pease, K. (1997) 'Crime Prevention', in M. Maguire, R. Morgan and R. Reiner (eds) *The Oxford Handbook of Criminology* (2nd ed.), Oxford: Oxford University Press.

Pease, K. (1998a) *Repeat Victimization: Taking Stock*, Crime Prevention and Detection Series Paper 90, London: Home Office Police Research Group.

Pease, K. (1998b) 'Changing the context of crime prevention', in P. Goldblatt and C. Lewis (eds) *Reducing Offending: An Assessment of Research Evidence on Ways of Dealing with Offending Behaviour*, Home Office Research Study 187, London: Home Office Research and Statistics Directorate.

Pease, K. (1999) 'The Probation Career of Al Truism', *The Howard Journal*, 38(1), 2–16.

Peay, J. (1997) 'Mentally Disordered Offenders', in M. Maguire, R. Morgan and R. Reiner (eds) *The Oxford Handbook of Criminology* (2nd ed.), Oxford: Oxford University Press.

Pence, E. and Paymar, M. (1993) *Education Groups for Men Who Batter*, New York: Springer.

Pennington, N. and Hastie, R. (1990) 'Practical implications of psychological research on juror and jury decision making', *Personality and Social Psychology Bulletin*, 16(1), 90–105.

Petley, J. and Barker, M. (1997) *Ill Effects: The Media/Violence Debate*, London, Routledge.

Philo, G. (ed.) (1996) *Media and Mental Distress*, Harlow: Longman.

Pitts, J. (1992) 'The end of an era', *Howard Journal of Criminal Justice*, 31, 133–48.

Polvi, N., Looman, T., Humphries, C. and Pease, K. (1991) 'The Time Course of Repeat Burglary Victimization', *British Journal of Criminology*, 31 (4), 411–14.

Porteus, J. (1977) *Environment and Behavior*, Reading MA: Addison Wesley.

Povey, D. and Prime, J. (1998) *Notifiable Offences England and Wales April 1997 to March 1998*, Home Office Statistical Bulletin 22/98, London: Home Office.

Power, A. (1989) 'Housing, community and crime', in D. Downes (ed.) *Crime and the City*, Basingstoke: Macmillan.

Poyner, B. and Webb, B. (1992) *Crime Free Housing*, Oxford: Butterworths.

Price, W.H., Strong, J.A., Whatmore, P.B. and McClemont, W.F. (1966) 'Criminal patients with XYY sex-chromosome complement', *The Lancet*, 1, 565–6.

Prins, H. (1995) *Offenders, Deviants or Patients* (2nd ed.), London: Routledge.

Quinsey, V.L., Harris, G.T., Rice, M.E. and Cormier, C.A. (1998) *Violent Offenders: Appraising and Managing Risk*, Washington DC: American Psychological Association.

Raine, A. (1993) *The psychopathology of Crime: Criminal Behavior as a Clinical Disorder*, San Diego CA: Academic Press.

Reed Report (1991) *Review of Health and Social Services for Mentally Disordered Offenders and Others Requiring Similar Services*, London: Department of Health/Home Office.

Reiner, R. (1992) *The Politics of the Police* (2nd ed.), Hemel Hempstead: Wheatsheaf.

Reiner, R. (1997) 'Media made criminality: The Representations of Crime in the Mass Media', in M. Maguire, R. Morgan and R. Reiner (eds) *The Oxford Handbook of Criminology* (2nd ed.), Oxford: Oxford University Press.

Reisser, M. (1982) 'Crime-specific psychological consultation', *The Police Chief*, March, 101–4.

Resnick, H.S., Kilpatrick, D.G., Dansky, B.S., Saunders, B.E. and Best, C.L. (1993) 'Prevalence of civilian trauma and post-traumatic stress disorder in a representative national sample of women', *Journal of Consulting and Clinical Psychology*, 61, 984–91.

Resnick, H.S., Veronen, L.J., Saunders, B.E., Kilpatrick, D.G. and Cornelison, V. (1989) 'Assessment of PTSD in a subset of rape victims at 12 to 36 months post-assault', unpublished manuscript cited in Rothbaum *et al.* 1992 (see below).

Robertson, G., Pearson, R. and Gibb, R. (1995) *The Mentally Disordered and the Police*, London: Home Office Research and Statistics Department.

Robins, L.N., Helzer, J.E., Weissman, M.M., Orvaschel, H., Gruneberg, E., Burker, J.D. and Regier, D.A. (1984) 'Lifetime prevalence of specific psychiatric disorders in three sites', *Archives of General Psychiatry*, 41, 949–58.

Robinson, J. (1988) *On the Demon Drink*, London: Mitchell Beazley.

Rock, P. (1998) *After Homicide: Practical and Political Responses to Bereavement*, Oxford: Clarendon Press.

Roesch, R., Zapf, P.A., Golding, S.L. and Skeem, J.L. (1999) 'Defining and assessing competency to stand trial', in A.K. Hess and I.B. Weiner (eds) *The Handbook of Forensic Psychology* (2nd ed.), New York: Wiley.

Rosenhan, D. L. (1963) 'On being sane in insane places', *Science*, 179, 250–8.

Rosman, J.P. and Resnick, P.J. (1989) 'Sexual attraction to corpses: A psychiatric review of necrophilia', *Bulletin of the American Academy of Psychiatry and Law*, 17 (2), 153–63.

Ross, L. (1977) 'The intuitive psychologist and his shortcomings: Distortions in the attribution process', in L. Berkowitz (ed.), *Advances in Experimental Social Psychology*, New York: Academic Press.

Rossmo, D.K. (1996) 'Targeting victims; serial killers and the urban environment', in T. O'Reilly-Fleming (ed.), *Serial and Mass Murder: Theory Research and Policy*, Toronto: Canadian Scholars Press.

Rothbaum, B.O., Foa, E.B., Riggs, D.S., Murdock, T. and Walsh, W. (1992) 'A prospective examination of post-traumatic stress disorder in rape victims', *Journal of Traumatic Stress*, 5, 455–76.

Rotter, J.B. (1966) 'Generalized expectancies for internal versus external control of reinforcement', *Psychological Monographs*, 80 (1, whole no 609).

Ruback, R.B. and Innes, C.A. (1990) 'The relevance and irrelevance of psychological research: The example of prison overcrowding', *American Psychologist*, 43(9), 683–93.

Rubenstein, H., Murray, C., Motoyama, T., Rouse, W.V. and Titus, R.M. (1980) *The Link Between Crime and the Built Environment; The Current State of Knowledge*, Washington: National Institute of Justice.

Rubin, Z. and Peplau, L.A. (1975) 'Who believes in a just world?', *Journal of Social Issues*, 31, 65–89.

Rutter, M. (1971) *Maternal Deprivation Reassessed*, Harmondsworth: Penguin.

Saunders, D.G. (1996) 'Feminist-cognitive-behavioral and process-psychodynamic treatment for men who batter: Interaction of abuser traits and treatment models', *Violence and Victims*, 11(4), 393–413.

Schachter, S. (1959) *The Psychology of Affiliation*, Stanford CA: California University Press.

Schneider, D.J. (1995) 'Attribution of Social Cognition', in M. Argyle and A.M. Colman (eds), *Social Psychology*, London: Longman.

Scourfield, J. (1995) *Changing Men: UK Agencies Working With Men Who Are Violent Towards Their Woman Partners*, Norwich: Probation Monographs.

Seligman, M.E.P. (1975) *Helplessness: On Depression, Development and Death*, San Francisco CA: W.H. Freeman.

Sennett, R. (1977) *The Fall of Public Man*, London: Faber.

Shaw, C. and McKay, H. (1942) *Juvenile Delinquency and Urban Areas*, Chicago: University of Chicago Press.

Shaw, M. (1999) 'A bereavement model of the emotional scars of chronic victimization', in Farrell, G. and Pease, K. (eds) (1999) *Repeat Victimization*, New York: Criminal Justice Press.

Sheldon, W.H. (1942) *The Varieties of Temperament: A Psychology of Constitutional Differences*, New York: Harper.

Shepherd, E. (1993) 'Resistance in interviews; the contribution of police perceptions and behaviour', in E. Shepherd (ed.) *Aspects of Police Interviewing*, Leicester: British Psychological Society.

Sherman, L.W., Gartin, P.R. and Buerger, M.E. (eds) (1989) 'Hot spots of predatory crime: Routine activity and the criminology of place', *Criminology*, 27 (1), 27–55.

Shipherd, J.C. and Beck, J.G. (1999) 'The effects of suppressing trauma-related thoughts on women with rape-related PTSD', *Behavior Research and Therapy*, 37, 99–112.

Sims, A. (1996) *Report of the Confidential Inquiry into Homicides and Suicides by Mentally Ill People*, London: Royal College of Psychiatrists.

Skinner, B.F. (1953) *Science and Human Behavior*, New York: Macmillan.

Skogan, W. (1981) *Issues in the Measurement of Victimization*, Washington DC: Department of Justice.

Smith, D.J. (1997) 'Ethnic origins, crime and criminal justice', in M. Maguire, R. Morgan and R. Reiner (eds) *The Oxford Handbook of Criminology* (2nd ed.), Oxford: Oxford University Press.

Smith, G.E. (1998) *Offender Profiling: its Role and Suitability in the Investigation of Serious Crime*, unpublished MA dissertation, University of Manchester.

Smith, L.J.F. and Burrows, J. (1986) 'Nobbling the fraudsters: Crime prevention through administrative change', *Howard Journal*, 25, 13–24.

Snyder, S. (1995) 'Movie portrayals of juvenile delinquency: Part II. Sociology and Psychology', *Adolescence*, 30, 325–7.

Sommer, R. (1987) 'Crime and vandalism in university residence halls: A conformation of defensible space theory', *Journal of Environmental Psychology*, 1–12.

Sorrensen, S.B. and Golding, J.M. (1990) 'Depressive sequelae of recent criminal victimization', *Journal of Traumatic Stress*, 3, 337–50.

Sparks, R. (1992) *Television and the Drama of Crime: Moral Tales and the Place of Crime in Public Life*, Milton Keynes: Open University Press.

Spivey, W. (1994) 'Stranger Rape: Some Characteristics of Offenses, Offenders, and Victims', unpublished MSc dissertation, University of Manchester.

Stanko, B. (1999) *Gender and Crime*, Harlow: Longman.

Steblay, N.M. (1992) 'A Meta-analytic Review of the Weapon Focus Effect', *Law and Human Behavior*, 16, 413–24.

Steketee, G. and Foa, E.B. (1987) 'Rape Victims: Post-traumatic stress responses and their treatment: A review of the literature', *Journal of Anxiety Disorders*, 1, 69–86.

Stephenson, C. (1992b) 'Better by design – Crime-fighter architect draws on experience', *Manchester Metro News*, 20 March 1992, 4.

Stephenson, G.M. (1992a) *The Psychology of Criminal Justice*, Oxford: Blackwell.

Stevens, J.A. (1995) 'Offenders in profile', *Policing Today*, August.

Stone, A.A. (1984) *Law, Psychiatry and Morality: Essays and Analysis*, Washington DC: American Psychiatric Press.

Stoner, J.A.F. (1968) 'Risky and cautious shifts in group decisions: The influence of widely held values', *Journal of Experimental Social Psychology*, 4, 442–59.

Stradling, S.G., Tuohy, A.P. and Harper, K.J. (1990) 'Judgemental Symmetry in the Exercise of Police Discretion', *Applied Cognitive Psychology*, 4, 409–21.

Straus, M.A. and Gelles, R.J. (1990) *Physical Violence in American Families: Risk Factors and Adaptations to Violence in 8145 Families*, New Brunswick: Transaction.

Sturman, A. (1980) 'Damage on buses: the effects of supervision', in R.V. Clarke and P. Mayhew (eds) *Designing out Crime*, London: HMSO.

Sutherland, E.H. (1939) *The Professional Thief*, Chicago: Chicago University Press.

Sutherland, E.H. and Cressey, D.R. (1970) *Criminology* (8th ed.), Philadelphia PA: Lippincott.

Swanson, C.R., Chamelin, N.C. and Territo, L. (1988) *Criminal Investigation* (4th ed.), New York: McGraw-Hill.

Sykes, R.E., Fox, J.E. and Clark, J.P. (1976) 'Socio-legal theory of police discretion', in A. Niederhoffer and A.S. Blumber (eds) *The Ambivalent Force: Perspectives on the Police*, Hinsdale: Dryden Press.

Tajfel, H.J. (1981) *Human Groups and Social Categories: Studies in Social Psychology*, Cambridge: Cambridge University Press.

Tetem, H. (1989) 'Offender profiling', in W. Bailey (ed.) *The Encyclopedia of Police Science*, New York: Garland.

Thomson, D.M. (1995) 'Eyewitness testimony and identification tests', in N. Brewer and C. Wilson (eds) *Psychology and Policing*, Hilsdale NJ: L.E.A.

Tilley. N. and Ford, A. (1996) *Forensic Science and Crime Investigation*, Crime Detection and Prevention Series Paper 73, London: Home Office.

Torrey, E.F. (1994) 'Violent behaviour by individuals with serious mental illness' *Hospital and Community Psychiatry*, 45, 653–62.

Trasler, G.B. (1987) 'Biogenetic Factors', in H.C. Quay (ed.) *Handbook of Juvenile Delinquency*, New York: John Wiley.

Trower, P., Bryant, M. and Argyle, M. (1977) *Social Skills and Mental Health*, London: Methuen.

Tseloni, A. and Pease, K. (1997) 'Nuisance phone calls to women in England and Wales', *European Journal of Criminal Policy and Research*, cited in K. Pease (1998) above.

Underwager, R. and Wakefield, H. (1992) 'False confessions and police deception', *American Journal of Forensic Psychology*, 10, 49–66.

Van Dijk, J.J.M. and De Waard, J. (1991) 'A two dimensional typology of crime prevention projects', *Criminal Justice Abstracts*, 23, 483–503.

Van Hooris, P., Cullen, F.T. and Applegate, B.K. (1995) 'Evaluating interventions with violent offenders: A guide for practitioners and policy makers', *Federal Probation*, 59, June, 17–28.

Vennard, J. and Hedderman, C. (1998) 'Effective Treatment with offenders', in P. Goldblatt and C. Lewis (eds) *Reducing Offending: An Assessment of Research Evidence on Ways of Dealing with Offending Behaviour*, Home Office Research Study 187, London: Home Office Research and Statistics Directorate.

Vennard, J., Sugg, D. and Hedderman, C. (1997) *The Use of Cognitive-Behavioural Approaches with Offenders: Messages from the Research*, Home Office Research Study No. 171, London: Home Office.

Von Hirsch, A. (1995) 'Proportionality and parsimony in American sentencing guidelines', in C. Clarkson and R. Morgan (eds) *The Politics of Sentencing Reform*, Oxford: Clarendon Press.

Von Hirsch, A. and Ashworth, A. (eds) (1992) *Principled Sentencing*, Edinburgh: Edinburgh University Press.

Vrij, A. (1998a) 'Nonverbal communication and credibility', in A. Memon, A. Vrij and R Bull, *Psychology and Law: Truthfulness, Accuracy and Credibility*, Maidenhead: McGraw-Hill.

Vrij, A. (1998b) 'Interviewing suspects', in A. Memon, A. Vrij and R. Bull, *Psychology and Law: Truthfulness, Accuracy and Credibility*, Maidenhead: McGraw-Hill.

Vrij. A. (1998c) 'Physiological parameters and credibility: The polygraph', in A. Memon, A. Vrij and R Bull, *Psychology, and Law: Truthfulness, Accuracy and Credibility*, Maidenhead: McGraw-Hill.

Vrij, A. and Winkel, F.W. (1993) 'Objective and subjective indicators of deception', *Issues in Criminological and Legal Psychology*, 20, 51–7.

Wagenaar, W.A. and Veefkind, N. (1992) 'Comparison of one-person and six-person line-ups', in F. Losel, D. Bender and T. Bleisener, *Psychology and Law: International Perspectives*, New York: Walter de Gruyter.

Walker, N. (1968) *Crime and Insanity in England* Vol. 1, Edinburgh: Edinburgh University Press.

Wallbott, H.G. (1996) 'Social psychology and the media', in G.R. Semin and K. Fiedler (eds) *Applied Social Psychology*, London: Sage.

Walters, D.G. (1998) *Changing Levels of Crime and Drugs: Intervening with Substance-Abusing Offenders*, Chichester: Wiley.

Walters, G.D. (1992) 'A meta-analysis of the gene-crime relationship', *Criminology*, 30, 595–613.

Webster, C.D., Menzies, R.J. and Hart, S.D. (1995) 'Dangerousness and Risk', in R. Bull and D. Carson (eds) *Handbook of Psychology in Legal Contexts*, Chichester: Wiley.

Weiner, B. (1980) *Human Motivation*, New York: Holt Rinehart & Winston.

Weingardt, K.R., Toland, H.K. and Loftus, E.F. (1994) 'Reports of Suggested Memories: Do People Truly Believe Them?', in D.F. Ross, J.D. Read and M.P. Toglia (eds) *Adult Eyewitness Testimony: Current Trends and Developments*, Cambridge: Cambridge University Press.

Weiss, J.M. (1973) 'The natural history of antisocial attitudes: What happened to psychopaths?', *Journal of Geriatric Psychiatry*, 6, 236–42.

Wells, G.L., Seelau, E.P., Rydell, S.M. and Luus, C.A.E. (1994) 'Recommendations for properly conducted line-up identification tasks', in D.F. Ross, J.D. Read and M.P. Toglia (eds) *Adult Eyewitness Testimony: Current Trends and Developments*, Cambridge: Cambridge University Press.

Wexler, H.K., Falkin, G.P. and Liton, D.S. (1990) 'Outcome evaluation of a prison therapeutic community for substance abuse treatment', *Criminal Justice and Behavior*, 17, 71–92.

Whitehead, J.T. and Lab, S.P. (1989) 'A meta-analysis of juvenile correctional treatment', *Journal of Research in Crime and Delinquency*, 26, 276–95.

Wilczynski, A. and Morris, A. (1993) 'Parents who kill their children', *Criminal Law Review*, 31–6.

Williamson, T.M. (1990) *Strategic changes in police interrogation*, unpublished PhD thesis: University of Kent.

Witkin, H.A., Mednick, S.A. and Schulsinger, F. (1976) 'Criminality in XY and XYY men', *Science*, 193, 547–55.

Wood, J., Wheelwright, G. and Burrows, J. (1997) *Crime against Small Businesses: Facing the Challenge*, Swindon: Crime Concern.

Wrightsman, L.S. (1991) *Psychology and the Legal System* (2nd ed.), Pacific Grove, California: Brooks/Cole.

Yancey, W.L. (1971) 'Architecture, Design and Social Control: The case of a large scale public housing project'. *Environment and Behavior*, 3, 3–18.

Yarmey, A.D. (1992) 'Accuracy of eyewitness and earwitness showup identifications in a field setting', poster presented at the *American Psychology–Law Society Conference*, San Diego, California, March.

Young, A. (1996) 'In the frame: Crime and the limits of representation', *The Australian and New Zealand Journal of Criminology*, 29(2), 81–101.

Zander, M. and Henderson, P. (1994) 'The Crown Court Study', Royal Commission on Criminal Justice Study No. 19, *Research Bulletin No. 35*, 46–8, London: Home Office Research and Statistics Department.

Zedner, L. (1997) 'Victims', in M. Maguire, R. Morgan and R. Reiner (eds) *The Oxford Handbook of Criminology* (2nd ed.), Oxford: Oxford University Press.

Zeisel, H. and Diamond, S.S. (1976) 'The jury selection in the Mitchell-Stans conspiracy trial', *American Bar Foundation Research Journal*, 1, 151–74.

Zimring, F.E. and Hawkins, G. (1995) *Incapacitation: Penal Confinement and the restraint of Crime*, New York: Oxford University Press.

Index